Julia Boyd is the author of *Hannah Riddell,*
Excellent Doctor Blackwell. She has travelled f

'Julia Boyd tells the fascinating tale of the foreign community surviving in Peking between the end of the Ch'ing Dynasty and Mao's communist revolution. It is a great story very well told – turmoil behind, turmoil ahead and turmoil all around.'

Chris Patten, Chancellor of Oxford University, Chairman of the BBC and former Governer of Hong Kong, author of *East and West: The Last Governor of Hong Kong on Power Freedom and the Future*

'Based on a treasure-trove of original sources, this book gives an enthralling insight into the expatriate community in Peking during the half-century before the triumph of Mao. Anyone who wants to understand China's relationship with foreigners, today as well as yesterday, should read it.'

Piers Brendon, author of *The Decline and Fall of the British Empire*

'A fascinating account sourced from many previously unpublished letters and archives. Boyd's characters flit on the surface of the city like water beetles, unaware of the depths below.'

Frances Wood, Curator of Chinese collections, British Library, author of *China's First Emperor and His Terracotta Warriors*

Julia Boyd

A DANCE WITH THE DRAGON

The Vanished World of Peking's Foreign Colony

I.B. TAURIS

LONDON · NEW YORK

Published in 2012 and reprinted in 2012 and 2013 by I.B.Tauris & Co Ltd
6 Salem Road, London W2 4BU
175 Fifth Avenue, New York NY 10010
www.ibtauris.com

Distributed in the United States and Canada Exclusively by Palgrave Macmillan
175 Fifth Avenue, New York NY 10010

ISBN: 978 1 78076 052 0

A full CIP record for this book is available from the British Library
A full CIP record is available from the Library of Congress

Library of Congress Catalog Card Number: available

Printed and bound by CPI Group (UK) Ltd, Croydon, CR0 4YY

MIX
Paper from
responsible sources
FSC
www.fsc.org   FSC® C013604

For John

CONTENTS

PLATES

PHOTOS

1. Sir Claude MacDonald, British Minister in Peking, 1896–1900
   (Published in *China of Today: The Yellow Peril,* London: Army & Navy
   Illustrated, 1900)
2. Emperor Street, Peking, 1901
   (Reproduced from *Ein Tagebuch in Bildern,* Courtesy of Toyo Bunko,
   Tokyo)
3. The American Minister Edwin H. Conger and his family approaching
   the Forbidden City, 1900
   (Courtesy of Library of Congress)
4. Camels outside the Peking wall
   (Courtesy of The Hon. Lady Bonsor)
5. The first steam engine to arrive at the station near Chien-men,
   1 November 1901
   (Reproduced from *Ein Tagebuch in Bildern,* Courtesy of Toyo Bunko,
   Tokyo)
6. Mrs Cecil Carnegie entertaining Manchu court ladies at the British
   Legation, 1906
   (Copyright and Courtesy of Queen's University, Belfast, Sir Robert Hart
   Collection, MS 15)
7. Allied victory parade at the Forbidden City, 18 November 1918
   (Courtesy of The Hon. Lady Bonsor)
8. Cecil Lewis and Doushka Horvath 'flying' on the Altar of Heaven, 1920
   (Sir Ian Axford Collection, Courtesy of Robert Axford)
9. General Dmitri Horvath in his study, *c.*1920
   (Sir Ian Axford Collection, Courtesy of Robert Axford)

MAPS

ACKNOWLEDGEMENTS

Many people have contributed to this book and I am deeply grateful to them all. Without the encouragement and input of Gordon Barrass and Dr Jim Hoare, I would never have started, let alone finished. I owe an immense debt to Dr Piers Brendon and Dr Frances Wood, whose constant support and interest have been vital to me. All four have been unfailingly helpful in directing me towards promising sources, suggesting improvements and contributing ideas. Any errors that have crept in are of course mine alone. Graham Greene has, as always, been extraordinarily generous with his time and advice.

Much of the material I have used comes from unpublished sources and private collections. I was particularly lucky to meet Daniele Varè's daughter, Gianmarina Grose, with whom I spent many happy hours transcribing her father's diaries. Lady Bonsor showed equal generosity in lending me copies of Lord Killearn's diaries – one of the most vivid records of the period. I thank her too for allowing me to reproduce photographs from her grandfather's albums. General Stilwell's grandson, Colonel John Easterbrook, and his wife Hanh welcomed me to their home in California and made available many fascinating family documents. Alexandra Blair generously loaned me Sir Malcolm Robertson's diary. The following individuals have shown great kindness in allowing me access to private papers: Virginia Fraser, Paul French, Ambassador Yasuhide Hayashi, the Horvath family, Adam Jordan, Kate Ker, The Viscount and Viscountess Killearn, Thomas Pinschof, Anton von Rosthorn, Benita Stoney, Sir Adrian Swire, John Travers Clarke, Sir George and Lady Young, Richard Warren, Helen Winnifrith, Peggy Wiles and Emmeline Wray.

I owe special thanks to my long-suffering American friends Louis Bradbury and Dr Nancy Sahli, who undertook research for me in New York and Washington. Also to Barbara Laughlin and Patrick Miles, for their translations of Russian text, and to Ambassador Nishigahiro, who, despite his demanding job as Minister at the Japanese Embassy, found time to translate Hayashi Gonsuke's autobiography for me. Robert Massam gave me invaluable assistance with the photographs.

Phoebe Bentinck, Ambassador Roland van den Berg, The Lady Biffen, Stephen Boyd, Sir Tony Brenton, Jennifer Chang, Jung Chang, Professor Paul Chen, Richard Davies, Paula Diamanti, John Gerson, Patricia Haines, Dr Gaynor Johnson, Ambassador Klaus Kappel, George Loudon, Professor Roderick MacFarquar, Professor David McMullen, Sally McMullen, John Moffett, Jon Halliday, Nicholas Maclean, the late Sir Robin MacLaren, Margaret Mair, Professor Allan Mazur, Dr Susan Pares, Lord Patten of Barnes, Tom Phillips, Desmond Power, Marian Ramsay, Dr Zara Steiner, Virginia Surtees, Dr Madhavi Thampi, Josephine Walker, Lady Weston, Lord Wilson of Tillyorn, Dalena Wright, Lady Youde and Dr Yuan Boping have helped in countless ways – I thank them all.

I have also been very fortunate to have received help from individuals working in the libraries and archives I have consulted while researching this book. Dr Richard Luckett kindly gave me access to Dorothea Richards' diary in the Old Library, Magdalene College, Cambridge, while the following staff went well beyond the line of duty in providing me with information, suggestions and photocopies: Julia Banks, Judy Burg, Sarah Campbell, Lorraine Coughlan, Bert Edstrom, John Entwisle, Patrice S. Fox, Carol A. Leadenham, Allen Packwood and his staff at the Churchill Archives Centre, Churchill College, Cambridge, and Dale Sauter, Carrie Lyn Schwier, Paul Smith, Anne Thomson, Debbie Usher and Reina Williams. Holly Wright was particularly helpful in providing me with photocopies of the Laurence Sickman material.

I owe Katy Talati a very special debt, since it was her own fascinating memoir – itself an important source – that first gave me the idea for this project.

Tatiana Wilde has been an astute and skilful editor. I thank her and everyone at I.B.Tauris who has been involved in producing this book.

Lastly, I thank my husband John – for his knowledge and memories of Peking, his fluent Mandarin, his patience with my lack of punctuation and, above all, for the wonderfully happy times we have spent exploring China together.

NOTE ON CHINESE SPELLING

In most instances, I have followed the transcriptions of Chinese names used in contemporary texts. Most are accurate or inaccurate renderings of the Wade/Giles Romanisation System developed in the mid-nineteenth century, the 'Post Office' transliterations or earlier systems. In some cases (Shanghai, Feng-tai), there is little or no difference between the old Wade/Giles and the current Pinyin Romanisation but in others, such as today's Jinan, which was Tsinan in the old 'Post Office' version or Canton/Guangzhou, the differences are considerable. The list below gives the modern equivalent of such names and terms:

Canton	Guangzhou
Chang Hsun	Zhang Xun
Chang Tso-lin	Zhang Zuolin
Chiang Kai-shek	Jiang Jieshi
Chien-men, Ch'ien-men gate	Qianmen
Ch'ien-lung emperor	Qianlong
Chihli	Hebei province
Prince Ching	Yikuang, Prince Qing
Ching-shan	Jingshan
Ch'ing Dynasty	Qing
Chou En-lai	Zhou Enlai
Choukoutien	Zhoukoudian
Chu Teh	Zhu De
Chungking	Chongqing
Feng Yu-hsiang	Feng Yuxiang
Fu Tso-yi	Fu Zuoyi
Hankow city	Hankou
Hatamen Street	Dongdan dajie
Hsien-feng emperor	Xianfeng

Hung-hsien Dynasty	Hongxian
Jung-lu	Ronglu
Kalgan	Zhangjiakou
Kansu province	Gansu
Kuan-yin	Guanyin
Kuang-hsu emperor	Guangxu
Dr Kung, H.H. Kung	Kong Xiangxi
Prince Kung	Yixin, Prince Gong
Li Hung-chang	Li Hongzhang
Li Lien-ying	Li Lianying
Lung-yu	Longyu
Mao Tse-tung	Mao Zedong
Nanking	Nanjing
Nankow Pass	Nankou
Ningpo	Ningbo
Pei Hai	Beihai
Pei ho river	Beihe
Pei Wenchang	Pei Wenzhang
Peitaiho	Beidaihe
Peitang cathedral	Beitang
Peking, Peiping	Beijing
Prince Puju	Puru
Shansi province	Shanxi
Shantung province	Shandong
Sian	Xi'an
Sun Yat-sen	Sun Yixian
Sung Chiao-jen	Song Jiaoren
Taku bar	Dagu
Tientsin	Tianjin
V.K. Ting	Ding Wejiang
Tsinan	Ji'nan
Tsinghua University	Qinghua
Tsingtao	Qingdao
Tsu-hsi, Tz'u-hsi	Cixi
Tsung-li yamen	Zongli Yamen
Prince Tuan	Zaiyi, Prince Duan
Tung Fu-hsiang	Dong Fuxiang

Tungcho pagoda	Tongzhou
Tung-chih men gate	Dongzhimen
Tung-wen kuan	Tongwenguan
Waiwupu	Waiwubu
Wanhsien	Wanxian
Whampoa	Huangpu
Weihsien	Weixian
W.W. Yen	Yan Huiqing
Yenan	Yan'an
Yuan Shih-k'ai	Yuan Shikai
Yung-lo emperor	Yongle

Although Peking was renamed 'Peiping' by the Nationalist government (1928–49), I have followed the practice of most foreigners at the time by continuing to use 'Peking'.

PROLOGUE

Peking is paradise ... I never felt better in my life.
—Alice Green Hoffman, 1925

Most Westerners went to China in the first half of the twentieth century to make money or to make converts. But those living in Peking were different. Forbidden by treaty to trade on any large scale, their small community was influenced not by the powerful businessmen in Shanghai and the other treaty ports, but by a colourful mix of diplomats and dropouts, intellectuals, artists, merry widows, Russian refugees and remittance men. Peking also had its fair share of missionaries, but as they were more involved in higher education than grass-roots conversion, they too tended to differ from the norm.

Peking's foreigners always considered themselves a cut above other China expatriates, in particular the philistine 'Shanghailanders'. After all, Shanghai, with its huge international settlement and Western architecture, had been a foreign enterprise from the start. But in Peking, the foreigners lived close to the emperor's palace, at the very heart of a great and ancient civilization, in a city that remained essentially untouched by the modern world. Furthermore, they were centre stage for the crucial events that were to shape China: the Boxer siege of 1900; the death (eight years later) of the last great representative of imperial China, the Empress Dowager Tsu-hsi; the 1911 revolution that sparked decades of civil war, most notably between Chiang Kai-shek and Mao Tse-tung; the long years of Japanese occupation; and finally the Communist victory of 1949. Given this context, it is hardly surprising that, for many foreigners, time spent in Peking against a setting of gently decaying splendour, acute poverty, exotic street-life and pungent smells was the defining event of their lives. For even the most insular among them knew that to have lived in Peking before war and modernisation destroyed its unique way of life forever was an experience never to be forgotten.

Despite this, remarkably few made any real effort to understand the country in which they were living. Oblivious to revolution and famine, the majority lived in a world apart, absorbed by their parties, ponies and club gossip. 'I note there is a great deal of cocktail drinking in Peking,' wrote Lord Northcliffe disapprovingly, in 1921, 'I don't know whether women drink cocktails in London but they certainly do here on the slightest provocation.'[1] There were of course exceptions, and by the 1930s (just as Japan was tightening its grip on the city) Peking had become a magnet for Western literati, many of whom fell so much in love with the city that they never wanted to live anywhere else.

For most foreigners, their first sight of Peking was a glimpse of its wall from the train as they travelled from the treaty port of Tientsin on the last 80 miles of their journey. After crossing the monotonous mud-coloured Chihli plain (stretching east of Peking to the sea) relieved only by equally mud-coloured villages and burial mounds, few ever forgot this first view of the wall rising out of the flatness against the darker backdrop of the Western Hills. New arrivals quickly discovered that Peking was in fact dominated by walls – encircling, dividing and concealing. Surrounding the whole city was the crenellated grey brick wall built by the Ming in the fifteenth century. It was 20 odd miles in circumference, 40 feet (12 metres) high in places and, as guidebooks liked to note, broader than Fifth Avenue. Gates (firmly shut between dusk and dawn) pierced the wall at intervals, the curving roofs of their elaborate towers partially offsetting its forbidding exterior. 'The most wonderful thing in Peking is the wall,' wrote an American visitor in 1912, 'that is what first holds your attention and you never for a moment forget it. There it stands, aloof and remote, dominating the city it was set up to defend, but not a part of it.'[2]

Since the Manchus descended from their homeland in the north-east to defeat the Ming in 1644 (and found their own Ch'ing Dynasty, 1644–1911), Peking had consisted of four distinct walled cities – the Tartar City, the Chinese City, the Imperial City, and, lying not just at the heart of Peking but of the whole Chinese empire, the Forbidden City. Here, in the 'Great Within', lived the emperor (until the last, Puyi, was expelled in 1924), protected and hidden from prying eyes by rust-coloured walls above which could be seen the glittering yellow tiles of the roofs. Deep in this complex stood his dragon throne – the ultimate symbol of imperial power.

But only a short distance from the Forbidden City, tucked into the south-east corner of the Tartar City, lay a cuckoo's egg – the legation quarter. It was in this diplomatic enclave, walled like its neighbours and occupying just under a square mile, that Peking's foreign community was concentrated between the Boxer siege and Communist victory. After the siege – an event of such intense drama that it was to affect foreign policy towards China for decades – the Chinese government was forced to accept that the legation quarter would now, in effect, be a miniature treaty port subject only to its own laws and administration and defended by foreign troops. The southern boundary of the legation quarter was formed by the Tartar City wall, but around its other three walls a large grassy area, the *glacis*, was created to give the foreigners yet further protection, at the same time providing them with a sports and parade ground. Even though, as the century progressed, increasing numbers of Westerners chose to live outside the legation quarter, its walls – loopholed for machine guns – always remained a striking symbol of the gulf between foreigner and Chinese.

Once safely inside the legation quarter's gates, the world was again instantly recognisable – the buildings and banks, the well-kept lawns, the clean, macadamised streets and social conventions all redolent of bourgeois Europe. The only Chinese permitted to live there were the legions of servants (in special uniforms), without whom the foreigners would have been quite unable to function. Others – tradesmen, teachers, merchants and the night soil coolies (who removed the contents of latrines[3]) – were provided with special passes. One British diplomat, in Peking during the 1930s, recalled how each May a long line of garden coolies would enter the embassy, each balancing potted plants from a pole across his shoulder:

> Having selected the plants in the colours desired, we instructed the coolies to plant so much of one colour here, of another there until we had 'painted' a gardenful and so created an instant garden in less than an hour.[4]

If inside the legation quarter all was reassuringly familiar, outside was a different story: 'You can't conceive what the horrible, fascinating streets of Peking are like,' wrote a visitor in 1903:

> Your rickshaw dashes in and out, bumps over boulders, subsides into ditches, runs over dogs and toes and the outlying parts of booths and shops, upsets an occasional wheelbarrow, locks itself with rickshaws coming in the opposite direction and at a hard gallop conveys you breathless, through dust and noise and smells unspeakable to where you would be.[5]

The colourful chaos of Peking's streets belied the formality of the city plan, laid out in the fifteenth century on strict *feng-shui* principles. Wide avenues ran in straight lines from north to south, east to west, wall to wall. But in their interstices lay a network of muddy lanes or *hutongs* filled with endless crowds of ragged Chinese in butcher blue, the interiors of their ramshackle shops overflowing with pigs, rickshaws, garbage and overpowering smells. While the mediaeval exoticism of Peking's streets was for many foreigners thrilling, the ubiquitous beggars and excrement, the corpses chewed by stray dogs, cruel public punishments and an all-pervading stench were also a powerful deterrent.

One place which always afforded refuge was the top of the Tartar City wall. Once up there, foreigners could walk for miles among the crumbling stones and weeds, far removed from the clamour and dirt below – as well as from the Chinese who were forbidden access. Seen from this elevated point, Peking was surprisingly green and tranquil. Looking north, the foreigners could gaze across the sweeping roofs of the Forbidden City to Coal Hill, where the last Ming emperor had hanged himself. To the south lay the Chinese City, where the victorious Manchus forced their new subjects to live and which over the centuries had retained its distinctive character. More dilapidated than the Tartar City, it remained until the mid-twentieth century a mixture of crowded streets and rural smallholdings. Foreigners rarely lived there but visited it for its restaurants and markets, theatres, sing-song houses, and for the Temple of Heaven where each December the emperor went to perform the rituals necessary to ensure a good harvest, and where, in its fine park among ancient cypresses and oaks, the Westerners enjoyed riding their short, ugly Mongol ponies.

If foreigners found Peking's smells unpleasant, they were enchanted by its sounds. Once the early morning fires had been lit, a great cacophony rose with the dawn as the daily round of bargaining, buying and hawking began. Equally charming were Chinese street names – Big Embroidery Street, Little Embroidery Street, Flower Street, Jade Street, Lantern Street, as were those of shops such as 'Ever Flourishing' or 'Broadly Ample'. One street in the Chinese City, the Liu-li Chang, was a particular favourite. Clustered there (as now) were the finest antique shops, and if there was one characteristic that distinguished Peking's foreigners from other expatriates, it was their passion for 'curios'. As Mrs Mascot exclaims in Harold Acton's novel *Peonies and Ponies*, 'in Peking we all have collections. One simply has to collect, you know. It's in the air, an epidemic that catches everyone sooner or later.'[6] By the 1920s many foreigners (the British and Americans being the biggest contingent) had also discovered the delights of Peking's courtyard houses. Although these single-storey dwellings differed greatly in size and status, they were all designed on the same pattern. Built in narrow, unpaved *hutongs*, they were from the outside entirely unprepossessing. Nor was there any hint of what lay within. Even when the studded red lacquer doors were swung open, all that could be seen was a screen, strategically placed to ward off evil spirits. But, beyond the screen lay a world of immense charm. Raftered rooms with filigree papered windows were arranged around a series of courtyards filled with the fragrance of flowering shrubs and the sound of songbirds in bamboo cages.

Courtyard houses and curios, flocks of musical pigeons with miniature flutes attached to their legs, picnics in the Western Hills, rickshaws (for some the most perfect transport, for others the most detestable), fading palaces, venerable Chinese gentlemen dressed in long silk gowns airing their caged birds, strings of woolly camels bringing coal into the city, temples, kites, colours, sounds and sing-song houses – the list of Peking's seductive charms was long. 'What I like about Peking,' wrote one long-term resident,

> is the feeling of being in the heart of Old China ... coming home at night sometimes in a rickshaw through dark and twisting little streets under magnificently starred skies, against which there loom, just like Chinese shadow pictures, the little curved roofs and gnarled trees covered with ravens' nests.[7]

But not everyone saw the point. Many foreigners, no matter how long they lived in Peking, were unable to reconcile themselves to the dirt, the food or the ever-present bed bugs. 'After fumigating three times and much use of kerosene, we find them in commercial quantities in all our beds,'[8] wrote one woman in 1926. Peking was considered to have a good climate even if the intense cold of winter and the sticky summer heat took their toll on the more fragile. Far worse, however, were the ferocious dust storms whipped up in the Gobi Desert that regularly blighted Peking in the spring. Then, the city's cherry and peach blossom, its green willows, roses and peonies were blotted out by sand mixed with filth from the streets. Compared with many places in the Far East, Peking was thought to be relatively healthy. Even so, people died 'in the most disconcerting manner' as one woman observed, adding, 'it's probably the nose blowing on the ground and spitting and urinating everywhere all the time'.[9]

The American sinologist John King Fairbank believed that the 'biggest fact' in China was the poverty.[10] This was equally true of Peking (where he lived 1932–5) even though it had a higher percentage of upper-class families than any other Chinese city. Raw poverty was everywhere, impossible to ignore. What puzzled foreigners was how ordinary Chinese maintained their sense of fun in such conditions. But while admiring their cheerful resilience, not many could see beyond the poverty – the outcome of incompetent government, civil war, corruption and foreign colonial attitudes – to appreciate China's true potential. And although it was a commonplace among them to talk about China as the 'sleeping giant' that would one day awake and astonish the world, few really believed that China would ever win a seat at the international top table. Peking's foreigners may have been more sensitive to China's cultural riches than the materialistic Shanghailanders, but for most of them it was a superficial homage that had more to do with personal gratification than acknowledgement of another civilization. The Westerners' deep-rooted sense of cultural superiority was clearly demonstrated by their reluctance to appoint Chinese to senior administrative positions or even as bishops in their own church. In this respect the normally conservative Vatican was a notable exception since in the mid-1920s it appointed many Chinese bishops – a policy dismissed by one British official as being 'ostentatiously indifferent' to current political questions.[11] The eminent geologist Dr V.K. Ting was in no doubt that the Western 'superiority complex' was deeply damaging, provoking a sense of inadequacy among his fellow Chinese professionals that caused them to become self-conscious and over-sensitive in the presence of foreigners.[12]

The fact was that even in 'civilized' Peking most Westerners regarded the Chinese – no matter how able, learned, aristocratic or wise – as cut-out figures in a topsy-turvy world quite divorced from their own. Life in Peking was in many respects like a visit to the theatre – entertaining, challenging, occasionally frightening but ultimately unreal. And, by convincing themselves that the Chinese operated under different criteria, the foreigners were able more easily to accept their suffering. As countless commentators had noted, it was clear that the Chinese did not feel physical pain as acutely as Westerners, so no doubt the same was true of their poverty. 'What is the point of organising coolies into labour unions?' one well-heeled American resident remarked.

What good have labour unions ever done to anybody? They've ruined America so that you can't get a decent servant in the whole country. Why can't all those people leave the coolies alone? They are quite happy as they are.[13]

Even more sensitive observers were apt to dwell on the 'aesthetics' of Chinese poverty like the diplomat who compared a coolie's naked torso to the mahogany of a Sheraton table sun-bleached to the colour of pale sherry.[14]

No Peking diplomat better sums up foreign attitudes to the Chinese than Sir Miles Lampson. Like many of his colleagues, he genuinely loved China (he even talked of retiring to Peking) but, as his diary entries reveal, he habitually saw himself in the role of indulgent parent guiding unruly offspring. 'These men are just like children when they are in the mood they were tonight,' he wrote after spending an evening playing 'Drunken Coachmen' with two senior Chinese ministers, 'really they are pleasant folk socially whatever their shortcomings as a race or as a government may be.'[15] It was these shortcomings – inadequate leadership, callous warlords, political ferment and lack of financial probity that gave even the most liberally minded foreigners their mandate to behave like colonial masters. In fact, there was often a considerable gap between official government policy and the views of expatriates. The Foreign Office's China policy tended to be far more liberal than that of the gunboat-loving British actually living in the country (especially in Shanghai). Rather surprisingly, the American philosopher and educationalist John Dewey, writing from Peking in 1919, remarked that although Britain was the leading power in China it was not the most aggressive, even suggesting that next to the United States Great Britain had been the most decent of all the great powers dealing with China. He made the additional point (all too familiar to British diplomats serving in Peking) that 'India was the only thing she really cares about and her whole policy here is controlled by that consideration with such incidental trade advantages as she can pick up.'[16]

Not everyone accepted the general view that China was too corrupt, too badly governed and too poor ever to change. As early as 1900, Sir Robert Hart, Inspector General of the Chinese Maritime Customs, was in no doubt that China would one day be a great power. And, at the very moment his country was bombing Shanghai in 1932, the Japanese Consul General remarked to Miles Lampson that it was quite possible in 100 years China would have absorbed Japan.[17] But even those who did predict China's future success were not immune to the patronising attitudes so prevalent among leading foreigners in Peking and which led so many of them into the trap of believing that they understood the Chinese better than the Chinese themselves. In consequence, few foreigners in the 1930s thought that Communism would prevail, believing the Chinese to be too individualistic, too humorous and too human to fall, as Winston Churchill put it, for such a 'silly system of economics or absurd doctrine of equality'.[18]

When Mao formally founded the People's Republic of China in Tiananmen Square on 1 October 1949, Peking was physically more or less intact, despite all the wars, sieges and occupations it had endured. It was left to globalisation and peacetime bulldozers to sweep away the city that the foreigners who are the subject of this book knew so well. But despite the dazzling skyscrapers and motorways of modern Beijing, it is still just possible for those with a nostalgic bent and a little imagination to wander through the legation quarter (where many of the old buildings survive), or the temples of the Western Hills so beloved by Peking's foreigners; to ride in the moonlight by pedicab under the walls of the Forbidden City; or to pause in some secluded corner of the Temple of Heaven, and for a fleeting moment catch a glimpse their world.

1
BOXERS V. BARBARIANS

By 14 August 1900, the foreign legations in Peking had been under Chinese attack for almost two months. But at 3 o'clock that afternoon relief finally came, when soldiers of the First Regiment of Sikhs and Seventh Rajputs – covered in mud but still resplendent in their scarlet turbans – poured on to the British Minister's lawn. Pathans, Cuttucks and the Punjab Infantry arrived soon afterwards, followed by the Royal Welch Fusiliers and Bengal Lancers – the latter magnificent on their Arab mounts. For the besieged it was the 'moment of a lifetime... better imagined than described'.[1] Within minutes, the war-shattered compound was transformed into a scene of joy and gratitude.

The commander of the British relief force, Lieutenant General Sir Alfred Gaselee, fearing that they had arrived too late, rode along Legation Street a little behind the vanguard. Catching sight of the American First Secretary's wife and her young cousin, he dismounted, then, taking Mrs Squiers' hands, said, 'Thank God, men, here are two women alive', and 'most reverently kissed Mrs Squiers on the forehead.'[2] A small blonde Englishwoman, overcome with emotion, threw her arms around the nearest Sikh[3] but Lady MacDonald, wife of the British Minister, Sir Claude, was more circumspect. Greeting a dishevelled naval officer (later to become an Admiral of the Fleet), she simply told him that she was delighted to see him. The young officer was surprised to find the besieged in such good condition, later observing that it was 'just as if we had run into a garden party. The lawn was crowded with ladies, looking very cool, clean and nice – rather an excited garden party but really like nothing else'.[4]

The Boxers' siege of the legations was the climax of a peasant uprising that, during the last years of the nineteenth century, had spread rapidly across northern China from its original base in Shantung. Its causes were many: foreign encroachment on Chinese territory, the introduction of Western technology, missionary interference in village life, famine, flood and the inability of the corrupt Ch'ing Dynasty to deal effectively with any of these issues. Calling themselves the 'Righteous Harmonious Fists', they were an amalgamation of various secret societies and martial arts groups. The foreigners dubbed them 'Boxers' because of the ritual exercises that they practised in public. The majority of them were young, male peasants (although there were also women's groups such as the 'Red Lanterns', 'Shining' and the 'Cooking-pan Lanterns'), who believed that their incantations and magic spells made them invulnerable in battle. In the circumstances, the Boxers might have been expected to turn on their Manchu rulers but instead, they chose an even more obvious target – the foreigners.

Although by the turn of the century there were 11 foreign legations in Peking,[5] the competition among them for Chinese concessions was so intense that their diplomats spent more time monitoring one another than they did China. Later, they were widely blamed for not anticipating the Boxer disaster, but even the vastly experienced Sir Robert Hart, Inspector General of the Chinese Imperial Maritime Customs Service, who by then had lived nearly 50 years in the country, did not fully grasp the reality of the threat. Just three weeks before the siege began he wrote, 'We have been crying, "Wolf" all the last fifty years and still life goes on as before.' But he added, 'Some day or other there is bound to be a cataclysm but as none can say *when*, it will probably be unprovided for and so will work very thoroughly and disastrously.'[6] On 20 June 1900, his prophecy came true.

With hindsight, the murder of a young missionary, Sidney Brooks, in December 1899 was a clear omen of the coming catastrophe. In the months following his death in Shantung, the diplomats received countless warnings from missionaries and Chinese converts, but the only authoritative foreigner to take them seriously was Bishop Favier, the Catholic Vicar-Apostolic of Peking. Further attacks on foreigners in the early months of 1900 still failed to stir the diplomats into action, even though by April, the Boxers were to be seen all over Peking flaunting their red sashes and knives.

On 20 May, just one month before the siege began, the 11 ministers formally debated Bishop Favier's plea that soldiers should be urgently summoned from Tientsin. Believing him unnecessarily alarmist, they decided instead to renew pressure on the Chinese government to deal with the situation. However, as the days went by, it became clear that far from suppressing the anti-foreign movement, the government was actively encouraging it, as no-one was more anxious to rid China of foreigners than the Empress Dowager herself, Tsu-hsi. She had risen to power nearly 40 years earlier, after the death of the Hsien-feng emperor in 1861. As the mother of his only son, she had been appointed one of eight regents when the five-year-old succeeded to the throne – a promotion that served only to sharpen her ambition. Emerging victorious from the power struggle that followed the boy's enthronement, she seized control of the Imperial Court and thus of the whole country. Having gained power, she had no intention of relinquishing it, though she knew that her authority could last only as long as her son remained a minor. Conveniently he died when only 17, probably of venereal disease, while his pregnant wife's death followed shortly after. Ignoring Confucian protocol, Tsu-hsi quickly nominated another minor as emperor, her nephew, and was thus able to prolong her regency. When years later the young Kuang-hsu emperor tried to exert his authority by supporting the political reform movement of 1898, his aunt crushed him utterly. From then until her death ten years later she remained in effect, the sole ruler of China.

Whatever the underlying tensions in Peking during the early summer of 1900 may have been, nothing marred the celebration of Queen Victoria's 81st birthday at the British Legation on the evening of 24 May 1900. Chinese paper lanterns swung from the trees, while the guests drank champagne and danced on the tennis court to music played by Sir Robert Hart's Chinese orchestra. The band, known as the 'I.G.'s Own', was the Inspector General's pride and joy. Barbers, shoemakers and carters were among the 20 odd musicians who had been lured from their former trades to don smart uniforms and learn to play Western instruments under the direction of a Portuguese conductor. By the late 1890s, no important social occasion in Peking was complete without the I.G.'s Own. Each Wednesday afternoon in the spring and autumn months, they gave an open-air concert on the Inspectorate lawn. Hart later recalled how well 'the lads' had played at the Queen's Birthday Party, adding: 'Little did we think that before that day month we should be flying for our lives to the protection of the Legation walls!'[7]

If outwardly all appeared calm, the foreigners were nevertheless increasingly fearful – and with reason. Chinese servants began to disappear without warning, language teachers did not arrive to give their lessons, threatening posters appeared on the streets, while reports of brutal attacks on Chinese Christians multiplied. As the tension mounted, so too did the heat and dust. Dining at the French Minister's house, Bertram Lenox Simpson, a Customs' employee, observed, 'We had Boxers for soup, Boxers with the entrées, and Boxers to the end.'[8] The burning of the railway station at Fengtai, a few miles outside the city walls, on 28 May, finally convinced the ministers to telegraph urgently for troops. But when some 400 men from America, Britain, Japan, Russia and Italy arrived two days later, they were too few, too poorly equipped and too late to slow down the anti-foreign momentum.

While missionary reports on the escalating violence became more frequent, the diplomats continued to dither. Then on 9 June, the Boxers burned down the racecourse – a potent symbol of the foreign presence in Peking. This, together with the disturbing news that the Mongol general Tung Fu-hsiang and his much-feared Kansu soldiers were encamped in the city, persuaded the ministers that the time had come to telegraph their governments. Sir Claude sent word to Vice-Admiral Sir Edward Seymour, whose ships, together with those of other foreign powers, were patrolling in Chinese waters off the Taku Bar near Tientsin. The following day he received confirmation that a substantial relief force, under the Admiral's command, was on its way to Peking by train.

Confidently expecting these troops to appear on 11 June, the diplomats sent hundreds of hooded Peking carts to meet them at the station. Nothing happened. After hours of waiting, the carts returned to the legations. Later that afternoon, Mr Sugiyama of the Japanese Legation, dressed in tailcoat and bowler hat, set out for the station in search of news. He had just passed through one of the Chinese city gates when he was attacked by Kansu soldiers, dragged from his cart and hacked to pieces. As one of the young British student interpreters noted in his diary,

> It is difficult to understand why more was not made of Sugiyama's death. News about it was flashed abroad, but it did not cause much of a stir beyond Tokyo. It seemed to take the murder of a European to raise a world-wide outcry …[9]

That murder eventually took place nine days later on 20 June. The events leading up to it were dramatic. Baron von Ketteler, the striking but confrontational German Minister, was not a man to pour oil on troubled waters.

As he walked down Legation Street on 13 June, he was outraged to see, sitting on the shafts of a cart, a full-fledged Boxer with his hair tied up in red cloth and a red girdle round his waist, sharpening a big carving knife on his boots. Such presumption was too much for the Baron, who set about him with his stick. When the Boxer ran off, von Ketteler had his young companion taken prisoner. A few hours later, as Lenox Simpson recorded, 'myriads of Boxers... armed with swords and spears, and with their red sashes and insignia openly worn... rushed into the Tartar city... slashing and stabbing at everyone indiscriminately'. That night, thousands of Chinese Christians were butchered or roasted alive and any building associated with foreigners was set ablaze. The streets rapidly filled with terrified people fleeing the nightmare. 'Everybody was panic-stricken and distraught... running, running, running.'[10]

The foreigners, meanwhile, hung grimly on to the expectation that their St George, in the shape of Admiral Seymour (rapidly nicknamed 'See No More'), would appear any minute to slay this terrifying Chinese dragon. It was probably as well that they did not know the true state of affairs. Seymour had decided to transport his forces from Tientsin to Peking by train – normally the quickest route. But these were not normal times. The Boxers had torn up the railway and disrupted his supply line. Less than 40 miles short of Peking, Seymour made the difficult decision not to press forward but to retreat to Tientsin – also now under attack by the Boxers. In the meantime, the admirals of the international fleet lying off the coast anxiously awaited news. As none came, they all, except for the Americans, decided to demand the surrender of the Taku forts flanking the mouth of the Peiho River. When this was rejected, the allies captured the forts on 17 June in a daring action that was at once interpreted by the Chinese government as a declaration of war.

Back in Peking, the telegraph wires had been cut, leaving the legations – now swollen with refugees – totally ignorant of events going on in the outside world. Unaware, therefore, that allied forces had taken the forts, each minister was astonished to receive, on 19 June, a red envelope containing an identical message from the Tsungli Yamen (the Chinese office for foreign affairs) stating that the diplomats and their dependents had until precisely 4 o'clock the following day to leave Peking but would be escorted to the coast by Imperial guards. This unexpected communication threw the ministers into a state of desperate indecision. Should they go and risk massacre or stay and be slaughtered? Polly Conduit Smith, a guest of the American First Secretary, Herbert Squiers, recorded how they restlessly moved, 'from one legation to another, arguing, talking – always talking'.[11] Finally, they voted to accept the Chinese ultimatum. However, Captain Francis Poole, who had recently arrived in Peking as a language student, thought they must be out of their minds. He set out the problem with chilling clarity:

> Heaven help us looking after all these helpless women and children through hostile country…it is impossible to get transport for 1000 souls and the Chinese escort would be useless to a long convoy in an unsettled country for 80 miles…*We must stay here and defend the legations.* [12]

Dr George Ernest Morrison, since 1897 Peking correspondent for *The Times*, agreed. Addressing the ministers, he did not mince his words, telling them that if they voted to leave Peking, the death of every man, woman and child would be on their heads.

His opinion carried weight, for not only were his reports on China highly respected, but he had also in recent days shown great courage in rescuing Chinese converts and stranded Americans alike. His physical exploits were legendary. As a teenager, he had walked alone across Australia, then, a few years later, survived a spear attack in Papua New Guinea. One piece of the spear had not been removed until many months later when Morrison reached Edinburgh, where he had gone to study medicine.

Like Morrison, von Ketteler was a man of action. Impatient with his colleagues' wavering, he decided to go himself to the Tsungli Yamen and stay until given a proper hearing. Taking an interpreter and a book to read (he anticipated a long wait), he set off in his sedan chair on the morning of 20 June. A few minutes later, he was dead – shot through the head. This shocking act was made more sinister by the fact that his assassin was not even a Boxer but a soldier in the Imperial Army. The ministers' dilemma was at least resolved. There could be no question of leaving the legations. The only problem now was how best to defend them.

By the time of Ketteler's murder, the legation quarter's population had risen to around 3,500. Added to its normal mix of diplomats, bankers and Customs Service staff were now missionaries with some 3,000 of their Chinese converts in tow, stranded tourists, engineers, hoteliers, journalists, academics, a Norwegian lunatic and even a group of Chinese schoolgirls. It was quickly decided that women, children and civilians would be housed in the British compound – the most spacious of the legations and the easiest to defend. It contained many houses and plenty of tall trees to give shade in the fierce summer heat. Although relatively large, normally it housed only 60 people. Now it had to give refuge to nearer 1,000. Carrying his mattress and pillow, the slight figure of Robert Hart was seen to pick his way carefully through all the confusion. As Hart's house was outside the defence lines, he was to lose everything (apart from his journals) – home, possessions and papers. It was a tragic outcome to nearly 40 years' service to the Chinese government. The problem of where to put the enormous number of Chinese converts was solved by Morrison, who persuaded a Manchu noble to give up his palace, the Su Wang Fu. The Fu, as it came to be known, played a key role in the defence of the legations, as did the Chinese Christians it sheltered. Despite being brought close to starvation (they were denied a share in the foreigners' food), they showed remarkable endurance, working all hours in appalling conditions.

On 20 June, as the 4 o'clock ultimatum drew closer, Sir Claude strolled out of the main gate of his legation with one of the sergeants. Together they looked at the sun glinting on the yellow tiles of the Imperial City wall and the 'Street of Permanent Peace'.[13] Another group of men gathered expectantly on the legation lawn, reminding one missionary of the moments just before the starting gun during the Eights Week boat races at Oxford. 'Five minutes more, three minutes more, two minutes more, and then firing was heard from the east…Sergeant Murphy ran up and saluted his senior officer. "Firing has begun, sir …" '[14] The phoney war was over.

***

The daunting task of defending several thousand civilians in less than one square mile against untold legions of belligerent Chinese now fell to the legation guards. With only 389 men and 18 officers, they were pathetically few. But they did at least have the support of 100 or so volunteers, several of whom were seasoned soldiers such as the Japanese military attaché, Colonel Shiba, and the language student Captain Poole.

The first major crisis occurred only a couple of days into the siege. An Austrian naval captain, who, as senior allied officer, had been placed in overall command, ordered his entire contingent of guards to abandon their respective legations and retreat to the British compound. This exigency had been planned for only as a desperate last measure and certainly not at this early stage. If the Chinese had taken advantage of the error, the siege would have been quickly over. As it was, the guards were immediately sent back to their posts and the situation retrieved at relatively small cost. Captain Poole was not impressed. 'What impossible people foreigners are!,'[15] he wrote in his diary. To the relief of those sharing this view (the German, French and Italian commanders emphatically did not), the very British Sir Claude MacDonald was hastily appointed commander-in-chief in place of the Austrian. International rivalry and a contorted chain of command made Sir Claude's already testing role a good deal harder. But, although he was not a man of brilliance or originality, his tact, cheerful composure and sound military instinct won grudging admiration even from the acerbic Morrison, whose early opinion had been anything but flattering: 'Surely the F.O. now recognise their folly in selecting an ill-read half educated infantry major, without brains, memory or judgment, for this most difficult post.'[16] By the end of the ordeal, he had changed his mind, 'He acted exceedingly well during the siege and was an example to all the other Ministers, especially to the French Minister who was a craven-hearted cur.'[17]

Having barely survived the Austrian's *faux pas*, the foreigners faced yet another calamity a few hours later – fire. Started just the other side of the British Legation wall, it seemed to Polly

> impossible that this enormous fire…would not in an hour or so completely burn us up…if I live to be a thousand, I could never see a queerer collection of people working together…coolies, missionaries, soldiers, and Ministers Plenipotentiary working and straining every muscle.[18]

A combination of a shift in wind direction and human valour eventually put out the fire, although another, started by the Chinese in the Hanlin Academy (immediately to the north of the British Legation), destroyed China's most precious library containing thousands of volumes of ancient scrolls and silk covered books.

Apart from the constant threat of fire, the besieged had to get used to the noise of whining bullets and exploding shells. Even the phlegmatic Poole felt the strain:

> Heavy rain, thunder, lightning, six hours attack firing from under cover. Was all night up, another rumour that the enemy was in the compound, brilliant flashes and rockets, fireballs, the elements and the enemy together. Flooded out in parts, a night of absolute hell.[19]

Although by the second day of the siege ground had already been lost with the abandonment of the Dutch and Belgian Legations, some comfort was drawn from the fact that the Boxers seemed incapable of aiming their weapons with any accuracy, most of their bullets and shells flying too high to do serious damage. Stripped of their 'magic', they were exposed as naive, untrained peasants. But even when joined by professional soldiers, the attacks remained curiously ineffective as the Chinese consistently failed to press home their advantage. After the siege, it became clear that this was due to the struggle between the anti-foreign camp surrounding the Empress Dowager and more moderate Chinese voices. Ultimately, it was this political disunity that was to save the legations.

Meanwhile, the besieged had only one question on their minds – when would the relief force arrive? In fact, Seymour's troops, many of them wounded, were struggling back to Tientsin, also under heavy attack, which they finally reached on 26 June. The foreigners' ignorance of Seymour's whereabouts was, a blessing, as morale might have collapsed completely had they known their rescuers were growing more distant with each passing hour.

In the absence of news, the foreigners tried to bring some order to their predicament by setting up committees. There was a general committee whose operations none could fathom, a fuel committee, a food committee, a sanitary committee, in fact, complained Lenox-Simpson, nothing but committees engaged in endless discussion, meeting in the safety of the British Legation.[20] However, a less cynical observer thought the resulting teamwork,

> ...a wonderful sight; everyone was slaving away with all his might...the Second Secretary, as master of the stables, was dashing about in his shirt, with his head tied up in a handkerchief, collecting fodder. M. Chamot, the hotel-keeper, and Fargo Squiers, the son of the American Secretary, who seemed to think the whole affair a huge joke, drove furiously to and fro, bringing in stores of all kinds. Mr Norris was barricading somewhere...the Second Secretary, was coal-hauling. The military people were organising and planning.[21]

Each day, the women produced the hundreds of sandbags needed to shore up the defences. As no material was considered too expensive, many were made of the finest silks, satins and brocades, contributing improbable splashes of opulence to the embattled scene. Drawing-room curtains and monogrammed bed linen were willingly sacrificed, while trouser-legs were found to be ideal for the purpose.

Ammunition, or lack of it, was the biggest worry, especially since each country used a different type of gun, making it impossible to share. A solitary piece of artillery and three machine guns were the total sum of the defence force's heavy weaponry. It soon became necessary to melt down every piece of metal that could be found – teapots, candlesticks, pewter pots and shell-cases – any scrap that might be converted into a bullet. Several weeks into the siege, an ancient French cannon was discovered abandoned in a shop in Legation Street. Ingeniously modified by an American gunner, it was mounted on a spare Italian gun carriage and fired off at the Chinese barricades. No doubt the belched black smoke and devastating blast intimidated the enemy more than its ineffective Russian shells. Nevertheless, the cannon, variously dubbed 'Old Betsey', 'Boxer Bill' and the 'Empress Dowager', was a symbol of international cooperation that did much to raise morale.

Even if ammunition was scarce, at least there was plenty of clean water, with a number of deep wells in the British Legation alone. Food was also reasonably plentiful at any rate for the foreigners to whom the possibility of sharing it with the Chinese seemed to have occurred only rarely. A bonanza of over 200 tons of wheat destined for the Forbidden City was discovered in a warehouse, adding to other stocks of grain and rice. This unexpected prize came with 15 mules, which, like the grain they had transported, soon ended up on someone's plate. A solitary cow was taken care of by Dmitri Pokotilov, who, as president of the Russo-Chinese bank, a director of the Russo-Chinese railway (and later Russian Minister), was one of Peking's more prominent foreign residents. Wounded early on in the siege, he became a familiar sight hobbling after the cow in his efforts to coax from her precious drops of milk for the many babies that each day grew visibly weaker. Polly found it hard to look at the 'pitiful collection of perambulators, huddled together... with limp, languid babies in them, some looking so ill that their parents must feel each day more of the siege brings their little ones nearer death'.[22]

Fresh meat was not a problem thanks to the many racing ponies and mules housed in the legation stables. To his great joy, Meyrick Hewlett, a student interpreter, thought he had saved his pony from the long arm of the food committee only to record in his diary a few weeks later, 'pony meat was running out and poor little "Memory" was sacrificed. I took leave of him just before he was shot'.[23] Early in the siege some variation of diet was possible owing to the tins and other foods salvaged from the two legation stores, Kierulff's and Imbeck's. But as it wore on, the foreigners were faced with an increasingly monotonous menu of rice and horse or mule meat. At least there was plenty of champagne in the diplomats' cellars – even if it was warm.

Such testing conditions bring out the best and worst in human nature. Many of the besieged dealt surprisingly well with their ordeal, while others, as Polly observed, completely disintegrated:

> People who, before the siege began, seemed to have reasonable intelligence, and if one had thought about such a thing, looked as if they would show up pretty well if they were put to it, have now gone to pieces entirely, lacking apparently the desire even to appear courageous. The men often make some trifling ailment an excuse to shirk all work for the common defence, and spend their time groaning over the situation and becoming more hateful daily to the men and women upon whom the real responsibilities of the siege are resting; while the women who have collapsed simply spend their hours, day and night, behind the nearest closed door, and await each fresh attack to indulge in new hysterical scenes.[24]

If the physical demands of the siege were unpleasant, many found the psychological strain worse. For even more terrifying than the prospect of a violent death was anticipation of the torture the foreigners could expect should the legations fall. In his *Times* report, Morrison graphically described Boxer atrocities: 'Women and children hacked to pieces, men trussed like fowls, with noses and ears cut off and eyes gouged out.'[25] At a low point in the siege, Polly wrote:

> The deaths are coming so frequently now that a final stand seems not improbable, and if when that is taken we continue to have the same percentage of deaths then we can well say our prayers. It is discussed quietly by the men that they will certainly kill their wives when that time comes...Apropos of this, I have in my pocket a small pistol loaded with several cartridges, to use if the worst happens. A Belgian secretary stole it from the armoury for me – 'in case you need it, mademoiselle.'[26]

Nevertheless, there were lighter moments. Gramophones provided music to soothe tattered nerves, while American missionaries gathered each evening outside the chapel to sing hymns or stirring songs such as 'Marching Through Georgia'. Madame Pokotilov's powerful renderings of operatic arias (she was a former St Petersburg diva) provoked particularly intense rifle-fire from the Chinese. Meanwhile the children, Polly observed, amused themselves with their newly invented game – 'Boxers', building their own small barricades with small sandbags and shouting '*Sha, sha*' (kill, kill).

If there were shirkers and cowards among the besieged, there were also heroes. Outstanding among these were the Chamots whose Hotel de Pékin was situated in a dangerously exposed part of the outer defences. Annie Chamot refused to take shelter in the British Legation, choosing instead to work with her husband cooking for the troops round the clock.[27] Paula von Rosthorn, wife of an Austro-Hungarian diplomat, also preferred the front line to being closeted in the British Legation with the other women. Frank Gamewell, an American missionary, was the most creative engineer among the besieged. He masterminded the fortifications which, with the help of the Chinese converts, he maintained throughout the siege. A man of unquenchable cheerfulness, Gamewell was everywhere at once and always where he was most needed. 'It's all right,' he would call out as he pedalled furiously round the defences on his bicycle dodging shells, 'it's never as bad as it sounds.'[28]

Given Western arrogance towards Asians, the most unexpected hero of the siege was a Japanese – Colonel Shiba. Captain Poole – not conspicuous for his love of foreigners – 'put Shiba on a golden pedestal for endurance and perseverance'.[29] The latter's tiny force of 24 soldiers suffered over 100 per cent casualties, since nearly half of them were killed while the survivors were all wounded more than once. The Japanese, together with Italian marines, were responsible for defending the Fu and its 3,000-odd Chinese refugees. Without Shiba's leadership and the gallantry of his men, the Fu would have fallen long before relief came.[30] Situated directly between the enemy and the British compound, the once beautiful palace was one of the two key positions vital to retain. The other was the Tartar city wall bordering the southern boundary of the legation quarter. If the Chinese had succeeded in mounting their big artillery on top of it, the foreigners would have been swiftly annihilated. But despite several dramatic moments, the wall remained under the foreigners' control.

As the siege wore on, there was no lessening of international tension. Polly noted how the besieged became increasingly disunited, the fiercest antagonism being directed at the British, '... for no other reason than that the other nations begrudge the strategical [sic] superiority of the English positions'. She hoped that the appointment of the American Secretary as Sir Claude's Chief of Staff would have a calming influence,

> ... for, should national feeling ever reach the top notch, this besieged area will separate – the Continentals on one side and the English and Americans on the other – and Heaven only knows how soon the end would come for everybody should this horror of military separation take place.[31]

The fact that the British and Americans openly referred to their allies as 'Froggie Dago', 'Sauerkraut Dago', 'Macaroni Dago' and 'Vodki Dago'[32] did little to improve international relations.

One woman particularly well placed to judge the niceties of national character was Jessie Ransome, a deaconess attached to the Anglican Mission in Peking. Working long hours in the small hospital that had been set up in the British Legation Chancery on the first day of the siege, she wrote:

> It was very curious and interesting to observe the way in which the different nationalities behaved. The Russians, for instance, were as a rule, most stolid and silent about their pain... the French and Italians were inclined to make the most of their wounds with a view to a little longer rest in hospital, while the British and Americans were usually in too great a hurry to make out that they were well enough to return to duty. But to both cases there were large exceptions. The only nationality of whose conduct one could predict anything with almost absolute certainty was the Japanese. They invariably were brave and cheery and made as light as possible of their pains... and used to be exceedingly kind to one another.

The makeshift hospital was remarkably successful. Despite serious shortages of everything – especially medical supplies – only 14 died of the 120 cases admitted. The two doctors (one German, one British) with a handful of skilled nurses ingeniously improvised the essentials needed to keep their patients alive. Women's underclothes, muslin curtains and fine linen sheets provided bandages, while suppurating wounds were dressed with bags of powdered peat and fine sawdust. Great attention was given to the patients' diet – 'sometimes a little "game" would be provided for some special invalid, in the shape of a magpie or a few sparrows, which were daintily cooked and served, no questions asked'.[33]

Jessie Ransome was an exceptional woman, but by the middle of July, she, along with even the most stalwart of the besieged, had had enough. Everyone was depressed; casualties were rising at an alarming rate; the Chinese were getting palpably closer as they inched forward behind their elaborate barricades. The all-important Fu had been reduced to a barely defensible rubble, while both ammunition and food supplies were sinking fast. The stench of dead bodies was intolerable as were the dense clouds of flies they attracted, the mosquito bites and the appalling sticky heat. However, as Sir Claude MacDonald noted, 'The night is darkest before the dawn.' And a dawn of sorts was about to break.

2

CLEARING UP

A devastating mine explosion under the French legation, combined with a particularly intense bombardment, led Sir Claude to describe Friday 13 July as the most harassing day of the whole siege. His young orderly officer wrote to his parents wondering if they were at the Eton and Harrow cricket match, adding, 'We are gradually being closed in upon and unless relief comes soon we shall be in an awful fix.'[1] The French Minister, Stéphen Pichon, reacted by burning his papers and writing in his diary, '*C'est le massacre final qui se prépare.*'[2] But just when even the most determined optimists had lost all hope, there was a surprising twist to the drama.

The day after the *dies horribilis*, the first of a series of messages from the Chinese authorities (who had not officially communicated with the legations since 25 June) was delivered to Sir Claude. It was from Prince Ching – an ineffectual moderate but a favourite with the foreigners. The letter promised safe passage to the foreigners if they abandoned their own military escort and placed themselves under the protection of the Tsungli Yamen. This offer was naturally greeted with derision but a second message, delivered soon afterwards, was not only more conciliatory but made the extraordinary claim that the Chinese government was doing all it could to protect the foreigners.

Cut off as they were from their own side, the foreigners were equally ignorant of events within the Chinese ranks. They had no means of monitoring the conflicting influences surrounding Tsu-hsi, on which their fate hung. Li Hung-chang, Viceroy at Canton, and Yuan Shi-kai, Governor of Shantung, were key figures who well understood the catastrophe China faced should she take on all the powers at once. Like many of their colleagues in the South, they had counselled the Empress Dowager to put down the Boxers and had pointedly chosen not to respond to her demands to send troops. These more worldly politicians had long since understood that – disagreeable though it may be – China's long-term interests lay in dealing with foreigners, not murdering them. But ranged against such temperate leaders were powerful conservatives like Prince Tuan, whose soldiers, having joined forces with the Boxers, were among the legations' most relentless assailants. The role of the Empress Dowager's loyal supporter, Jung-lu, commander of the Imperial troops in Peking, is harder to fathom. At first he supported the Boxers but was later widely believed to have imposed restraint on them by choosing not to deploy heavy artillery and by keeping the attackers short of ammunition.

It was no coincidence that on 14 July, the day that Sir Claude received the first message, the anti-foreign camp suffered a major defeat when Tientsin fell to the allied forces. Furthermore, the Empress Dowager received an unwelcome memorial from 13 of her southern viceroys and governors urging her to protect the foreigners and suppress the Boxers. Furiously back-pedalling, the Imperial Court now published a number of appeasing decrees as well as reiterating their claim that they were doing everything in their power to protect the foreigners.

The besieged, meanwhile, could only guess at the politics. All they knew for certain was that on 17 July a curious truce came into being. At first they lived, as a missionary put it, in a 'state of amazed suspense, every hour saw a new marvel'.[3] Not only were their tormentors now smiling and waving at them from their barricades but before long, they were trading eggs and even rifles. One of Hart's bandsmen talked his way into the British compound in search of medical help for his severed ear. A dog with messages tied round its neck trotted back and forth between the Chinese and Japanese, while Sir Claude sat smoking on the Tartar wall with an enemy officer. The Tsungli Yamen sent gifts of fruit, vegetables, ice and flour in the name of the emperor, leading some of the more enterprising among the besieged to set up melon clubs. 'The luscious gourd was allowed its proper season to cool in the well; then, brought forth with care, it was duly scooped and seasoned with claret.'[4] While some ate melons and others boated on the canal, the British played cricket. It was, however, soon clear that the cease-fire was not universally supported. To the south and east, where Prince Ching and Jung-lu were in command, it seemed genuine enough. But from Prince Tuan's domain, to the north and west there was only a worrying silence.

Any dialogue with the Chinese authorities – however opaque – was of course welcome. But more important for the foreigners' morale were the messages, which from 18 July began to filter through from Tientsin. There, the allied authorities – uncertain whether or not the besieged were still alive – were taking their time to organise a new relief force. Determined not to repeat the Seymour debacle, they were slowly amassing an army big enough this time to do the job properly. It did not help that four of the powers were already fighting wars – the British in South Africa, the Americans in the Philippines, the Russians on the Manchurian border and the French in Indo-China. Japan, geographically the closest, was able to send by far the biggest force thus immediately antagonising her arch-enemy, Russia. Germany, meanwhile, anxious to be present at the denouement of a drama launched so spectacularly by the murder of its envoy, was transporting troops from Europe as fast as possible. In the event, they arrived too late to play a significant role, but von Ketteler's assassination gave the Kaiser the moral advantage when it came to choosing a supreme commander. With some reluctance, the other powers agreed that the honour be given to the Prussian Field Marshal, Count Alfred von Waldersee. As this unusual army was being summoned from all corners of the globe, the Pope gave it his blessing, observing, 'these soldiers … are embarking on the first war since the days of the Crusades actually made in the cause of civilization'.[5]

Back in Peking it was clear that by 27 July, the truce was beginning to crumble. In fact, a former governor of Shantung, Li Peng-heng, rabidly anti-foreign and a great favourite of Tsu-hsi's, had arrived at the Imperial Court to inject new heart into the reactionary cause. Appointed deputy commander of the Northern Armies, he purged the imperial advisors who had advocated dialogue with the foreigners. Under this fresh xenophobic influence, the legation quarter yet again came under heavy attack. Depressing though this was, the besieged were at least still in contact with the outside world. The Tsungli Yamen continued to send messages daily, some so routinely diplomatic that it might have seemed to the casual observer that China's relations with the foreign envoys were entirely normal. But, as Sir Claude sat at his desk responding to elaborate Chinese condolences on the death of the Duke of Edinburgh, a shell burst into his room shattering all the windows. Hart, having received equally incongruous letters

from his Chinese employers, one day tossed a message of his own over the legation wall addressed to his tailor in England: 'Send quickly two autumn office
suits and later two winter ditto with morning and evening dress, warm cape
and four pairs of boots and slippers.'[6] The clothes arrived on 26 October.

As the legations' outer defences collapsed, the Bell Tower (built to
commemorate Queen Victoria's Jubilee) became the centre of the foreigners'
shrinking world. Here a confusing string of messages – not all of them genuine –
from their would-be rescuers were posted for everyone to see. On 1 August
they heard that the relief force was about to march and ten days later came
the news for which they had waited so long, 'Strong force of Allies advancing.
Twice defeated enemy. Keep up your spirits.'[7] It was signed: General Gaselee.

On his arrival in Tientsin from India on 27 July, Gaselee had galvanised the
allies into action. The relief force consisted of roughly 20,000 men, the Japanese
contributing the lion's share of around 10,000. Given the normal mistrust and
suspicion that exists between nations, it was a remarkable coalition. It was also
an exotic one. There were French Zouaves in red and blue, blond Germans
in pointy helmets, Italian Bersaglieri with tossing plumes, Bengal cavalry on
Arabian stallions, turbaned Sikhs, Japanese, Russians and English.[8] Adding a
touch of glamour were the three Maharajas present.[9] The Dutch, meanwhile,
provided their own expeditionary corps of ten men and one sergeant.[10]

This impressive army started for Peking at dawn on 4 August, marching up
both banks of the Peiho River. The different contingents may have been allies
in name but were hardly so in spirit. Like athletes on their starting blocks, each
yearned for the glory of being first through the Peking wall. Their political masters, meanwhile, were nervously calculating the odds, knowing full well that,
should the Ch'ing Dynasty collapse, whichever nation had the most troops on
the ground would reap the greatest territorial rewards. But for the individual
soldier, whatever his nationality, the real problem was how to survive the appalling conditions on the march. Suffocating temperatures and lack of drinking
water were to prove far more dangerous than the Chinese. The Japanese and
Russians coped best with the heat but the Americans, 'thanks to the silly felt
hats they wear, had an awful time'.[11] The Russians were admired for their skill
in living off the country – if not for their sanitary arrangements. As usual the
Japanese won plaudits for their dash, courage and capacity for forced marches,
one American private commenting, 'The Japs are America's best friends. They
are as bold as lions.'[12] As for the Indian troops, some thought them cruel and
not up to scratch, while others considered them amongst the bravest soldiers

in the world. Although everyone had a different view of everyone else, all were united in despising the French: 'the dirtiest and filthiest soldiers here [and] the only ones who have shirked', recorded a US marine.[13]

After three days, the smaller groups returned ignominiously to Tientsin leaving only the Americans, British, Japanese and Russians still in the field. The race to be first into the legation quarter intensified, involving a good deal of plotting. In the end, to the profound irritation of the others, it was the British (despite having marched consistently in the rear) who won the crown – more by good luck than strategic brilliance. Led by English officers, the Indian soldiers stumbled their way through the unguarded water gate in the Tartar wall, along a sewer and into the legations. Here, Sir Claude MacDonald – immaculate in flannels and waxed moustaches – stood waiting to greet them. The siege was over.

At least it was for the legations. It took a further two days before Bishop Favier and his decimated Christian flock were rescued from the Peitang Cathedral just a couple of miles to the north-west. It was the Japanese – the only non-Christians among the relief force – who accomplished the task. The Peitang had suffered far greater hardship than the legations. The 3,500 individuals under the Bishop's protection were nearly all Chinese and included hundreds of women and children. There had been less food, no truce and only 43 French and Italian sailors to defend them. Their survival was largely thanks to the inspirational leadership of their military commander (killed two weeks before relief arrived), the 23-year-old naval lieutenant Paul Henry, and of the Bishop himself. Described by a British officer as 'a splendid specimen of the Church Militant [whose] bravery is equalled by his modesty',[14] Favier later lamented:

> It is almost a pity that we were not all massacred. We should have died martyrs, and it would have spared us the pain of seeing our work of nearly half a century destroyed … but we have energy and we will begin again.[15]

***

> What a tangled wilderness of ideas! What a conglomeration! Will law and order ever come out of it? There are eight foreign armies established in the very capital of China. The emperor, empress dowager, empress and their court have left all and fled to parts unknown. China is without her ruling head.[16]

So wrote Sarah Conger, wife of the American Minister who, unlike most survivors of the siege, was to remain in Peking with her husband for some years. Many foreigners had looked forward to the Empress Dowager's public humiliation and felt cheated when they learned of her successful escape along with most of the court. She fled the Forbidden City through its northern gate in the early hours of 15 August – allegedly disguised as a peasant. The unfortunate emperor – his favourite concubine having been dispatched down a well – was given no choice but to accompany his aunt. Although the imperial convoy had a large military escort, its progress was hampered by thousands of refugees for whom there was no food and – with the wells full of decomposing corpses – little water. But once it became clear that the foreigners were not in pursuit, Tsu-hsi regained her confidence and began to enjoy the novel experience of seeing her country and people at first hand. After spending three weeks in Taiyuan (where, only a couple of months earlier the governor of Shansi had watched the decapitation of 45 foreigners), the 'Tour of Inspection' continued to its ultimate destination, Sian, reaching it on 26 October.

In Peking, meanwhile, there was little to report but misery. An American missionary described the horror:

> Dead bodies of soldiers lay singly or in heaps, in some instances covered with a torn old mat, but always a prey of the now well-fed pariah dogs…the huge pools of stagnant water were reeking with putrid corpses of man and beast; lean cats stared wildly at the passer-by from holes broken in the fronts of shops boasting such signs as 'Perpetual Abundance', 'Springs of Plenty', 'Ten Thousand Prosperities…' One might read over the door of a place thrice looted, and lying in utter ruin, the cheerful motto, 'Peace and Tranquillity.'[17]

After the initial euphoria, many siege veterans felt a sense of anti-climax. As one British diplomat put it: 'The joy and excitement of the relief have given way to disgust and confusion all round.'[18] They did not even have the comfort of mail since, as it was assumed they were all dead, it had been turned back at Tientsin. The foreigners had regained their lives but the structures and organisation that had enabled them to survive the siege had been replaced by new uncertainties and a disorder that at times bordered on anarchy. Nigel Oliphant, an employee of the Imperial Chinese Bank (whose brother had been killed in the siege and who had himself been wounded), captured the atmosphere of ennui and drift in his diary:

I found my first night in a Chinese house rather stuffy and uncomfortable...
it is anything but an ideal residence as the insect population is enormous and
aggressive... A long heavy day. I was up at 5 am, meaning to go out... but the
weather was so wet that I had to stay in... no letters have come as yet... nor
any stores, and not even our highest authorities can tell us when anything is
going to happen or what is going on between here and Tientsin... With infinite
difficulty we got three minute eggs, two hens and three small chickens... still
raining steadily... I went to the Carriage Park to try and get some loot from the
Indian troops, but got nothing except a few rotten bracelets... In spite of the
rain it is vilely hot and muggy.[19]

Against this backdrop of desolation, the allies planned a victory parade. And,
to drive home the point, they decided to hold it at the very heart of Imperial China – the Forbidden City. Journalists were banned from attending –
except for one. Henry Savage Landor, who had asked permission to cover the
event but was turned away by the American commander General Chaffee
with the words, 'There are things in this world that are sacred! The Imperial
Palace is one of them.'[20] The Russian general, Linievitch, was more amenable.
Delighted to spite the Americans, he at once invited Landor to ride with him
at the head of the whole procession so that the latter was able to savour fully
the moment when the huge studded wooden gates of the Forbidden City were
swung slowly back on their 'rusty and squeaky hinges'. Recalling the experience
(if somewhat fancifully), he wrote:

When one thought that for five centuries, since this Palace was built these gates
had barred the way to all civilising influence, when one realised that, whatever
had occurred outside in the way of intercourse with foreigners, none had ever
penetrated these sacred walls. It is excusable if one felt somewhat proud to be
the first of one's race to set foot inside this Forbidden City.

Once the armies were through the gates and assembled in the marble courts,
the British artillery fired a 21-gun salute. 'The spell was broken the deed was
done,' wrote Landor, 'what Celestials had kept most sacred for 500 years, foreign devils desecrated in two seconds.' There followed a great parade led by
the ministers:

They were an extraordinary looking set, dressed up in the quaintest of
costumes... In front stood prominent the lumbering bony figure of Sir Claude
MacDonald, in an ample grey suit of tennis clothes and a rakish panama slouch

hat, which he wore at a dangerous angle. He walked jauntily with gigantic strides, moving his arms about as if preparing for a boxing match. To his right the Russian Minister seemed quite reposeful by contrast…Next to him came the Representative of the French Republic, in a garb which combined the requirements of the Bois de Boulogne on a Sunday with the convenience of a tropical attire on a weekday. Mr Conger, the American Minister stood ponderously behind, dressed in white cottons and military gaiters, while a horde of secretaries, students and interpreters in various fancy garbs, made part of the distinguished crowd.

A Russian military band enthusiastically played each national anthem but fell silent when it was the turn of their hated enemies, the Japanese, described by Landor as 'those wonderful and absolutely perfect little soldiers and officers who have astounded the world by their bravery and strategic skill'. After the Americans slouched by Landor noted how everyone had to suppress laughter at the goose-stepping Germans, while the bedraggled French could scarcely walk. With the parade over, the foreign dignitaries repaired to a garden where on six small plates were spread a few stale foreign biscuits, walnuts and dried fruit. Several court attendants stood 'with sulky faces and long gowns reaching to their toes' serving out boiling tea. 'There was a rush for both tea and eatables and the conquering allies walked off even with the plates and cups!'[21]

But the foreigners were after more than cheap crockery. The numerous eyewitness accounts of the pillaging in the weeks following the allied capture of Peking make depressing reading. One American correspondent, Jasper Whiting (working for the London *Westminster Gazette*), indignantly recorded:

> The looting of Peking was the most extraordinary as well as the most outrageous proceeding connected with the Boxer troubles. It was not confined, however, to any set of individuals or to any nationality, nor was it confined to the men. I was told upon the best authority that it was started by women. Within five minutes after the doors of the British Legation had been thrown open to admit the Allied Troops, two French ladies…rushed out of the gate and raced each other to a certain shop in Legation Street, which they had frequented in calmer times, and which they knew to be deserted. In ten minutes they were back, their arms loaded down with silks and embroideries and furs and jade, a triumphal smile upon their faces, both well repaid for the privations they had endured during the past few weeks.[22]

Whiting described the looting as a 'disease', moreover one so contagious that even Polly Condit Smith succumbed. She had tried to resist, nobly refusing a beautiful sable offered to her by a Russian diplomat. But when she saw the same fur eagerly accepted by another woman without a qualm, her 'soul was torn with conflicting emotions'. A few hours later, a Belgian (the same who had so recently given her a revolver) presented her with a tortoise-shell bracelet set with handsome pearls taken off the arm of a Chinese officer he had just killed. Polly confessed, 'I surprised myself by promptly accepting it.'[23] Herbert Squiers' reputation for 'acquiring' works of art cast such a shadow over his subsequent career that it prevented him from becoming minister in Peking or standing for the governorship of New York. The excuse everyone offered, Whiting noted, was that if they didn't take it someone else would.

On 17 August, just three days after the relief, Morrison reported on the looting to *The Times*, describing how the French and Russians now controlled sections of the Imperial City where it was believed the Imperial treasure was buried. The Japanese, he claimed, had seized a hoard of half-a-million taels of silver. Meanwhile, the British dealt with the problem by legalising it. All pillaged goods in their sector (Peking had been divided into eight, one for each of the allies) were officially auctioned every afternoon at the legation, the proceeds going into a fund for the soldiers. Morrison was quick to wire *The Times* about one particularly outrageous piece of looting – the removal of the astronomical instruments from the city wall. Erected by the Jesuits, they had for more than two centuries been one of Peking's chief glories. Now half were shipped off to Paris and the other half to Berlin. As Morrison pointed out, 'They are so beautiful that even the Chinese, who wrecked every other evidence of foreigners within reach, left the instruments untouched throughout the recent outbreak.'[24]

The looting was bad enough but the wanton cruelty worse. The Boxers having long since discarded their scarlet clothing were indistinguishable from other working Chinese, many of whom lost their lives to trigger-happy allied soldiers. Ordinary Peking citizens, in a desperate attempt to survive this second wave of brutality, were seen everywhere destroying Boxer symbols and replacing them with hastily contrived allied flags – the Japanese, as the most easily reproduced, being the most common. Outside Chinese doors hung banners proclaiming, 'May I come under the protection of your flag?' and 'I protected a missionary, please protect me' or, more originally, 'I am a damned good Christian.'[25] Stories of rape and torture were rampant, each nation accusing the other of the most despicable acts. Among the foreign soldiers there was a belief that as the Chinese were sub-human, any atrocity committed against them was justified. When it came to violence there was little to choose between Boxer and barbarian.

***

But, in contrast to the horror on Peking's streets, the foreigners were for the first time able to enjoy the cultural glories of the city. Once the gates of the Forbidden City had opened, they flooded through them, eager to see the many courts and buildings of the Imperial Palace and to feast their eyes on the fabled jades and porcelains, the lacquer, woodcarvings and bronzes, the immense mirrors and richly embroidered silk hangings. They were particularly curious to see the private apartments of the Empress Dowager, where in the words of an English officer, 'in the usual spirit of tourists, to whom nothing is sacred, many would romp on her bed or sit on the emperor's gilded chair so that they could boast of once having occupied the Throne of China.'[26]

The resourceful Polly was among those determined to see the Imperial Palace before leaving Peking and, like Landor, approached General Chaffee for permission. To her surprise, he refused her, pounding his fist on the table and claiming that there were sights of war there that no American girl should see. Polly thought this:

> ridiculous, as the sights of war referred to were simply the heaps of corpses...He was right, inasmuch as these were not pretty things to see; but as I had been in the midst of war for two months, and seen all these things many times I did not feel that it was just in him to deny me the privilege now of being able to get a bird's eye view of this wonderful park.

She too turned to the Russians for help and was consequently escorted through the Forbidden City by a posse of Cossacks. Once inside its walls, Polly was so overwhelmed by the 'magnificent simplicity' of the landscape gardening that she rapidly forgot the putrefying corpses outside:

> We crossed the wonderful white marble bridges which spanned the artificial waterways, and the glorious lotus-flowers were all in bloom on the banks...They are such gorgeous, big flowers they are like the Chinese architecture – wonderful in big, sweeping lines. We rode on through this semi-cultured landscape, where every detail was so carefully attended to that the ensemble was a complete joy to the senses, and after the eight weeks we had been barricaded in our Legation district this park seemed like heaven.[27]

The new Summer Palace, 12 miles west of Peking and built by the Empress Dowager on money intended for China's new navy, was another magnet for the foreigners. Consisting of numerous picturesque temples and pavilions set around a lake it was, as Sarah Conger described it, a dreamland of rocky hills, glistening yellow tiled roofs, grottoes, marble terraces with white, carved marble balustrades, large bronze statues and gardens with flowering shrubs and spreading trees.[28] Landor, in turn, was struck by the vast quantity of clocks and mechanical toys he saw crammed into the Imperial apartments:

> Puppets of abnormally-proportioned eyes, mouth and legs, which spun round wildly when they were wound up; articulated crowing cocks, artificial Swiss humming-birds, speaking dolls...German painted vases that would set on edge the teeth of the most inartistic were prominently displayed in the company of jade vases of exquisitely refined shape and proportion, cloisonné work of delicate finish and enamels of mellow, refined and harmonious tints.[29]

But of all Peking's mysteries so suddenly revealed, none excited the foreigners' awe more than the Temple of Heaven set in its great park, twice the area of the Forbidden City. Once a year, the emperor came to worship at the white marble Altar of Heaven. For a week he performed intricate rituals and acts of purification, which, if completed successfully, were China's best hope for a good harvest. Louis Viaud, better known as the French novelist, Pierre Loti, was shocked to find Indian cavalry encamped in such a sacred place, noting how their horses trampled and fouled the temple grounds. But much worse, on the Altar of Heaven itself, '...there rose whirlwinds of disgusting smoke, the British having chosen this place to burn their livestock which had died from foot and mouth disease'.[30]

Loti, who liked to wear make-up and was only five feet tall, was one of the more unusual figures to be caught up in the Boxer troubles. A vivid recorder of post-siege Peking, he was an acknowledged influence on Marcel Proust and in 1891, had been elected to the Académie Française. He was also a professional naval officer and as such, one of the thousands of additional troops drafted into Peking after the siege. On a bleak October day in 1900, as the sleet turned to snow, he stood before one of the city's great gates waiting to enter:

> The wall of Peking crushes us. It is a giant 'Babylonian' structure...intensely black under a dead morning light of snow and autumn. It thrusts into the sky like a cathedral and stretches unchanging into the distance for miles and miles. Not a soul approaches this city, no one. Not a blade of grass grows along these walls; the soil is rutted, dusty and as sinister as ashes, with shreds of clothing lying

about, bits of bone and a skull. And, from the top of each black crenellation, a
crow salutes us with a deathly croak as we pass.

Loti goes on to describe how he and his companions, dejected and chilled to
the bone, stood there longing to see some sign of life when,

> from a gate in the colossal enclosure there emerges an enormous slow brown
> animal padded with wool like a giant sheep – and then two, three, ten of them:
> a Mongol caravan that flows towards us in this infinite silence broken only by
> the cawing of crows. In an endless file, the massive camels of Mongolia sheathed
> in fur…with manes like lions, process past…their feet sink deep in the dust
> deadening any sound of their tread. The silence is unbroken by their passing;
> the Mongolians who lead them, cruel distant figures, throw us furtive, hostile
> glances.[31]

For the Chinese trying to rebuild their lives, as for the many thousands of
foreign troops garrisoned in Peking, it was a long, cold winter. But slowly life
began to creep back onto the streets, so that by January 1901 Sarah Conger
could write: 'We cannot any longer call Peking a deserted city. The Chinese
are gaining more confidence, and so are we.'[32] Captain Casserly noted further
signs of returning normality – rickshaw coolies arguing about the fare, crowds
refusing to make way for foreign officers, the rattle of Peking carts and the endless trains of coal-bearing camels. Wandering down Hatamen street with his
Indian army colleagues, he saw jugglers, dancing bears, peepshows, fortune-
tellers, peddlers of all kinds and an old clothes merchant hammering nails into
a bare patch of wall so that he could hang up his wares including a tarnished
gold-embroidered mandarin coat with 'a suggestive rent and stain that spoke
all too plainly of the fate of the last owner.'[33]

Having exhausted the looting and carried out punitive expeditions, the
allied soldiers were put to work cleaning up the city, with the result that,
for a while at least, the fearful stench usually hanging over Peking receded.
The British, meanwhile, extended the railway by cutting through the wall
and bringing it to a new terminus close to Chien-men. This was in the face
of bitter opposition from the Chinese to whom the dragon was a symbol of
Peking. By piercing the wall, the British had sliced into the dragon's flesh, causing its blood (the city's wealth) to ooze away. Sarah Conger was one of the few
foreigners to understand the railway's significance to the Chinese, describing
how after the destruction of an ancient cemetery they were forced to carry

the bones of their ancestors away in baskets, adding, 'this railroad work of the foreigner must be to them a most heartrending affair.'[34]

By the summer of 1901, the foreign troops had nearly all gone. Shortly before von Waldersee's own departure in June, the French hosted a gala dinner to mark the end of the occupation and herald a bright new chapter in China's relations with the powers. It took place on a warm, May night in an old palace which, Loti noted, had been especially lit for the occasion:

> Strange lanterns some of glass dripping pearls, others of rice paper in the form of birds and lotuses... People are coming and going in festive costume – officers from all the European nations and Chinese in long silk robes wearing the official hat from which cascade peacock feathers. A table is set for seventy and we await the various guests. Followed by little processions, they arrive from the four corners of Peking, some on horseback, others in carriages or rickshaws or sumptuous sedan chairs. Preceded by their red visiting cards, the Chinese dignitaries arrived, Li Hung-chang, the Chief Justice of Peking, the Empress Dowager's representative – all expressionless and followed by a horde of silk-clad servants. Western uniforms blend with mandarin robes, pointed hats and coral buttons. The presence of Chinese among barbarians at the heart of the Imperial City is one of the strangest incongruities of our time... Towards the end of this bizarre, essentially blasphemous feast when the roses are starting to dip their heads in the great precious vases, our general, winding up his champagne toast, addresses himself to these yellow princes, 'Your presence among us,' he says, 'proves sufficiently that we have come here not to make war on China but simply on an abominable sect.' The Empress' representative thereupon picks up the ball with all the flexibility of the Far East and without a wrinkle shifting on his yellow courtier's mask, he, who has been a crafty and dedicated Boxer, replies, "In the name of his Imperial Majesty I thank the European generals for having come to lend assistance to the government of our county in one of the gravest crises it has ever encountered." A moment of stupefied silence and the glasses are drained.[35]

Loti was not alone in believing that the Boxer uprising had delivered a death blow to the old Peking – the city that with its enigmas and hidden treasures had for so many centuries both fascinated and frustrated foreigners. But now the barbarian genie was well and truly out of the bottle and for the next half century it would prove impossible to push it back.

3

RETROSPECT

The allied occupation of 1900 was not the first time that Peking had been
overwhelmed by Westerners. In 1860, the emperor's old Summer Palace, the
exquisite Yuan Ming Yuan, partly built by Jesuit architects in the seventeenth
century, was burned and looted by an Anglo-French expeditionary force under
the command of Lord Elgin. This seemingly mindless act of vandalism was
born out of deep frustration with the Ch'ing authorities' steadfast refusal –
despite treaty agreements – to allow British and French diplomats to live
in the capital. As was so often the case, Britain's chief motivation was trade,
but France was also keen to establish diplomatic relations in order to protect
the growing number of its missionaries working in China. However, since
the middle of the eighteenth century, when Britain's merchants in Canton
had first pressed for a representative in Peking authorised to negotiate on
their behalf directly with the central government, all attempts to establish a
permanent mission in Peking had failed, most memorably Lord Macartney's
in 1793 and Lord Amherst's in 1816. Despite such setbacks, the Westerners
refused to give up, for as British diplomat Bertie Freeman-Mitford (later Lord
Redesdale) commented:

> It used to be a cardinal article of faith ... during the fifties, that if once we could
> throw Peking open to foreign diplomacy all would be well ... We should be in

touch with the Emperor and his Court and we could not fail to convert the most recalcitrant of mandarins to the adoption of our Western civilization: perhaps China might become a Christian country.[1]

To the Chinese, however, the very idea of non-subordinate foreigners living permanently in Peking was not one to be taken seriously, despite their having been forced to agree to it in principle. Their response to the problem was simply to ignore it. But Lord Elgin was not put off so easily. In the summer of 1860, he sent British and French interpreters (under flag of truce) to talk to the Chinese who instead of negotiating, tortured and killed a number of them. For Elgin, this was the last straw. Determined to make the point once and for all, he now ordered the small force that had landed in Tientsin on 1 August to enter Peking and destroy the old Summer Palace which lay a few miles to the west of the city. A more disastrous beginning to formal diplomatic relations with China would be hard to imagine. Nevertheless, in the absence of the emperor (who had fled north with Tsu-hsi and most of the court to his hunting lodge at Chengde) and with the Yuan Ming Yuan still smouldering, Lord Elgin and Baron Gros (for France) signed the 'Convention of Peking' on 24 October 1860 with the emperor's younger brother, Prince Kung. This treaty explicitly and unequivocally stipulated the right of British and French representatives to take up residence in China's capital city. After two Opium Wars,[2] three treaties[3] and the sacking of the old Summer Palace, Western diplomats had at last arrived in Peking.

A few days after signing the treaty, Elgin summed up his feelings in a letter to Lord Carnarvon:

> Here I am at last…This place is not in itself very much worth the trouble we have taken to get to it, and the existing Chinese Govt. hardly deserves the pains which we have been at to establish relations with it. But whatever may be the issue of the civil conflict now raging in China, whatever be the Dynasty which gains the upper hand, we may I think, be assured that the British Treaty of 1858 supplemented by the Convention of 1860 will be the bases on which the relations of this great Country with Christendom will hence-forward rest. Whether for good or for evil China is now opened up to Christianity and Commerce.[4]

Prince Kung was even less enthusiastic: 'We humbly believe that the various barbarians have the habits of curs and swine. The English barbarians are the most unrighteous and uncontrollable.'[5]

Although the Chinese had done everything possible to prevent Western diplomats from establishing themselves in Peking, the city was well used to foreigners. Cosmopolitan traders had operated there for centuries; tribute missions arrived regularly from distant lands while colonies of Russians, Indian Buddhist monks and, most notably, Jesuit priests had, at various times, flourished. But until October 1860, resident barbarians – wherever they came from and whatever their rank – had kowtowed. This time it was different. Europeans had succeeded in forcing themselves on Peking with all the diplomatic trappings of their own culture. For the first time in the city's long history, foreigners with inflated notions of equality would be living permanently within its walls – a mere stone's throw from the dragon throne itself.

In the West, diplomacy was considered a hallmark of the civilised world but in China it had come to mean something very different. Beginning with the Treaty of Nanking in 1842, the Chinese had been forced to sign one unequal treaty after another. Humiliating concessions such as the opening of treaty ports (where extraterritoriality entitled foreigners to live under their own laws), the import of opium, the expansion of missionary work and the ceding to Britain of Hong Kong had fully exposed China's weakness in the face of foreign pressure. Furthermore, in 1844, 'the most favoured nation' clause had been inserted into a treaty signed with the United States,[6] ensuring that any agreement ratified with one power would automatically be extended to the others. In light of all this, it is not surprising that for the Chinese, the word 'diplomacy' had become synonymous with foreign aggression. As China had no wish to trade with the West, to use its technology or to adopt its religion, it could see no useful purpose in opening diplomatic relations with inferior nations. It wanted simply to be left alone, undisturbed and unmolested. But to the West, hungry for trade and focused on progress, this complacency in the face of China's crying need of modernisation was incomprehensible. The gulf between China and the West was too wide to be bridged by the 'Convention of Peking' but the treaty did ensure that the two civilisations would now be dealing directly with each other – whether the Chinese liked it or not.

And they emphatically did not. But once the immediate politics had been dealt with, attention turned to more practical matters – most pressingly, the need to find suitable quarters for the new missions. The Chinese, with a certain irony and a flickering hope that they might yet keep their unwelcome guests outside the city wall, at first suggested building on the site of the devastated Summer Palace. When this was rejected, they then instinctively looked to a part of Peking that had a long association with barbarians. For centuries, an area just to the south east of the Forbidden City had housed tribute bearers from the vassal states of Korea, Burma, Mongolia and Annam. To all parties, therefore, this seemed a natural place for the French and British to install themselves. Each country was offered a fine palace but both were so dilapidated that it was decided that the ministers, Alphonse de Bourboulon and Frederick Bruce (later Sir Frederick), younger brother of Lord Elgin, would winter in Tientsin, while junior members of their staff remained in Peking to take charge of the renovations.

On the morning of 26 March 1861, de Bourboulon watched as the tricolour was hoisted above his new mission. At 3 o'clock that afternoon, Bruce rode into Peking escorted by a detachment of Sikh cavalry so that by evening, with the Union Jack also flying high, the British legation doctor, David Field Rennie, was able to record: 'Thus has been peaceably consummated the establishment of the representatives of England and France at Peking.'[7] The next day he noted:

Now is commencing the most difficult part of a permanent English residency at Peking, namely the satisfying of the Chinese that we are a tolerably harmless and well-intentioned people inclined to live with them on terms of amity rather than the contrary.[8]

There then followed a period – meticulously documented by Rennie – during which both Chinese and foreigners made tentative attempts to understand each other better. The 35-year-old doctor, delighted by every aspect of his novel surroundings, quickly came to like the Chinese whom he believed were 'little understood and much misrepresented'[9] – a view not shared by many of his colleagues. Certainly, misunderstanding and curiosity at every level marked the early days of the diplomats' presence in Peking. While the Europeans grappled with Confucianism, Chinese governance and the intricate layers of ritual surrounding the Imperial Court, the Chinese were forced to revise notions of the British as maritime monsters who walked like penguins on webbed feet.[10]

The first European women to appear on the scene were Madame de Bourboulon and Mrs Reynolds, the British legation housekeeper. Each time they appeared in public, crowds would gather around them, eager to catch their first glimpse of a foreign female. Scottish by birth, Catherine de Bourboulon was an unusual woman. A talented equestrian, she took to riding side-saddle through the streets of Peking, much to the astonishment of the Chinese who were mystified as to where she had put her other leg. When the time came for the de Bourboulons to leave Peking, instead of taking the long sea voyage home, they decided to return on horseback, riding across Mongolia and Siberia all the way to Moscow. At 6 o'clock on the morning of 17 May 1862, a large crowd of mandarins, diplomats and curious Chinese gathered in front of the French legation to see them off. Dressed 'like a man' in a grey coat trimmed with black velvet, blue pantaloons, riding boots and a flamboyant feathered hat, Catherine de Bourboulon must have seemed like a creation from another planet. Just as the extensive caravan of camels, mules, supplies, servants and litters (one of them containing Catherine's Pekingese dogs[11]) was about to move off, the servants let go a barrage of firecrackers. Catherine's horse promptly bolted, carrying her off to some distant part of Peking, while the rest of the entourage scattered in utter chaos. Eventually, with the animals recaptured, carts righted and Catherine having found her way back, the couple embarked on their remarkable adventure.[12]

Less glamorous than Madame de Bourboulon, Mrs Reynolds nevertheless matched her for pluck. A middle-aged Welsh woman, she came to Peking from Shanghai to take up the job of housekeeper to the British legation, bringing with her two turkey cocks that aroused even greater curiosity than she did. Each day she emerged from her quarters in 'The Hall for the Nourishment of Virtue' to shop in the marketplace. Although she soon learned how to argue and barter with the tradesmen, they could still on occasion fool her with a lump of wood cleverly disguised as a fine ham – or a 'plump' fowl stuffed with straw and pebbles.[13]

Misunderstandings between two peoples of such different cultures were inevitable. Some were amusingly trivial such as when (because of a small tonal mispronunciation) 240 lbs of eels, instead of the expected Mongolian potatoes, were delivered to the British Minister. But others were potentially more serious. The Peking authorities became greatly disturbed when a long line of carts was seen entering the British and French legations filled with packing cases containing household furniture for the diplomats but which they assumed hid merchandise. Had their suspicions been correct, the legations would have been in breach of the treaty terms that strictly forbade any foreign commerce in Peking.

But as confidence grew between the Chinese authorities and the diplomats, such difficulties were sorted out with increasing ease. In the early

1860s, the government even had reason to be grateful to the foreigners (most famously General 'Chinese' Gordon) for their help in quelling the 15-year-long Taiping rebellion that had caused such widespread misery in China and, by some calculations, as many as 20 million deaths. Although the emperor still refused to return to Peking, remaining at his hunting park at Chengde, 150 miles away, every move the foreigners made was reported back to him. Meanwhile, the daily business of dealing with them was left in the hands of Prince Kung, together with five senior officials. These men supervised 'The Office for the Management of the Business of All Foreign Countries' – the Tsungli Yamen – officially opened in 1861. Revealingly, it was originally intended only as a temporary measure to deal with the immediate crisis. Equally significant was the fact that its building (formerly the office of the Department of Iron Coins) was intentionally shabby, leaving no one in any doubt of its inferiority to other government offices. Foreigners were often kept waiting long hours there, sometimes in the bitter cold: 'I was three hours at the Yamen yesterday,' wrote Robert Hart, 'and came back almost as stiff as a winter sheep from Mongolia.'[14]

But despite their reluctance to accept the Europeans as a permanent fixture, Prince Kung and his colleagues made genuine attempts to understand something of the West. In response to the Prince's request to see some English poetry, Thomas Wade, the then Chinese Secretary at the British Legation (later minister from 1871 to 1883; first Professor of Chinese at Cambridge University and co-compiler of the Wade/Giles system of Romanization for the Chinese language), presented him with translations of *Auld Lang Syne* and *Childe Harold's Farewell to His Page*. Prince Kung's reaction to Byron is unrecorded but interest in literary expression was by no means confined to the ruling class. A Frenchman writing in the 1860s noted the surprising number of Chinese who owned portable printing presses. From these flowed a constant stream of political protest, poetry and philosophy that were posted on every available space:

> One could say that the streets are libraries: Not only are courts, pagodas, temples, shops, front doors, private houses, passages covered with comment of all kind but tea-cups, plates, vases, and fans become anthologies of poetry and proverbs. In the poorest villages, where even the barest necessities are lacking, one will always find posters.[15]

On 8 July 1861, with the arrival of the first Russian Minister to Peking, Colonel de Balluzeck, and his wife, a third treaty power flag was added to those of Britain and France followed a year later by the Stars and Stripes. The American Minister, Anson Burlingame, so impressed the Ch'ing authorities that in 1867 they asked him to head a delegation to Europe and America with the aim of improving China's image in the West. In the wake of Burlingame's efforts, Chinese diplomatic representatives were sent to Paris and London in 1871 and to Washington in 1878. Once the four treaty powers were established in Peking, other nations were naturally eager to follow suit. For a few years, the government managed to keep them at bay but by 1900, a further seven foreign missions had taken root in the capital.

***

Although, as the century wore on, dialogue between the Peking authorities and the diplomats gradually grew more relaxed, the same cannot be said of Chinese relations with the missionaries. On the contrary, missionaries were increasingly the focus of anti-foreign feeling throughout China and especially in Shantung. For a start, they were the only foreigners that ordinary Chinese (not living in Peking or one of the treaty ports) were likely to meet. And by the end of the century, many were established deep in China's interior, preaching a message utterly at odds with Confucianism and its core practice of ancestor worship.

By the summer of 1900, there were perhaps three-quarters of a million Chinese converts to various Christian denominations (Catholics taking the lion's share), while missionaries made up one-quarter of the total foreign community.[16] For those at the bottom of the heap such as rickshaw pullers, camel drivers and canal boatmen, the missionaries' very real achievements in educating the poor, delivering medical care and raising the status of women counted for little. Rather, they saw Christianity as an insidious foreign evil bringing with it competitive imports, and inventions like the steam engine and steamboat, designed only to deprive them of their traditional livelihood. They also detested the protection missionaries gave to their new converts in village disputes and – as they saw it – the duplicitous way they bought private houses for conversion into churches. Nor did rumours of child torture and wild orgies help or the fact that Chinese Christians no longer took part in traditional local festivals. To the majority of peasants, therefore, it seemed that the missionaries were destroying the very roots of their society. Moreover, this threat was set against a backdrop of devastating natural disasters that were also blamed on the foreigners. As the years passed, violence against missionaries became more frequent, the most notorious incident being the murder of 16 French men and women (including ten nuns) in Tientsin in 1870. While missionaries based in Peking faced less physical danger than their rural colleagues, they found it harder to make converts so the baptism of an official in the Tsungli Yamen in the 1880s came as a welcome boost to morale.

Before the arrival of the French and British in 1860, the longest surviving foreign colony in Peking was a small Russian ecclesiastical mission. It supported the descendants of some 50 Albazinian prisoners, captured in skirmishes on the Sino-Russian border in the late seventeenth century. They had been allowed to settle in the north east of the city near the Lama Temple, where they had prospered, many of them serving in the Imperial Guard. Although by the 1860s they were physically indistinguishable from the Chinese, they continued to practise the orthodox faith of their Russian forebears. Meanwhile, Russia's trade relations with Peking (dating back to Ming times) were strengthened in the 1727 Treaty of Kiakhta, which also made provision for four Russian students to live in Peking to study Chinese languages. It was this rudimentary language school that formed a convenient precedent for what, in Ch'ing terms, was a radical initiative – an interpreters' school (the Tung-wen kuan). It was founded in 1862 as part of the 'self-strengthening' movement, the name given to China's efforts to confront foreign pressures and prop up the crumbling Ch'ing Dynasty. The government may not have liked the idea of its citizens learning foreign languages, but the unequal treaties had made China's need for its own interpreters all too plain. Key to the school's development was the involvement of an American missionary, W.A.P. Martin. Under his direction it soon evolved into a fully-fledged college where a modern curriculum, including astronomy, mathematics, physics, chemistry and international law, was introduced.

The 'Convention of Peking' restored to France two cathedrals built in the seventeenth century by the Jesuits – the Nantang (southern cathedral) and its companion in the north of the city, the Peitang. When Rennie visited the latter in 1861, he discovered that there were nine Chinese priests in Peking caring for some 5,000 Chinese converts. The cathedral's Dutch abbot, he observed, 'was dressed in every respect like a Chinese mandarin...his costume was very complete, though his pig-tail was rather of the kind called a "rat-tail" amongst horses'.[17] Such attempts on the part of missionaries to identify so totally with their converts provoked a good deal of amusement among

Chinese and foreigners alike, although others, like the scholarly A.E. Moule, believed such missionaries to be the 'true pioneers of civilization' on whose shoulders fell the responsibility of carrying the reputation of foreigners into the heart of the country.[18]

On 13 June 1861, Rennie noted in his diary that Robert Hart, the then acting Inspector General of the Customs Service, had been informed by the Tsungli Yamen that: 'The emperor knew his name.'[19] For a foreigner there could be no higher compliment, but then Hart was no ordinary foreigner. Credited with having created 'one of the most striking monuments ever produced by the genius and labour of any individual Englishman'[20] and described in 1928 as 'the man who remains the most interesting foreign personality that ever figured in China,'[21] he occupies a unique place in the history of China's relations with the outside world. Hart's 'monument', the Imperial Chinese Maritime Customs Service, was a remarkable segment of the Chinese administration over which he had complete control for more than 45 years. By the treaties China had signed with Britain, France, Russia and America in the 1840s, foreign merchants were required to pay tax on their goods. Because collection of these duties became difficult during the Taiping occupation of Shanghai, the Chinese authorities agreed in 1854 to employ a few foreigners to help. That same year, the 19-year-old Hart arrived in Hong Kong as a fledgling member of the Chinese Consular Service. He spent three-and-a-half years in Ningbo (one of the original five treaty ports) studying the language – a task made easier by his acquisition of a Chinese mistress who bore him three children. In 1859, Hart was transferred to the Customs Service and by 1863, at the still tender age of 28, he was living in Peking as Inspector General – a post (for his last three years in name only) he was to hold until his death in 1911.

Ahead of its time, the Customs Service was, in effect, an international civil service that by the end of the nineteenth century was employing around 700 foreigners from some 20 different countries as well as 3,500 Chinese. As the dominant trader in China, Britain provided the majority of foreign staff, but Hart, who kept an iron grip on recruitment, was by no means partisan. Writing in 1893 he stated: 'The next ten men for appointment will be American and Continental: too many English comparatively just now!'[22] And then in 1895, 'We are badly off for able Britishers – the Americans, Russians, German and French in the Service are far more "go ahead" and also fitter and better educated!'[23] The revenues Hart was responsible for collecting made a vital contribution to China's economy not least by providing security for foreign loans. But apart from its prime tax-collecting function, the Customs also operated the postal system, built lighthouses, conducted hydro-graphic surveys and published statistics and books on a wide range of subjects, and also funded the Interpreters' School. As Hart was the chief deliverer of all this and much else, it is not surprising that his Chinese employers referred to him as 'our Hart'.[24]

The small, spare Ulsterman of modest background was equally admired – if not always loved – by the foreigners. Charles Addis, a British banker, who knew him well, left a thumbnail portrait:

> A marvellous man and yet such an insignificant shy man and of bald conversation. Fond of the ladies (pretty ones) in a rather a fawning sort of way...He never goes out, lives surrounded by files...Lives by rule; rises early; 10 minutes to the classics; 10 minutes to the cello etc. etc. Sleeps every afternoon for an hour. Begins a book and will tell you to a minute when he will finish it...a dreamer of dreams...a marvellous organiser and the machinery of the enormous service is almost perfect...an undoubted egoist; Hart must be in everything...Will nourish an injury for years...No friends, no confidants. Never takes exercise...Now he is Sir Robert and has had the refusal of the British Ministership. He is one of the first men in China, but it is too late and he finds himself unable to mix freely with the men now his equals. And so he lives on in solitude.[25]

Addis, the 11th child of a Free Kirk minister, was himself among the earliest non-diplomatic foreigners to live in Peking. His employer, the Hong Kong and Shanghai Bank, had been founded in 1865 but it was not until 20 years later that it managed to secure a foothold in the capital. In 1886, Addis arrived in Peking 'hot and dusty', having ridden the 85 miles from Tientsin on horseback.

> It was a lucky chance that brought me here and I may bless my stars that ever I took a fancy to Chinese study. Only that could have raised me over the heads of 30 or 40 seniors and sent me at a jump from humble clerk to Acting Agent at Peking...I have a fine house, stables, servants, mule and cart, coal and oil (heavy items during the severe winter) newspapers, furniture, house and table linen etc. all supplied by the Bank. I was in charge of an Agency at 25 years of age – the youngest agent in China.[26]

While Addis went on to do great things elsewhere, it was his colleague Guy Hillier who truly became the Bank's man in Peking, living there for 33 years from 1891 until his death in 1924. Initially he had found professional conditions far from ideal. The Chinese authorities tried to thwart him at every turn, while even his own employers viewed their Peking branch as a tentative experiment unworthy of serious investment. Furthermore, the native bankers complained bitterly, accusing him of illegal commercial activity. Despite all these difficulties, Hillier was captivated by Peking, noting the use of carrier pigeons by Chinese bankers to communicate exchange rates and the sight of Burmese elephants (stabled in a nearby temple) enjoying a dip in the city's moat.[27] By the end of the century, with China's 'self-strengthening' programme in its latter stages, the government had come to accept the Bank's presence and more especially, the foreign loans it could provide.

So it was against this background of increasing international activity in Peking that the Boxer uprising – like some giant Chinese firecracker – was flung at the small foreign community almost but not quite destroying it. The immediate disastrous effect was plain for all to see. Less clear was how the foreigners would fare in the longer term. Would the Chinese opt for a modern dialogue with the West or retreat into xenophobia?

4
IMPERIAL SUNSET

Most foreign survivors of the Boxer siege understandably left Peking as soon as they could – but not all. A number stayed on, determined, despite their experiences, to remain in China at such a pivotal moment. As the dust settled, the burning question was whether a reform movement of the kind the Empress Dowager had so decisively stamped out in 1898 might yet breathe life into the corrupt and incompetent Ch'ing Dynasty, or had imperial rule, after 2,000 years, finally run into the sand?

Of the ministers present during the siege, only three – the American, Edwin Conger, the Russian, Michel de Giers and Stéphen Pichon (now hailed in France as a great hero) – remained to negotiate the peace treaty known as the 'Boxer Protocol'. From the Chinese perspective, this was just one more unequal treaty, since its prime purpose was to extract punitive reparation from China and make clear the futility of any future attempt to confront the powers. With the Court still in voluntary exile, Li Hung-chang and Prince Ching were appointed to represent the government. Realising the weakness of their position, they made little difficulty, but discussions nevertheless dragged on for nine long months as a result of bickering between the allies. The new British Minister, Sir Ernest Satow, found the whole process deeply frustrating. But finally on 7 September 1901 the Protocol was signed. Having rubbed China's nose in her Boxer folly, the powers were now free to get on with the more serious business of competing over concessions and their respective spheres of influence.

Apart from demanding a formal Chinese apology, the death penalty for the guilty and the banning of state examinations in cities where foreigners had been murdered, the Protocol stipulated an indemnity of 450 million taels (approximately 110 million pounds) to be paid over 39 years (which, had it run its course, with interest, would have amounted to nearly a billion taels). Additionally, the legation quarter was to be fortified and expanded while the Tsungli Yamen, renamed the Waiwupu, would become the significantly upgraded Office for Foreign Affairs.

Although most foreigners considered the terms of the Protocol perfectly appropriate, even lenient, others were not so sure. Hart, despite having been 'horribly hurt by all that has occurred',[1] was uneasy about the size of the indemnity: 'China will be sorely put to it! I must try my best to do it in the cheapest and least crippling way ... but I doubt if the powers will be accommodating.'[2] He also had the foresight to remark that as China would itself one day be a great power, it was worth taking care with the Boxer settlement so that the China of the future 'might have something to thank us for and not to avenge'.[3] Even young diplomats, like Jack Garnett, with robust imperialist views, could see the point: 'Of course the Chinese loathe us: so should we the Chinese if our country were invaded by foreign concession hunters trying to get the right to build railways in all directions and exploit mines in every county.'[4]

As the 'Boxer Protocol' did little to ease anti-foreign feeling, the rapid rebuilding of a secure and enlarged legation quarter was a high priority. New buildings soon arose from the ashes of the siege, but were now encircled with a high wall. Outside this sloped the glacis, a generous grassy area, intended to give the foreigners added protection but which served more to emphasise their isolation. By 1902, the legation quarter had, in effect, become a foreign concession, guarded by foreign troops and similar to those found in all the treaty ports but one in which the Chinese themselves were no longer permitted to live. Not everyone approved of these developments. Satow and Hart were among those who believed such heavy-handed measures would in the long run prove counter-productive.

Thirty-year-old Garnett arrived in Peking to take up his post as Second Secretary at the British Legation in November 1905. In an early letter home he wrote:

The whole of our quarter covers a very large area and seems like a fortress, sentries of every nationality on every legation wall and at every gate, bugles going at all times of the day, officers and soldiers going about in every direction, the chapel yesterday, too, was full of soldiers and officers.[5]

The impressive new defences did not, however, offer protection from the enemy within. Having lost all his possessions to the Boxers, the unfortunate Hart now had to fight an equally obdurate foe – the Italians. Stealing a march over his fellow diplomats in the middle of the night, the Italian Minister, the Marquis Guiseppe Salvago Raggi, staked out a large area for his new legation that included the Inspector General's beloved rose garden. This diplomatic incident was eventually smoothed over but Hart clearly considered it an outrage equal to any he had suffered from the Boxers. At the age of 66, he might reasonably have decided the time had come to pack his bags and go home. But although he had for many years considered retiring, his sense of duty, love of the job and, perhaps more to the point, the power it wielded, always persuaded him to stay. Possibly, the thought of living with Lady Hart, the wife he had not seen for 20 years (she had returned to England in 1882), was another deterrent. Whatever the reasons, the Empress Dowager's reluctance to let him go and the difficulty involved in finding a suitable successor provided all the incentive he needed to remain in Peking.

On 7 January 1902, Hart was among the large crowd of foreigners gathered on the wall at the main gate Chien-men to view the long anticipated return of the Imperial Court. As Morrison reported to *The Times*, the entire 700-mile route had been converted into a smooth, even surface of clay 'soft and noiseless underfoot'. Every obstacle and stone had been removed and as the imperial procession approached, gangs of men were to be seen frantically brushing the surface with feather brooms.[6] If the Court's procession back to the capital resembled some great mediaeval pageant, the last lap of the journey was completed in that hated symbol of foreign modernity – a steam train. Could this, wondered some observers, be symbolic of China's belated evolution from mediaeval isolation to the contemporary world? When Hart later asked the Empress Dowager what she thought of the train ride, she replied that she had enjoyed it so much that she might even go to Europe.[7]

Aware that they were witnessing an extraordinary event, the foreigners watched fascinated as the Son of Heaven and his aunt emerged from their yellow chairs to allow the emperor to perform the prescribed rituals at the small temple dedicated to the god of war, tucked between the outer and inner structures of Chien-men. Their emotions must have been mixed when they saw the small, elderly woman, so recently intent on their murder, now graciously smile and wave at them as they looked down at her from their vantage point on the wall. Hart simply commented: 'The Court got back Tuesday last and all looks promising ... several good Edicts have come out since: I hope the new era is coming in but the Indemnity is a terrible deadweight to carry!'[8] Sarah Conger was more effusive:

> This was a wonderful day ... it must have been a mighty Hand that lifted the heavy, blood-stained curtain between China and the eleven nations and made it possible to lay down animosities and extend friendship's hand warm with pledges of forgiveness and good will.[9]

A little more than a year later, in April 1903, Gertrude Bell (traveller, archaeologist, Middle East administrator and much else) described to her father another imperial entry into Peking – this time on the emperor's return from the Western Ch'ing tombs:

> First came mounted men carrying huge banners, pale pink with dragons on them and scarlet ... then a motley collection of soldiers in sailor hats very much battered and their pigtails wound round their heads (they look for all the world like very determined old maids) and then the Emperor's yellow chair. He got out just below us and went into a little temple to the god of war ... to offer sacrifice: a little wizened man with a head far too big for his body. He got into his chair and was carried away. Then an interim of court followers carrying baskets of provisions slung over poles. They take everything with them when they go from palace to palace – every stick of furniture and food for 10 times the immense number of people that go with them, because so much vanishes by the way. And finally the Empress's procession, much more numerous than the Emperor's: banners, and mounted men and a lot of princes in yellow jackets and last the Empress's yellow chair. She got out too at the temple and walked in, brave in blue and mauve, supported on either side by a Manchu dignitary or a eunuch or something. When she came out, she stood for a long time in the temple court and examined the foreigners on the wall through opera glasses, bowing and waving a blue handkerchief to those whom she knew. She saw my camera too and gave it and me a special greeting all to ourselves. Then she was helped into her chair, handed a tray of refreshments, an imperial yellow tray, and was carried away ... wasn't that an amusing thing to have seen?[10]

As a mere 'globetrotter', Gertrude Bell had been unusually lucky to glimpse the Manchu Court in all its splendour – an experience every foreign resident in Peking coveted. Those fortunate enough to take part in an imperial audience recorded every detail, knowing full well that the dynasty was unlikely to survive beyond the Empress Dowager. And once the Manchus – however irrelevant and anachronistic – were finished, the link with China's ancient past would be gone forever. There was intense rivalry between the legations – especially their women – over access to the Court. The aristocratic Lady Susan Townley (daughter of the Duke of Albermarle and wife of the First Secretary at the British Legation) had all the confidence of her class when it came to such matters. 'The Empress,' wrote Bell, 'has given [her] extraordinary marks of favour – all the other Legations are rampant with jealousy.'[11] However, the controversial Lady Susan (her extra-marital love-life had caused havoc at the embassy in Constantinople) faced serious competition from the homely, missionary-minded wife of the American Minister, now dean of the diplomatic ladies. Sarah Conger's credentials were impeccable. A veteran of the siege, she had consistently preached sympathy and support for the Chinese throughout her time in Peking and, as Hart noted, she and her husband had far more Chinese acquaintances than any of the other diplomats.[12]

Both women fell under the spell of the Empress Dowager, each claiming a unique intimacy with her. Conger believed her meetings with Tsu-hsi – so full of 'womanly significance'[13] – to be a material contribution to the healing of relations between China and the powers – 'Can we not catch glimpses of a distant union as the rungs in the ladder take us upward?'[14] And how could she not feel deeply moved when the Empress Dowager took her hands in her own and, controlling her tears with difficulty, pleaded, 'It was a grave mistake and China will hereafter be a friend to foreigners.'[15] At an imperial audience, the well-meaning Mrs Conger even took it upon herself to make a political speech. This was not the British way of doing things and Satow noted crossly in his diary that it seemed to him quite wrong for diplomatic ladies to play a political role.[16]

Lady Susan's account of the Court is more down to earth, though it is clear that she too came under its spell. But whereas Sarah Conger could see only beauty and sincerity in all things imperial, Lady Susan's eye fell upon certain incongruities. The banquet table, for instance, laid with the most exquisite porcelain, 'was covered with shiny American oil-cloth, the ground of which was black, besprigged with coloured flowers', while each of the guests was given a napkin 'hailing evidently from Manchester of coarse cotton, mauve in colour and adorned with a large white floral design'.[17] Nor was Lady Susan impressed by the protocol that forced her Chinese interpreter

> as often as Her Majesty spoke to him ... to go upon his knees to listen, rising
> again to transmit the remark to us or *vice versa*. I could not help feeling sorry for
> the poor man after an hour of this very hard exercise, and noticing the perspira-
> tion streaming from his forehead I forbore to say several things I had in mind![18]

While Mrs Conger talked of better times to come, Susan Townley sat cross-legged with the Empress Dowager on her bed chatting about clothes and clocks. Tsu-hsi, a passionate devotee of Chinese theatre, was herself an instinctive actor who played the role of sorrowful leader misled by disloyal subordinates to perfection. But, despite all the fine words and professed friendships, it seems unlikely that her fundamental antipathy to foreigners had much changed.

Sarah Conger could boast one imperial triumph that even Lady Susan could not equal. In 1903, she persuaded the Empress Dowager to allow an American artist, Katherine Carl, to paint her portrait, so that it might be displayed the following year at the Louisiana Purchase Exhibition in St Louis. Since por-traits in China were normally only painted after the subject's death, this was a diplomatic coup. Inevitably, Hart was drawn into the exercise: 'I have just wired for 8 yds of canvas (Painter's) 2 yds wide. The Empress D told Carl to get "Hart" to wire to "Campbell" for it – the quickest way!'[19] Hart was delighted by the eventual outcome, although he did not find the artist an easy guest!

> Miss Carl left the Congers and moved in here today. She is very breezy – quite
> a Tornado in fact, and I fear the solitude which suited both my health and my
> work will now be interfered with to anything but the advantage of either.[20]

In the finished painting, the Empress Dowager's robes and jewellery, her striking Manchu headdress and fingernail guards are all sumptuously depicted, but of the personality behind the formal mask, there is not the slightest hint. The face is a masterpiece of blandness. This was not entirely the artist's fault. The conditions under which she was forced to work were hardly conducive to penetrating insights of character. Although it was to be a very large por-trait, rough preliminary sketches – considered insulting to Her Majesty – were unacceptable, the light, filtered through paper windows, was entirely inadequate while neither shadow nor perspective was allowed to shape the imperial countenance. According to Carl, the business of stretching the canvas nearly brought the whole project to a premature end:

> Owing to the size of the canvas I was compelled to stand on a stool six feet high (they had no ladders), and with the huge stretcher before me. An army of eunuchs stood around to assist me, presided over by a head eunuch...It was held at the corners by eunuchs, also on stools; one eunuch held the tacks, another the hammer, etc...and at every failure to comprehend my directions the working eunuchs were rebuked and threatened with the 'bamboo'...Her Majesty was greatly exercised when she learned I had done it myself. She said I should have made the eunuchs 'stretch four or five,' until they learned to do one properly.[21]

The court astrologers had decided that 11 o'clock on 5 August 1903 was the most auspicious time to begin the portrait; so just as Carl picked up the charcoal to make her first stroke,

> ...eighty-five clocks...began to chime, play airs, and strike the hour in eighty-five different ways...For a few moments I heard the faintest ticking of the clocks as if they were great Cathedral bells clanging in my ears, and my charcoal on the canvas sounded like some mighty saw drawn back and forth.[22]

Although Carl had been initially told she would be given only two sittings, in the event Tsu-hsi was so taken with the whole venture that she stayed nine months, spending long periods in both the Forbidden City and Summer Palace. The astrologers, as precise about endings as they were about beginnings, announced that the portrait must be finished at 4 o'clock on 19 April 1904. Before embarking on its long journey to America it was viewed at the Waiwupu by the diplomatic corps in full dress-uniform. Too precious to be carried by ordinary bearers, the 'sacred picture' was conveyed from the foreign office to the station outside the wall on a specially built railway. By then, Tsu-hsi had become so enamoured with her own image that she suggested Carl spend the rest of her days in Peking painting her over and over again. Politely declining, Carl returned to America, where in 1906 she published an account of her unique experience – *With the Empress Dowager of China*.

For the diplomats, audiences at court now became a regular event. In 1906, Sir John Jordan presented his credentials to the emperor – the last British Minister to do so. Jack Garnett accompanied him:

> It was a drenching morning and the streets of Peking swimming in water and mud. Luckily the chair-bearers dropped none of us in the various holes we traversed.

Because the Minister was presenting a royal letter we entered the Forbidden City by the 'Great Pure Gate' or main entrance up which no foreigner may proceed except on such a purpose. As King Edward's letter was addressed to the Emperor, the old cat was not present though it is generally supposed that she assists from behind the screen at the back of the throne. The Emperor sat on a high gilt throne at the end of the Audience Hall a yellow table covered with a black tablecloth in front of him and looks frightfully worn and ill and childish. He was terribly nervous. On either side of the hall were ranged a row of Imperial princes some fifty of them all looking frightful scoundrels and prepared to cut our throats. Having announced his arrival in English and Chinese, Sir John ascended the throne and handed the royal letter to the Lord of Heaven...we then retired backwards nearly tripping up over our own swords and partook of drinks in the Imperial schoolroom. We then returned to the Legation but the rain was so bad that the splendour of the procession was spoilt by the chairs being covered over with mackintoshes and the mounted escort being wrapped up in sombre coats. The rain was also good enough to come through the chair and spoil my gold lace.[23]

The emperor struck most foreigners who met him as a sad, pathetic figure. In audiences he was always seated behind his aunt, appearing bored, even vacant. Some concluded he was an opium addict. 'I could not help noticing how small and frail the Emperor looked sitting on the edge of his big chair with his hands folded palm upwards in his palm, and the toes of his dangling feet turned in,'[24] Susan Townley observed. Indeed, his life was by all accounts so wretched that he possibly no longer cared when at last, but too late, the Empress Dowager accepted the urgent need for constitutional reform.

In 1905, a group of five Manchu princes and Chinese officials was despatched around the world to discover the exact nature of the elusive elixir called 'constitutional government' that made other countries so powerful. Perhaps if in some way it could be introduced to China, the deadly thrust of the foreigner could be parried and the Manchus restored to their former glory. The group's departure coincided with Japan's victory over Russia in a war triggered by the two countries' competing ambitions in Manchuria. That foreigners should be fighting for supremacy in the ruling dynasty's own homeland was an especially painful reminder of China's weakness and humiliation.

Returning in 1906, the Commission recommended far-reaching changes. Not only were existing ministries to be reorganised, new ones invented and the power of the governors-general curtailed, but also – and most radical of all – a national assembly convened. That same year, various aspects of Chinese life that were particularly horrifying to foreigners, such as death by slicing and torture during trials, also became illegal. Jack Garnett reported that the Court was even discussing 'whether the pigtail ought to go or not. Opium smoking and foot binding are to be abolished by Imperial edict but they are still squabbling over the pigtail'. [25] Further reforms in the pipeline included schools for women, the development of an urban police force and the restructuring of local government.

For the rebellious-minded Sun Yat-sen in exile in Japan, and for many of the thousands of Chinese students who had gone there to study (the traditional Confucian state examinations were abolished in 1905), such reforms were not radical enough. Japan was the natural role model for these young men (and in increasing numbers, women), since it had itself so successfully grafted a modern constitutional government onto an ancient imperial system. The proof had been its unexpectedly easy victory over China in 1895 and now again over Russia ten years later. The message was clear – modernisation worked. And Japan, linguistically, culturally and geographically so much closer to China than the West, was the obvious place for young patriots to go to discover how they too could drag their country into the twentieth century.

Against this background of Manchurian disintegration, simmering rebellion and a host of other nightmarish problems, the Empress Dowager lived on in her fantasy world. Surrounded by flocks of fawning princesses and eunuchs, she glided over the Summer Palace lakes aboard her imperial barge, through carpets of lotus flowers and under exquisite marble bridges. Cocooned in obsequiousness, it is conceivable that she really did believe 'she was the cleverest woman who has ever lived'.[26] But as she posed imperiously for her portrait seated upon the dragon throne, a mantle of pearls cascading over her shoulders, perhaps she wondered whether even she was clever enough to save her dynasty.

Certainly the foreign community was in little doubt that after Tsu-hsi's death China would erupt into chaos and bloodshed. As Garnett wrote:

Everything looks gloomy as far as Peking is concerned. The Manchu dynasty is loathed everywhere and the Chinese are longing to get rid of them. Any involvement of the mob is as much anti-dynasty as anti-foreign. The question is will the Court try again, as in 1900, to divert all the hatred from their own head to the foreigners? I rather hope so since personally I am spoiling for a row![27]

Threat of another attack was never far from anyone's mind. 'Sir Ernest gave a Chinese dinner the other night,' Garnett wrote, 'it was one of the days on which the supposed massacre of the legations was to have taken place. By a Machiavellian stroke of policy, Sir E had asked the Minister of Police!'[28]

The foreigners had other worries too. Just as China's vast territory seethed with discontent in the dying years of imperial rule, so too, as Jack Garnett noted, did the legation quarter in its rather smaller province:

> Poor Peking society! They take things very seriously. A few bachelors gave a large dinner party at the Club and they had a dance afterwards. The hosts were the Belgian Minister, an Austrian Secretary, a Russian Secretary and a Russian officer and the manager of the French Bank. The guests were fifty in number for the dinner and the rest of Peking was asked to come in after dinner. The feuds in consequence of the unfortunate party have been legion. The French Minister declined to attend the dinner because he hadn't been asked to be one of the hosts! The Austrian Commandant of the guard refused to come in afterwards because he said he ought to have been invited to dine, while the Austrian Minister and his wife refused to dine because on seeing the table arrangements they considered they weren't properly placed: the consequence is that the Austrian Secretary host has broken off all social relations with his Minister and the Minister's wife...a great many more people refused to go in afterwards because they thought they should have been asked to dine, others because the invitation reached them very late.[29]

Peking was not at this stage a popular posting. Most of the diplomats did not speak Chinese and few had any real interest in the country. Outside the legation quarter there was no 'society', and once the main sights had been absorbed, there was little to do except ride, play sport, walk on the wall and indulge in scandal and petty squabbles. 'You ask me how I like Peking,' wrote one young diplomat,

> it is extremely interesting and there is an immense amount of work to do; were it not for this life would not be bearable. Social intercourse of a congenial kind is entirely lacking. One has one's work and one's books and a great variety of exercise, riding, golf, fives, hockey skating, bowls fencing, boxing and lawn tennis. I am glad to have come here but I shall be heartily glad to get away.[30]

The majority of diplomats posted to Peking in the first decade of the twentieth century shared this view. Once the novelty of China had worn off, many of them suffered from intense boredom – especially with each other. Shortly after succeeding Sir Ernest Satow in 1906, Sir John Jordan and his wife gave their first dinner party. Garnett recorded the occasion:

> Lady Jordan hardly opened her mouth during dinner and looked so bored. So did the French Minister on her left and the Russian Minister on her right: the latter went to sleep during the long dinner. I felt inclined to do the same and didn't dare leave the ladies after dinner because they had nothing to say to each other. However, even that didn't help matters much. The cold inside the drawing room was almost as severe as that out of doors.[31]

The menu – usually 12 courses – was virtually the same at every dinner party regardless of nationality. Any diplomat bold enough to offer his guests Chinese food would have been considered dangerously eccentric. Two adventurous women globetrotters (their brother had just published *In the Footsteps of Marco Polo*[32]) asked to be taken to a Chinese restaurant so that they might taste some real Chinese food, 'and a very terrible ordeal it was', recorded Garnett, 'poor things, they stood it very bravely!'[33] The guest list at legation parties was as predictable as the food: 'On Monday evening I dined at the Japanese Legation,' wrote Garnett:

> It was a party of twenty and we had all parted in the Jordans' house only an hour before. So you can imagine how brilliant our conversation was. In the evening we had a mad dinner party at the Doctor's twenty yards from my house and kept up the silliness till after midnight. Today I had a large luncheon party and we have continued our silliness. Indeed we see each other so often there is nothing to do but to be silly![34]

Foreigners living in Peking envied the social whirl of the treaty ports. With any major commerce forbidden in the capital, their little circle was deprived of the stimulus a vibrant business community would have provided. It also suffered from a lack of women – a fact that bothered Garnett. 'At Christmas we were a party of twenty-five. We tried dancing afterwards but one can't get far with only four ladies one of whom must play the piano and another of whom doesn't dance.'[35] Paula von Rosthorn (wife of the Austro-Hungarian Chinese Secretary) was markedly different from most legation women. For a start, she spoke Mandarin and despite the Boxer siege (during which she had manned a gun), she and her husband formed genuinely close friendships with the Chinese. Unusually for a diplomat's wife, she liked to go to the market herself, where once a week she presented a coin to an elephant cared for by her gardener who would then select the three ripest bananas in exchange for the money.[36] While women of strong character like Paula von Rosthorn or Sarah Conger threw themselves into Peking life, others loathed it from the very start. The wife of one minister made her views plain by refusing to unpack, while Princess Borghese (married to the Italian chargé d'affaires, Prince Livio Borghese) wept for days on end after their arrival in March 1907. 'Almost the whole of female Peking is leaving in the course of the next two months,' Jack Garnett lamented in March 1907, 'and as we get few recruits we shall soon become like the monasteries of Mount Athos.'[37]

However, an event occurred that summer that cheered everyone up. The Paris newspaper, *Le Matin*, had in January issued an intriguing challenge:

> Is there anyone who will undertake to travel this summer from Paris to Peking by automobile?

For Prince Scipione Borghese – mountaineer, traveller and passionate motorist – it was irresistible. The brother of Prince Livio Borghese, he arrived in Peking in May (the race had been reversed so as to avoid the rainy season) with his splendid 40HP Itala motor car and his equally splendid mechanic, Ettore, who, 'when he has nothing special on hand, stretches himself out under his motor-car, and contemplates it piece by piece, bolt by bolt, screw by screw – in a long, strange colloquy with his machine'.[38] The third member of the Italian team was a journalist, Luigi Barzini, who already knew China, having covered the Boxer siege seven years earlier. Prince Borghese, rich and meticulously prepared for the race, could hardly have offered a greater contrast, with another of the contestants, a convicted French con-man, Charles Godard, who earned his living by performing 'Wall of Death' motorcycle stunts at fairgrounds. Penniless but still determined to enter the 'raid', he raised money under false pretences and by selling the spare parts of the car he had been commissioned to drive – a 15HP Dutch Spyker. Three more Frenchmen also entered the race, driving between them a pair of 10HP De Dion Bouton cars and a flimsy 6HP motorised tricycle called a Contal Cyclecar.

The challenge they had undertaken was no ordinary one. Motor cars had only been around for 20-odd years, while the route they were to follow was largely unexplored. Immediately before them, just to the north-west of Peking, lay the formidable Nankow pass, and after that, the great rolling Mongolian prairie. Then, if they survived the Gobi desert, there was the vastness of Siberia to traverse before reaching Europe and finally Paris – a journey in all of some 10,000 miles. The foreign community thought them quite mad and were divided into those who believed the cars would never start and those who expected them to come to grief on the pass.

In the event, it was neither mechanics nor mountains that nearly halted the race. The authorities, having reluctantly accepted the 'fire chariot' (railway engine) as a fact of life, were even less enthusiastic over this latest Western invention – the 'fuel chariot'. To a Chinese bureaucrat, the idea that even a barbarian should want to drive one of these absurd machines overland to Paris for the sheer fun of it was inconceivable. Convinced that there must be some sinister ulterior motive, the Waiwupu refused to produce the necessary passports. Prince Borghese, not in the habit of being told what he could or could not do, announced his intention of going anyway, while the ministers entered into a flurry of unproductive negotiations. Meanwhile, ignoring Chinese instructions that their automobiles were only to move if drawn by mules, the motorists drove furiously round the streets of Peking frightening humans and beasts alike. Pragmatically, the Waiwupu concluded that the quickest way to rid Peking of this latest foreign horror was to let the race go ahead. Just before it was due to start, the passports miraculously appeared.

Trains from Tientsin brought in crowds of Europeans eager to witness the historic event. They were not disappointed. Punctually at 8 o'clock on 10 June 1907, the elegant Madame Boissonnés, wife of the French First Secretary, dropped the starting flag and the cars lurched forward amid a cacophony of firecrackers, military bands and roars of enthusiasm from the crowd.

> We advance at a foot-pace. Cavalry officers ride on either side of us…And now the band ceases…the farewell voices fade in the distance…"Forward?"
> – "Forward!" cry the drivers…and the motors gradually increase their speed. Behind us the officers urge their horses to a gallop; but the distance grows between us, and they are left out of sight. And over the road lined by the Chinese soldiery…our five motor-cars alone remain, pursuing each other through the capital of the Chinese Empire at a speed which it has never known before, and which it may perchance never behold again.[39]

Borghese claimed that one aim of the race was to prove how close the motor car had come to replacing humans and animals. In fact, the teams of coolies required to pull the cars over the Nankow pass took five days to cross the mountains – far longer than the average camel train. But in the Gobi, it was a different story. Following the telegraph poles and the recently laid trans-Siberian railtrack, Borghese crossed it in only four days – nearly two weeks less than it normally took a caravan. After many extraordinary experiences, narrow escapes and much skulduggery, four of the cars arrived in Paris, headed by the triumphant Itala, on 10 August, two weeks ahead of its rivals and just 60 days after leaving Peking. The unfortunate tricycle did not survive the Gobi Desert (its team of two was rescued by Mongolian tribesmen) and is probably still there.

Whether or not the Empress Dowager showed any interest in the race is not recorded, but she did herself own a large collection of motor cars. Many of these she had received as gifts from Chinese dignitaries on their return from the West. One such vehicle had been lavishly adapted to form what was, in effect, a Dragon Throne on wheels. Tsu-hsi never went anywhere in it or indeed in any of her other automobiles for one simple reason – the chauffeur. As it was of course impossible for him to have his back to her or to be seated in her presence and as not even the cleverest eunuch could work out how to drive a car backwards in the kneeling position, the Empress Dowager remained stationary.

Standing among the crowd at the start of the great race, Barzini noticed 'a dignified old gentleman of short stature, with a striking Chinese-looking little white beard and a penetrating, lively energetic eye'.[40] It was one of the last Peking events at which Sir Robert Hart was present. Having once observed that he would 'prefer to go to Heaven... *via* London rather than direct',[41] he had begun to realise that time was running out even for him. Furthermore, in 1906 an imperial edict had created a new Board of Customs Affairs with a Chinese director general. Although this was a demotion for Hart and a clear sign of things to come, surprisingly, the Foreign Inspectorate continued to operate until the Communist victory in 1949. Even Hart never expected it to survive that long.

Whatever Hart's shortcomings – and many of his colleagues would have cited an excessive love of power among them – his devotion to China was beyond question. Given all the political pressures and competing national interests to which he was exposed in his long career, his integrity in maintaining both his independence and loyalty to his employers was commendable. He rarely lost sight of the special character of his position or of the trust that had been placed in him. When the Duke of Manchester lobbied him about a staff appointment, Hart explained why he was unable to help:

> The Chinese Govt. has given me a very peculiar imposition. My Communion says 'We only know *you* – appoint whom you please – call them what you like – pay them as you see proper: only knowing you and giving you these full powers, *you* are responsible for all your subordinates and for all their doings.'[42]

The message was clear. Robert Hart was incorruptible and no one (not even a duke) was going to tell an Ulsterman how to run the Customs Service. Although he turned down the offer to become British Minister in 1885, he was indispensable to his own government. *The Times* claimed that the last instruction always given to each new British Minister leaving for Peking was: 'When in doubt consult Sir Robert Hart.'[43] His close friend W.A.P. Martin summed him up:

> He looms up like the Tungcho pagoda, which, rising from a level plain, becomes a part of the landscape, and attracts the eyes of all who turn their faces towards Peking. If he has not...extended the boundaries of his own country, he has done more than any other man to avert the destruction of another empire.[44]

For nearly 40 years, Hart had written once a week to his friend and colleague in London, James Duncan Campbell. In September 1907 in one of his last letters to him, he wrote: 'China is going in for new methods, new measures, and new men, and it would be interesting to remain provided one was fit to take an acting part...that, however, is not my case and I ought to step aside.'[45] In April 1908, as Hart left Peking for the last time, the railway station overflowed with brilliant uniforms and military bands. His guard of honour stretched down the platform as far as the eye could see – American marines, Italian sailors, Dutch marines, Japanese soldiers, pipers from the Cameron Highlanders as well as three detachments of Chinese soldiers in smart new khaki uniforms. The I.G.'s Own played *Auld Lang Syne* and, as the train pulled away with Hart bowing modestly to the cheering crowds, the bands struck up in unison *Home Sweet Home*. He did not return to Britain empty-handed. Apart from his fortune (Morrison estimated that he had earned in total around a million pounds), he was loaded with honours from all over the world ('Fancy me an Ulsterman with a Papal decoration!').[46] The Chinese, however, trumped the lot by appointing Hart, together with three generations of his forebears, to 'The Ancestral Rank of the First Class of the First Order'. It was the only time such an honour was bestowed on a foreigner. Even after returning to Britain, he retained his title of Inspector General until his death in 1911.

A year before he left Peking, Hart had written: 'Around us on all sides there is unrest and anxiety and the materials for a conflagration are accumulating: nobody can say what will happen and the disappearance of either Empress Dowager or Emperor will fix the mine.'[47] Just seven months after Hart's departure, both 'disappeared' within hours of each other. On 15 November 1908, the woman who had dominated China for half a century died, it was said, of eating too many crab apples at a picnic given in honour of the Dalai Lama. The day before, the Kuang-hsu emperor had been murdered with arsenic poisoning, possibly by his aunt or the chief eunuch. The moment so long anticipated and dreaded by Peking's foreign community had at last arrived. As one young British diplomat put it: 'God help foreigners and Manchus!'[48]

5
CHANGING CHINA

In the event, the Empress Dowager's death, politically at least, proved a damp squib. The Empire did not collapse, nor were the foreigners all massacred. On the contrary, just one month later, Lady Jordan wrote to Jack Garnett (who was crossing Siberia), 'How extraordinary it is to think that the great crisis has passed and we are as calm as if nothing had happened.' She went on:

> The wife of the American Commandant professes to be very much disappointed with China at present. She says her chief object in life was to see the late Empress Dowager. She only married Colonel Barnett in order to see her and now the Empress is dead and cannot be seen and George does nothing but spoil the children and spoil the furniture![1]

But even if the expected revolution failed to materialise, it was clear that the Ch'ing Dynasty was on its last legs and that Tsu-hsi's deathbed decision to name yet another infant – her great nephew Puyi – as the new emperor would do little but hasten its extinction. Faced with this inevitable fact, many foreigners, despite their patronising attitude to the old China, now mourned its passing. But others like Dr Morrison, acutely aware that they were living in Peking at a crucial moment in the country's history, looked impatiently to the future.

On 9 November 1908, a few days before the imperial deaths, Morrison wrote, 'The Emperor is suffering from constipation and the Empress Dowager from diarrhoea, so the Imperial balance is struck.'[2] Thus reassured, he left the next day for a shooting trip on the Yellow River and was therefore absent from Peking for the big story. To have missed such a startling event for so trivial a reason was an intense professional blow to Morrison, whose reputation as the authoritative Western voice on China (especially since Hart's departure) extended far beyond *The Times* readership. Courted everywhere by the good and great, Morrison was, as one of his biographers put it, the most famous Australian after Dame Nellie Melba. Australian though he might be, more significantly Morrison was a committed apologist for the British Empire, believing profoundly in its mission to spread good government across a troubled world. Although exasperated by, as he saw it, the lack of talent among British diplomats in Peking, he always worked hard to boost Britain's influence in China – not merely for commercial gain but because he was convinced this was also in the best interests of the Chinese themselves.

In 1894, Morrison had undertaken a remarkable solo expedition across western China. Travelling up the Yangtze to Chungking he had then made his way, largely on foot, to Burma – a distance of 1,600 miles. Dressed as a Chinese, complete with pigtail, the tall, fair, unmistakably Anglo-Saxon Morrison had accomplished this 'pleasant journey' unarmed and speaking not a word of the language. His published account of the adventure[3] was well received and led directly to his being offered a job by *The Times* as its special correspondent in Peking. Arriving there in 1897, in the wake of the Sino-Japanese war, he soon established himself professionally, building up an impressive network of contacts. The city itself, however, was a disappointment: 'The life here is singularly unattractive. Nor have I lived in a more God forsaken place than this. There is no female society, no pleasure of any kind whatever.'[4] Nevertheless, it was to remain his home for the next 20 years. Politically, there was much to absorb him. It did not take him long to identify Russia as the key enemy – both of Chinese and of British interests in the region. His support of Russia's adversary, Japan, was so blatant that when fighting between the two countries finally broke out in 1904, it was nicknamed 'Morrison's war'.

Morrison was already a respected commentator on China at the outset of the Boxer uprising, but his graphic accounts of the siege and personal heroism had by the end of it turned him into a celebrity. As the result of a fabricated story by a Shanghai-based journalist claiming that the foreigners had all been massacred, he had enjoyed the curious experience of reading his own obituary, which, along with those of Hart, MacDonald and others, had been published in *The Times* on 16 July 1900:

> No newspaper anxious to serve the best interests of the country has ever had a more devoted, a more fearless, and a more able servant than Dr. Morrison... throughout the last three critical years in China, it is to Dr. Morrison that the British public has looked...for the earliest and most accurate intelligence concerning events in which the interests of this country have been so largely and often, we fear, prejudicially involved. With extraordinary judgement, amounting almost to intuition, in an atmosphere which he used himself to describe as 'saturated with lies', he discriminated with unfailing accuracy between what was true and what was false...

Gertrude Bell, one of many women to fall under Morrison's spell, wrote to her father about him:

> He is A Person. You feel no doubt about that from the first moment you see him. He has a big calm manner; he speaks softly – softlee, as he would say, for he has what I take to be a slightly Australian accent...you could not guess more of his mind than he wanted to you to know...He has a sledgehammer judgement that comes crashing down on every form of incapacity and an equally strong appreciation of every kind of 'capacitee'...He works very slowly and with great difficulty, takes four or five hours over a single telegram, writes and rewrites before he is satisfied...Peking rings with his praises, not loud but deep; for thoughtful and gentle kindness there must be few people like this big quiet man and I should think when he makes a friend he never loses him.[5]

The admiration was not mutual. Of Bell, Morrison wrote: 'My God she'd talk the leg off an iron pot and she has the cheek of the devil.'[6] Fearless and supremely confident of his own views, his scornful judgement of others was one of his less endearing characteristics.

Despite Morrison's reputation as an authority on China, he could neither speak nor read Chinese. He dealt with this not so insignificant problem by employing Edmund Backhouse – arguably the most notorious foreigner ever to live in Peking – as his translator. Backhouse's remarkable career might never have come to light had it not been for Professor Hugh Trevor-Roper (later Lord Dacre), whose detective work in the 1970s[7] unravelled an extraordinary web of subterfuge and lies. Out of Backhouse's murky history only one solid fact emerges – his genius for languages. Apart from this, he had little to offer when, at the age of 25, he first arrived in Peking in 1898, only a few months after Morrison. He had left Oxford without a degree and three years earlier had been declared bankrupt – his extravagance and love of jewellery belying his Quaker background. Exactly why he chose Peking is not clear, although he seems already to have had a good grasp of Chinese. Without a job (there was talk of his joining the Customs but it came to nothing), the opportunity to work with Morrison translating documents and newspapers was a welcome break.

Although Morrison did not pay Backhouse, he acted as his patron and was probably responsible for his being offered a teaching post in 1903 at the recently opened University of Peking. Certainly, in the early days of their acquaintance, he greatly admired the effete young Englishman, telling Gertrude Bell that he was the ablest person he had ever met and that the Chinese dictionary on which he was then working would be 'the wonder of the age'.[8] Unlike most foreigners at the time, both men lived outside the legation quarter in courtyard houses. They were near neighbours and during the decade in which they worked so closely together, they developed a warm friendship. It is hard to imagine two collaborators more different from one another. On the one hand, was the blunt, virile Australian, a genuine hero, relishing his role on the imperialist stage; while on the other, lurked a reclusive, homosexual Englishman, a fantasist on an epic scale who over the next 40 years was to dupe governments, universities, banks and businesses with breathtaking nerve.

Their partnership continued to work well until 1908, when Morrison's absence at the time of the imperial deaths caused a crisis. Naturally, *The Times* wanted to publish such a dramatic story as quickly as possible. But John Bland, the old China hand who normally deputised for Morrison, was sick and unable to deliver. It was Backhouse who came to the rescue, helping Bland to file a full and authoritative account. From this time, Backhouse's ties to Morrison began to loosen as he transferred his loyalties to Bland and others. By now it was not only his gift for languages (including Mongolian) that was in demand within the foreign community. His apparent close contacts with high-ranking Manchus and knowledge of complex imperial procedures provided invaluable inside information to the many agents in Peking competing for concessions.

Backhouse, realising that his own expertise might combine profitably with Bland's literary and business skills, suggested that they write a book together.

When *China under the Empress Dowager* was published in 1910, it was an unexpected success, largely because for the first time it recorded the Boxer uprising from the Chinese perspective. As Robert Hart had observed in 1901,

> It would be interesting to get a really reliable Chinese account of Palace doings –
> and Peking doings – during 1900. As it is we are all guessing and inferring and
> putting this and that together, but we have not got at the facts yet.[9]

Now it seemed these were at last forthcoming. The new evidence not only made plain Tsu-hsi's active support for the Boxers but also Jung-lu's vital role in restraining them. Events long shrouded in mystery were satisfactorily clarified, all thanks to a diary kept by a Manchu official named Ching-shan, discovered by Backhouse in the anarchic post-siege days.

Like Morrison, Backhouse had also taken refuge in the British Legation during the Boxer troubles but unlike the Australian he had not had a good war. After contriving to strain a muscle early in the siege, he had disappeared from view, spending the remainder of it immersed in his *Goodrich Chinese Pocket Dictionary*. After it was all over, he emerged (fully recovered) to join in the looting. Backhouse's own house had been destroyed but he was allocated quarters in Ching-shan's house. When the allied troops poured into Peking, the old man's wife and concubines had committed suicide while he met his own end down a well – pushed by his son. It was in this house, as Backhouse was later to recount in great detail, that he found the diary.

In fact, it was a forgery but one so accomplished that not only did it convince Backhouse's co-author Bland (who had a good knowledge of the language) but also many distinguished scholars – some of them even Chinese. Not everyone was taken in. Morrison knew it was a fake from the start but without any hard proof was not prepared to condemn it publicly. His views though were widely known and sparked a controversy that rumbled on until 1976 when Trevor-Roper convincingly demonstrated that the diary was a fake and Backhouse the forger. So plausibly did Backhouse weave fact and fantasy together, that even now the historical record remains clouded by his input. Furthermore, Ching-shan's diary was by no means his only grandiose deception. To quote Trevor-Roper, he 'palmed off forged scrolls on libraries, forged contracts on manufacturers, forged "curios" on individuals, forged letters of recommendation, forged reports of high-powered interviews, imaginary arms, imaginary battleships, imaginary libraries, imaginary pearls, all explained by elaborate, detailed self-glorifying fantasies'.[10]

Having so carelessly missed the Empress Dowager's death, Morrison made sure that he was in Peking to report her funeral. This did not take place until a year later when the court astrologers decided that the right moment had come to move her body from the Forbidden City to its final resting place in the Eastern Ch'ing tombs. Tsu-hsi had taken a keen interest in her mausoleum, inspecting it with increasing regularity, as she grew older. Built at staggering cost, it had been near completion in 1897 when she had ordered its destruction on the grounds that its teak pillars were too modest in scale. Several months before her funeral procession set off from Peking on its four-day journey, paper effigies of her favourite possessions – clocks, dressing tables, pipes and dolls – and entire companies of paper soldiers (in modern European uniforms) had been burned so that they would be ready and waiting for her in the after-life.

Near the Tung-chih men, the eastern gate of the Tartar City through which the cortège was to pass, the Waiwupu erected a stand from where the foreigners were invited to view the spectacle. Several mandarins stood by ready to receive them and collect their entrance tickets. Tickets, the Chinese had long since concluded, were an essential part of European civilisation. When in 1900 the Boxers had taken over the railway station to prevent the foreigners from escaping, their first action had been to destroy all the tickets in the belief that no foreigner could travel without one. In all likelihood, the scholarly-looking Backhouse was also present that day on the stand to bid farewell to the woman with whom, so he later claimed in his pornographic memoir, *Décadence Mandchoue*, he had shared wild orgies.

A Dutch tourist, Henri Borel, described how in a biting wind, the Westerners bared their heads and bowed as very slowly the catafalque drew closer:

It was square covered in yellow fabric with a huge golden ball on top. It advanced in stately fashion, carried by a hundred or so coolies on long bamboo poles...preceded by hundreds of yellow banners and standards, pajongs and pennants, carried high in the sky on poles coloured red and gold. In the sunlight the approach of this golden cavalcade seemed an apotheosis of mystic colour. The soldiers along the route presented arms, the military guards of the legation saluted. All was as still as death. Not a drum roll was heard. The thousands along the ridges of the hills were silent. It was as if a goddess were being carried by – solemnly swinging to and fro. A lama priest indicated the rhythm for the funeral stride of the coolies with a small wooden rattle, a little ball beating upon a piece of parchment, making a dry sepulchral sound in the depressing silence.[11]

In front of the bier, walked the Regent, Prince Ching, and the Manchu nobility and the Grand Eunuch, Li Lien-ying, who had so ruthlessly resisted any hint of reform within the court. In his arms he carried his mistress's favourite Pekingese dog.

Four days later, on 9 November 1909 at precisely 7 o'clock the Empress Dowager's coffin was placed on a richly jewelled couch, amid sacrificial vessels of carved jade, massive vases and gold incense burners. The sumptuousness of Tsu-hsi's funeral was in stark contrast to that of the emperor which had taken place six months earlier. Morrison had also witnessed this but had been so unimpressed by the scruffy Manchu cavalry mounted on half-starved ponies and the unkempt bearers with their broken umbrellas and tattered banners that he had not even thought it worth reporting to *The Times*. But, however shabby the Kuang-hsu emperor's funeral, at least in death (he was buried many miles away from his aunt in the Western Ch'ing tombs) he was finally free of the woman who had made his life such a misery. In a sobering epilogue to the Empress Dowager's *folie de grandeur*, in 1928 her tomb was dynamited and robbed. Some days later she was found by a group of Manchu nobles lying on her face, naked to the waist, her silken trousers pulled down and her dyed hair dishevelled. When, very gently, they turned her onto her back, they found her face 'wonderfully pale, but the eyes deeply sunken...like two black caverns'.[12]

***

> Will not some hear the voice of the Master calling them to go out and take the place of those called higher, to shepherd the flocks now scattered and bereaved, and to gather the fruit of the life-work as well as of the terrible suffering and death of our native and foreign brethren and sisters who have gone to their reward?[13]

Written in December 1900, when memories of Boxer atrocities were still vivid, this plea to the faithful did not go unheeded. Remarkably, despite the cruel fate of so many missionaries, recruitment to the missionary field soared after the siege. In fact, incentive had never been stronger for, despite inter-denominational squabbling, the missions were united in the belief that the real 'yellow peril' lay not in Asia's potential military menace but in its heathenism. And if Christendom allowed such a force to develop 'without straining every nerve to make it Christian, the results...may be as fateful as they will have been deserved'.[14] So strain every nerve the missionaries did, although the isolation, deprivation and dangers many of them faced were formidable.

In his book, *China*, the Reverend (later Bishop) Frank Norris (whose barricades during the siege had won widespread admiration) summed up Chinese religions for his missionary readers:

> **Buddhism**, with its countless images, its foreign language, its unworthy monks, has for centuries had a vast influence on China, and an influence not for the good.

> **Taoism**: A mystical philosophy mixed up with wide-reaching superstition, with its innumerable spirits and its many unknown terrors, has likewise played but an evil part in the religious life of the nation.

> **Confucianism**: In spite of its freedom from actual idolatry, in spite of its lofty moral teaching, in spite of, or perhaps because of, its influence in making what we call 'ancestral worship' the most prominent of all religious rites in China, has not only failed to raise, but rather tended to lower to a more materialistic level, the spiritual traditions of the Chinese people.[15]

Such a disparaging analysis must have made it easier for missionaries to convince themselves that with enough faith, hard work and courage (and funding), it could only be a matter of time before Christianity triumphed across China. But in reality it was to prove an uphill struggle. In more than a century of evangelising, they converted less than 1 per cent of the population. To counter Chinese indifference, a number of missionary boards set up schools and dispensaries in the belief that a more pragmatic approach would produce better results. After all, one commentator reasoned, 'The man who has successfully healed the body has some reasonable hope to expect that the patient will accept the medicine that he offers to cure the soul.'[16] In the years immediately after the Boxer uprising, these (mostly Protestant) missionary schools became immensely popular. Patriotic Chinese students enrolled in them, eager to discover, if not the gospel, the secrets of Western success which they might then deploy to modernise and rebuild their own country. The fact that these schools did so much to foster Chinese nationalism did not prevent the missionaries being later condemned as enemies of the revolution.

Britain may have been the dominant foreign power in China at the turn of the century but its church, in terms of conversions and investment, lagged far behind the Catholics and Americans. As Norris lamented, unlike other missions in Peking, the Anglicans had, by the outbreak of the Boxer uprising, only converted a handful of Chinese. The Bishop of North China and Shantung had an impressive title and a vast diocese, but little else. Even before the siege, the bishop's gallant operation had been run on a shoestring. Now, with their buildings destroyed and their few converts scattered, the Anglican survivors in Peking (two missionaries had been killed and two had died) had the depressing task of beginning all over again. One of their chief problems was the waning British interest in China once the siege had ended, and in consequence, lack of funding. Nor was morale helped by the knowledge ('enough to make missionary blood run cold') that one enterprising Birmingham firm was manufacturing heathen idols for export to China.[17]

It was all so different for the Catholics and for the Americans. In the years following the siege, the former made vigorous efforts to recover lost ground (apart from the Peitang, there were three other Catholic churches in Peking alone), expanding their operations into every province. Frank Norris was envious of their resources but also critical of their methods: 'The Roman Church in China has been not inaptly termed the largest "secret society" now in existence,' he wrote about the time of the Empress Dowager's death. He found it particularly galling that while the Catholic missions could boast 'no great colleges or educational centres...no preaching-rooms or hospitals, save here and there', they were winning more converts than anyone else. And '*after only forty days* instruction', he added indignantly.[18] In the United States, meanwhile, evangelistic fervour was turning mission work in China into nothing short of a national crusade.[19]

One encouraging feature of the post-siege decade was a new interest in women's education. The American missionary and siege veteran, Luella Miner, founded the first women's college in China – the Peking Union College for Women.[20] Given the low status of women, this was an important milestone. Among its early alumnae were the National Secretary of the YMWCA, a distinguished poet, social workers and the first female principals of secondary schools. That these women were able to achieve so much in a society where attempts to ban foot binding were still only partly successful was largely thanks to foreigners of Miner's calibre. Of the many Western women who campaigned against foot binding, none did so more vigorously than Alicia Little. An outspoken critic of foreign arrogance in China, she was elected in 1895 to be the first president of the Anti-Foot Binding Society of China; she spoke all over the country to groups of Chinese officials, determinedly keeping the organisation free from Christian affiliation so that it might have more influence among Chinese men. Mrs Little wrote a number of novels about life in China, where she herself lived for 20 years (1887–1907). Gertrude Bell met her at a dinner party in Peking in 1903 but was not impressed:

> She is a truly awful lady. She wore a mustard coloured dress which was exactly the same colour as her skin so for some time I did not notice she had a low gown on. She has a very vivacious manner and a heavy black moustache. Her husband doesn't count. [In 1898 Archibald Little was the first person to navigate the Yangtze by steamship.] Dr. Morrison says her books are pretty feeble but as they are popular he hopes she will write many more for he rejoices to see any interest about China.[21]

Individuals like Alicia Little and Luella Miner made a genuine attempt to understand the society in which they had chosen to live. Others, like a young First Secretary at the British Legation, were so confident of their native superiority that it came as a shock to discover how quickly the Chinese were able to assimilate Western culture:

> The demand for Western teaching is growing fast. I looked in on several classes in the American Methodist Episcopalian Mission College and was particularly interested in the Shakespeare lesson, taught by an American. I could not help asking whether Chinese could really take an intelligent interest in foreign authors; he assured me that they did and told me a story of one of his pupils whom he had taken through Longfellow and Tennyson and when asked which he preferred the man replied that he quite liked Longfellow but that 'Tennyson was more musical and a deeper thinker; he appeals more to the Chinese mind!!'[22]

In 1909, The Rt Reverend Lord William Gascoyne-Cecil (second son of the prime minister, Lord Salisbury, and subsequently Bishop of Exeter) was commissioned by an Oxford and Cambridge committee to explore the possibility of establishing a major new university in China. Although this particular scheme came to nothing, the eccentric Lord William (he allegedly fed crumpets to rats), together with his wife, Lady Florence, threw himself into the task with enthusiasm. 'He asks the most difficult questions,' complained Jack Garnett:

> At the soup stage he put an awful poser to me; I quickly passed it on to Sir John [Jordan] who had to refer it in turn to Morrison who did a bit of a bluff. At the Temple of Heaven Lord William stumped us all again wanting to know the meaning of every stone and slab

Garnett did not approve of such people, 'If they want to know so much, why don't they read books?'[23]

Garnett also had the job of organising the visit of another troublesome Christian visitor – General Booth of the Salvation Army. The latter insisted on an Imperial Audience but as Garnett pointed out:

> It is impossible to translate into Chinese his position and the title 'General'. He doubtless thinks that he will be able to converse freely with their Majesties and perhaps convert them to 'salvation'. He little knows the stony statuesqueness of an Imperial Audience. I can't imagine the Dowager Empress with a poke bonnet on her head and a tambourine in her hand. Foreigners who do not know what 'General' Booth is will be sure to think he is one of England's greatest generals come to conclude a secret military convention with this decaying nation – which will be humorous.[24]

But by 1907, it was not just well-meaning Christians who wanted to visit Peking. Tourism was growing fast, as Garnett noted.

> We have a vast number of globetrotters here just now; the place just crawls with them. Cook's have just sent up a man to enquire into the usefulness of establishing an agency here, and I suppose this place will shortly be advertised among Cook's tours. I am glad to have known it before that time.[25]

The increasing number of foreign visitors to Peking reflected a popular belief that China, following Japan's example, had at last begun to transform itself into a modern state. As Lord William Cecil put it:

> China has fundamentally altered. She used to be absolutely the most conservative land in the world. Now she is a land which is seeing so many radical changes, that a missionary said, when I asked him a question about China, "You must not rely on me, for I left China three months ago, so that what I say may be out of date." China is now progressive; yes, young China believes intensely in progress, with an optimistic spirit which reminds the onlooker more of the French pre-revolution spirit than of anything else. And this intense belief in progress shows itself at every turn; the Yamen runner has become a policeman, towns are having the benefit of water-works, schools are being opened everywhere, railways cover the land.[26]

Lord William called his account of his travels *Changing China*, and, although jaded diplomats like Garnett still regarded the country as 'decaying', there were plenty of other articles and books published around 1910 with titles such as *The New China* or *The Changing Chinese* to establish the contrary.[27] But if by 1910, foreign influence on Peking was becoming ever more noticeable, it is much harder to chart Peking's effect on the foreigners. Genuine friendships formed on an equal basis were rare, while the miscegenation that had been common when Robert Hart was a young man in Ningbo does not seem to have occurred much in the capital. A Danish diplomat summed it up: 'I am sometimes invited to dinner by mandarins but there it stops, we are too different in all our ways and thoughts to make any real friendship.'[28] And while outside the walls of the legation quarter the world may have been changing fast, life within them remained remarkably constant. On the day the Empress Dowager died, a Russian diplomat arrived for the first time in Peking and, to his evident delight, discovered:

> … the charming society of foreign diplomats who, in the middle of the Chinese capital, had arranged a purely European mode of living. Exiled from everything to which they were accustomed, and having little to do, the diplomats turned their lives into a perpetual merry-go-round of parties. Every Legation tried to eclipse the others: a ballet in the Russian Legation, where the charming daughter of the Minister was a comet surrounded by stars; a musical at the French Legation, where the beautiful wife of the French Minister danced the bolero to the music of Ravel; a fancy dress ball in the French bank with everyone under the influence of champagne, exotic costumes, Chinese lanterns in the garden, and romance in the air. I always wondered what the solemn Chinese servants who moved about with refreshment trays must have thought of the representatives of a higher civilization. Probably nothing that would have been to our credit. These parties were purely foreign affairs and unless it was an official dinner party in honour of the Chinese Foreign Minister one hardly saw any Chinese guests among the crowd. One got the impression that the foreign diplomats had been sent to China for the sole purpose of amusing themselves.[29]

Most missionaries – despite their closer daily contact with the Chinese – also lived in a very different world from that of their converts. The truth was that while the Chinese were striving to understand the West better and to find a way forward for their beleaguered country, the majority of foreigners, having scaled the Great Wall, explored the Ming tombs and watched the sun set over the Western Hills, gladly retreated to the familiar world of bridge, whisky and legation gossip.

6

REPUBLICAN DREAMS

On 10 October 1911, three years after the death of the Empress Dowager and ten since the signing of the 'Boxer Protocol', the revolution that was to sweep away more than 2,000 years of imperial rule finally broke out. It started in Wuhan[1] (650 miles south of Peking), which, with its volatile mix of industrial workers, students, Yangtze boatmen and disaffected soldiers, had for some years been ripe for rebellion. Spurred into action by an accidental bomb explosion, the revolutionaries seized an arsenal and put the Manchu governor to flight. China's most famous rebel, Sun Yat-sen, was at the time thousands of miles away in America, where he first learned of the successful revolution from a Denver newspaper. Since his earliest insurrection in 1895, he and his followers had regularly tried to topple the Ch'ing Dynasty, each attempt ending in disaster. This time it was different. Meeting little resistance, the rebellion quickly spread to Shanghai and key central provinces, causing panic at the court in Peking.

There, in a last-ditch attempt to save the dynasty, the Regent, Prince Chun (brother of the late Kuang-hsu emperor), summoned the man who had done so much to suppress the Boxers in 1900 – Yuan Shih-kai. This involved considerable loss of face since Chun had exiled him after the Empress Dowager's death, in revenge for his betrayal of Kuang-hsu and the 1898 reform movement. But it was now clear that the general and his well-trained Northern Army were all that stood between the Manchus and destruction. Yuan, fully aware that he held all the cards, took his time to respond but, once given full command of the army and appointed prime minister, agreed to return to Peking.

The foreigners' fears that the revolution would engulf them proved unfounded, but they were far from complacent. Percy Loraine, a young British diplomat, arrived in Peking the day after it broke out, 'just in time for all the excitement'. He summed up the general view:

> So far, the revolutionaries' attitude towards foreigners has been worthy of all praise, but this is emphatically not because they like the foreigner but because they fear him and understand that if they put his back up his vast interests in the country will compel him to intervene for their protection and so spoil the revolution and rob its leaders of the fruits. All the men who really know this country and whose opinion is worth listening to are unanimous in declaring that the latent hatred of the foreigner is still as strong among the mass of the Chinese as it was 50 or even 11 years ago.[2]

Although Loraine, like many of his colleagues, sympathised with the revolutionaries in their efforts to rid themselves of a 'rotten and unworthy administration', he had little confidence in their ability to put a more effective government in its place – let alone safeguard the foreigners or their property. The Danish Minister, Count Preben Ahlefeldt-Laurvig, was equally sceptical:

> We have really passed through an awful time here in Peking – street fights, looting, incendiarism etc. Personally I had the pleasure of hearing the bullets whistling past my ears when I went out in the Chinese City to fetch the married Danish families. You can simply not imagine the scenes of cruelty and barbarity we have witnessed. All sensible people are already longing to go back to the autocracy. I am afraid what we have seen is only the beginning, and I am pleased that Mary and my kids are returning in the spring. A place where you meet decapitated corpses and half decomposed heads at every street corner is certainly not a place for women and children.[3]

Although the foreigners respected China's imperial past, they had little time for the latter-day Manchus. They did, however, hold Yuan Shih-kai in high regard. As Governor of Shantung he had put down the Boxers and created China's first modern army, and was genuinely sympathetic to a wide range of reforms. And unlike any figure in the current government, he exuded authority. Dr Paul S. Reinsch (American Minister 1913–19) was struck by his energy: 'His eyes...alive with interest and mobile, were always brightly alert. They fixed themselves on the visitor with keen penetration, yet never seemed hostile.'[4] Yuan's 'energy' however, did not extend to physical exercise. As the foreign affairs vice-minister, W.W. Yen,[5] recorded, even within his own house he was always carried upstairs or to the gate in a sedan chair. Yen, who spent a good deal of time in the company of Peking's sport-obsessed foreigners, also noted that, 'the fundamental difference between the old Chinese and Occidental philosophy of physical well-being was that while the latter called for exercise to develop energy, the former advocated as little physical motion as possible to conserve the same.'[6]

Attitudes to physical fitness apart, Yuan was someone with whom diplomats like Reinsch and Jordan felt they could do business. So it was with high expectations that the foreigners gathered on the Tartar city wall (as they always did for any major event) to watch Yuan Shih-kai's formal return to Peking on 13 November 1911. Among them was Alice Bowden-Smith, a former Cambridge University student, who had come to China with the intention of setting up a school for upper-class girls. She later recalled the event:

> One day and one night remain vividly in memory. The day is the one on which Yuan Shih-kai came back to Peking, after his long period of exile. It was the only moment at which Peking seemed to rise to a sense of national feeling. On that November afternoon, the streets, from the station to the Premier's residence, were lined by silent waiting crowds, and in the lanes even the women were asking, 'will he really come?' And when the strong enigmatic figure actually passed along the thoroughfares the news thrilled through the city as with a common pulse.[7]

Under Yuan's command, the imperial troops quickly gained ground against the southern revolutionaries but their victories were not decisive. Furthermore, it was soon clear that Yuan had no wish to prolong hostilities. In reality, he was no more interested in the Manchus' survival than he was in seeing a republic or even a constitutional monarchy established. It is hard to establish whether at this stage he was already planning to make himself emperor, but what is clear is that he intended to keep power firmly in his own hands. First, he had to balance the revolutionaries and imperialists against each other – a feat he accomplished with impressive skill.

A few weeks after Yuan arrived back in Peking, Sun Yat-sen returned to China. On 1 January 1912, he was inaugurated in Nanking as the first provisional president of the Chinese Republic. He knew, though, that despite the revolutionaries' popular support, their position was too weak to gain control of the whole country. So, within hours of taking up office, he telegraphed Yuan, convinced by his former foe's overtures of peace and apparent conversion to republicanism, to tell him that the presidency was his when he wanted it. As Loraine had commented six weeks into the revolution, 'the situation is assuming complications which will severely tax human ingenuity to unravel when settling day comes'.[8]

For the Manchus, that day came a month later, on 12 February 1912, when the new Empress Dowager (Kuang-hsu's widow), after intense negotiations with Yuan Shih-kai, signed the abdication. Standing in the throne room of the Forbidden City, in the presence of the six-year-old emperor, Puyi, and hundreds of sobbing, prostrate eunuchs, Lung-yu, with tears streaming down her face, read out the imperial edict that brought to an end over 2,000 years of Chinese Empire:

> It is not fitting that We should withstand the desires of the nation merely for the sake of the glorification of Our House. We recognize the signs of the ages, and we have tested the trend of popular opinion; and We now, with the Emperor at Our side, invest the nation with sovereign power, and decree the establishment of a constitutional government on a republican basis...[9]

In the light of what was to happen (only six years later) to the Russian imperial family, the Manchus were treated extraordinarily well. The emperor kept his title and his court, received an annual income of four million dollars and was allowed to go on living in the Forbidden City. He even retained ownership of his priceless possessions. This generosity is less surprising when seen in relation to Yuan's own ambitions. If he was to accede to the dragon throne, he had no wish to see it stripped of its wealth and dignity. 'Republican in title he was,' wrote Reinsch, 'but an autocrat at heart. All the old glittering trappings of the empire he preserved.'[10]

The day after the abdication, Sun fulfilled his promise by handing over the presidential office to Yuan, on condition that the capital was transferred to the revolutionaries' stronghold – Nanking (southern capital). This city had special significance for them. It had been the Ming capital in the fourteenth century, whereas the Manchu capital, Beijing (northern capital), was, in the words of one Chinese intellectual, 'where all weird carbuncles and chronic diseases of this sinful world are concentrated'.[11] But Yuan declined to move, arguing that the north was too unstable for him to abandon. In fact, he never had the slightest intention of leaving his own power base. When, several weeks after the abdication, Sun sent a delegation to Peking to press the matter, revolt broke out among Yuan's own soldiers – a coincidence many suspected Yuan had himself engineered.

On the night of the 'mutiny', the diplomats were as usual entertaining each other. But as machine-gun fire began to drown out their conversation, the guests, Abrikosov among them, rushed on to the wall to see what was happening:

> The night was calm and we could clearly hear the shots in different parts of the city. Fires had started in two or three places; the clamour of many voices drifted toward us. There was a certain excitement among the ladies in evening dresses and their escorts but no one was afraid. I must say that in this respect the diplomats were generally courageous, filled more with curiosity than with anxiety for their own safety even at times of real danger. Thus they viewed the disorders as a new entertainment.[12]

Brave or not, ever since the Boxer uprising, Peking's foreign community had lived in constant fear of another attack. Now, on the freezing, moonlit night of 29 February 1912, with shooting and fires breaking out all over the city, it seemed clear that history was about to repeat itself. 'If we had to pass through the fire once again,' wrote Dorothea Soothill (later Lady Hosie), 'would we play as courageous a part as our noble dead?'[13] Spent bullets fell at her feet as she helped Lady Jordan receive the refugee families now pouring into the legation. Abrikosov watched a 'grinning' Cossack conduct a group of Russian Jewish prostitutes to safety, while the Danish Minister led a party to rescue Robert Hart's sister-in-law, Lady Bredon, from her house in the Tartar City. But, as she herself later recounted, her gallant saviours, having drunk all her champagne (to save it from looters), forgot why they had come and left without her.[14]

As legation guards were mobilised, provisions counted and beds installed in every conceivable corner, the sense of Boxer siege *déjà vu* was unnerving, though Morrison as usual revelled in the crisis:

> My house was so lit that I could see to read and the crackling of the burning buildings was quite sufficient to keep me awake...Sorry affair happened but since it took place I would not have missed it for anything.[15]

However, when everyone awoke the next morning, they were surprised to discover the worst was over. News that elderly Chinese gentlemen were airing their cage-birds on the city wall was encouraging, while Abrikosov discovered that he was able to ride to the Temple of Heaven as usual despite passing under dozens of freshly decapitated heads swinging from the trees.[16] Although many Chinese were dead, no foreigners had been hurt and scarcely any of their property damaged. Yuan even put out a proclamation apologising for the anxiety caused: 'To you strangers in a strange land, I wish in particular to convey my sincere regret for the untoward incident and the very natural anxiety you felt.'[17]

Having thus established that for security reasons he must remain in Peking, Yuan was inaugurated as the second provisional president of the Chinese Republic on 10 March 1912. Morrison was one of the few foreigners present:

> Yuan came wobbling in like a duck looking fat and unhealthy, in a Marshall's uniform, loose flesh of his neck hanging down over his collar, hat too large for him, nervous and uncomfortable...was handed document in large letters which he read nervously – the oath –...Admirable order no confusion...No more kowtowing. Now shake hands. No more queues. No more Chinese official dress – Chinese dressed most simply.[18]

Although most foreigners supported Yuan's leadership, few believed that China was yet ready for democracy. John Bland (Backhouse's co-author, now back in England) expressed a common view when he wrote:

> Recognising the indifference of China's masses towards all political theories, and bearing in mind the deep-rooted economic causes of unrest which must continue to afflict the nation until, by slow educative process, the existing social structure can be modified to meet its new environment, we perceive that only by the iron hand of authority can the nation be preserved at peace with itself and with its neighbours.[19]

Morrison, on the other hand, was so convinced by both the republic and its new president that in September 1912, he resigned from *The Times* to become Yuan's political adviser. Congratulations flowed in. Sir Edward Grey, Britain's Foreign Secretary, wished him every success in his efforts to help China through her difficulties; an American colleague wrote that the appointment was the first sign of intelligence the Chinese had shown for a long time, while Reginald Johnson who was to become tutor to the deposed emperor, Puyi, seven years later, added, '*The Times*' loss is China's gain.'[20] Not everyone was convinced.

Morrison's old foe Bland remarked, 'For a man who does not speak Chinese to be adviser to a man who does not speak English, is a position unique in its way.'[21]

For Yuan, desperate to win recognition from the powers and well aware of Morrison's influence on Western opinion, it was a shrewd move. Morrison had long since proved himself one of China's most effective ambassadors, never missing an opportunity to promote the country's progress to an often sceptical British public. Shortly before the revolution, in a letter to Lady Blake, wife of the Governor of Hong Kong, he outlined some of the changes taking place in Peking:

> I find that the city is being transformed. Macademised roads are being made everywhere: every important house is lit with electric light: the streets are lighted by electricity: there is an excellent telephone system: there is a postal service with delivery eight times a day. The police force cannot be too highly praised – a well paid, well equipped, well disciplined body of men…All the ministries are now either stationed in western buildings, some of quite imposing size…or will be soon. There is a good water supply, and I have no doubt before long we shall have electric tramways. The Chinese here are taking largely to the use of modern things…There is a large trade in English bed-steads. All over the city you find rubber-tyred rickshaws. Building is going on all over the city…[22]

By the time of the revolution, horse-drawn glass carriages had replaced sedan chairs and even Peking carts with their nail-studded wheels were less commonplace. Cars, although still rare, did not provoke quite the 'excitement among the natives' as when Count Otani, the dashing leader of a Japanese Buddhist sect, had raced his motor car all over the city only a few years earlier.[23]

Communications had also dramatically changed life for the foreigners. Gone were the days when, cut-off from the outside world for much of the winter, Hart could write: 'We are in Christmas week here; the river is frozen and we don't expect any mails to arrive before the 29th, the last in was that of 20th October.'[24] The trans-Siberian railway had reduced the journey to Europe to a fortnight, while an ever-extending railway system had vastly improved travel within China. Furthermore, a telegraph system operated by a Danish company and nicknamed 'the lifeline' now stretched across Asia to Britain and France.

But Peking's integration into the twentieth century did not please everyone. Many foreigners, having reviled the city's backwardness, now referred nostalgically to 'dear old Peking'. The Dutchman, Henri Borel, felt badly let down as he lunched in the modern dining room of the British-run 'Hotel des Wagon Lits' in 1908:

A glass of sherry, a cigarette, a French newspaper. Am I in Paris or Peking? Round about me are exactly the people one sees at Ostend, Biarritz, Wiesbaden, Cairo …smart business people and empty *desoeuvres*. What in Heaven's name are these people doing in Peking? "How do you like Peking?" I hear someone ask. "Oh, awfully nice" – the shrill high voice of a lady – "So pretty; so interesting. Yesterday we did the Ming Tombs near Nank'ou; oh it was lovely, lovely!" Thus appears Peking to me, the holy city of the Emperors, the Sons of Heaven, tarnished by the snobbery of white globe-trotters and loafers, who have forced themselves by the fuming, screeching train through its sacred ramparts, which can no longer shield its virginity. And outside to the right and to the left, louder than the buzzing of voices, I hear the hammering and knocking going on for ever – as if the Modern had conquered, and were triumphantly erecting a new, vulgar, cosmopolitan town in the ancient holy fortress of the Tartars of the North.[25]

Borel's theme was a common one – repeated regularly throughout the century by foreigners who, while urging change on China, actually hated it when it happened. 'How horrible,' William Rockhill (American Minister, 1905–9) said at the sight of young Chinese officials in Western clothes. 'European dress is intolerable on them, and it is so with all these attempted imitations.'[26]

Apart from the disturbances on the night of 29 February 1912, life within the legation quarter remained remarkably untouched by the revolution. Although the ministers representing the powers and their Chinese secretaries (professional foreign sinologists) had plenty of work, most of their colleagues were under employed. 'Diplomatic bag goes today therefore a great deal to do – an hour's work!'[27] wrote the Italian diplomat, Daniele Varè, in his diary entry for 21 January 1913. Recently arrived from Rome, he and his wife were quickly absorbed into a way of life that in its essentials had hardly changed in 50 years. Varè, who was to spend more than a decade in Peking, was also a writer who, with his light touch, perfectly caught the curious world of the legation quarter – a world in which boredom and fear were kept at bay by ponies, parties and gossip.

For many foreigners, their daily ride on a squat Mongolian pony (whose natural bad temper was allegedly aggravated by the smell of Westerners[28]) was still a central part of life, supplemented by race-going, paper chases, lengthy luncheons and the club's speciality, 'sherry with an olive'. Evenings continued to be devoted to parties and rumour; 'Dinner at the Haxthausens', wrote Varè: 'All Peking talked with Mrs Olé (approximately 140 kilos) with whom I sat quite a while on the sofa. De Lucca said that we looked like Jonah and the whale.' And a few nights later:

> One young Russian officer, all smiles and spurs, danced deliciously, always gazing into the eyes of his partner and every now and then falling to his knees at her feet. She was in a black dress with white boots. An Englishman – mad as a hatter – tried to imitate him.[29]

The Russian legation was a frequent source of scandal. When Madame Korostovets, wife of the minister, left for Russia after her husband had tried to elope with 16-year-old Miss Ping, the entire diplomatic body – from the doyen, Sir John Jordan, to the youngest attaché – came with flowers to the railway platform to bid her farewell.[30] Several years earlier it had shown equal sympathy to Dmitri Pokotilov's mistress after she was badly burned. The accident occurred when, having appeared before the minister's bachelor guests as 'a winter nymph of the forest' dressed in nothing but cotton wool, she hovered too close to the Christmas tree candles. The genial Abrikosov merely commented, 'Reputations were ruined with great ease, but this was done in such a good-natured way that no one took offence.'[31]

Sir John Jordan (yet another of the many Ulsterman to make a career in the East) was of a different stamp. For a start, unlike most of his colleagues, he was a professional sinologist who had spent his entire career in China and Korea. At a time when in diplomacy, social class and private income still counted for more than specialist knowledge, his appointment as British Minister (lobbied for by Morrison) was in certain quarters considered eccentric. Some of his staff were initially appalled that their 'Chief' came from the Chinese Consular Service rather than the smarter Diplomatic Service. As Varè put it, 'He had a personality that was worthy of study, though he was not what you would call a superior man; only an admirable public servant.'[32] Jordan was in Peking longer than most diplomats, representing Britain – the biggest foreign presence in China – for 14 years (1906–20). Varè summed him up:

> I do not profess to know what passed in Sir John's mind, but it seemed to me that his world consisted of the British Empire and China, with Russia and Japan

looming in the background (sometimes inconveniently near) and a lot of other powers fussing round and interfering in matters which did not really concern them and which they imperfectly understood. Germans and French he looked upon as tiresome, and Americans as spoilt children. Swedes, Spaniards and Portuguese were merely *Banderlog*.[33] And I think he would put Italians in the same category... Lady Jordan was very shy. To be First Lady in Peking was a sore trial to her. But she did her work conscientiously and paid calls and left cards and dined out and opened bazaars, and entertained everybody, doing her best to pretend that she liked it.[34]

Among the foreigners living in Peking at the time of the revolution, there were (in addition to the missionaries) a number of individuals drawn there by altruism. Dorothea Soothill was born in China, the daughter of a missionary (who later became Professor of Chinese at Oxford University). Educated at Newnham College, Cambridge, she persuaded her former fellow student Alice Bowden-Smith to accompany her and her mother to Peking with the aim of setting up a school for aristocratic girls. Their rationale was that while education was now available for girls at the lower end of the social scale, none was on offer to Manchu princesses. Moreover, Alice Bowden-Smith (whose admiral father had been present as a midshipman at the taking of the Taku forts in 1860) strongly believed that the British owed China for 'forcing ourselves upon her when she wanted none of us'.[35] Thus, with exquisite timing, the young women opened their school for Manchu girls in September 1911 – just one month before the revolution.

This was trying, since in the new republic there were technically no princesses or peeresses to educate. Abandoning the school, Miss Bowden-Smith stayed some months in Tientsin to whose foreign concessions many Manchus fled after the revolution. 'It was curious,' she observed, 'to see a Manchu Princess settling with her family and her eunuchs into one of a row of German villas.' She also recorded the delight that many Manchu women took in the 'sensation of being almost scandalously emancipated'. When Alice returned to Peking a few months later, she noted:

> Externally the old Peking has gone. Vanished are the shabby retainers who used to canter after the officials' carriages. Where one used to catch sight of gorgeous official embroideries, one now sees close-cropped men in Western clothes. Queues are fast disappearing. Only in the Imperial City round the glittering yellow roofs of the Palace, lying now like some brilliant fungus, excised for ever

from the body politic, the life of the old oriental court goes on as it did in Baby-lon...The Past has lost its grasp.[36]

***

Official foreign attitudes to the new republic were, above all, governed by national interest. Imperial Russia's reasons for not wishing to see a republic succeed on its own doorstep were obvious, while Japan's expansionist agenda required that China remain weak and defenceless. To the European countries, what mattered most was not what form of government the Chinese chose to adopt, but its ability to protect their investments and provide a stable environ-ment for commercial growth. As one British diplomat observed: 'It does not take nearly nine years of Foreign Office life to realise that not only we but the army and navy and the larger half of the public service generally are, *au fond*, mainly there for the purpose of safeguarding and furthering the interests of British trade...For good or for ill trade rules the world.'[37] Only the Americans, the first major country formally to recognise the Chinese Republic in May 1913 (to the dismay of the others), took a loftier line, as Reinsch made plain:

> It was not for what the *entrepreneurs* could get out of China, nor yet for what China could get out of us, that my policy as American Minister was directed to this complementary meeting of two civilizations. It was because I saw millions perishing wretchedly whose birthright in the higher arts and amenities of living is at least as rich as our own – perishing for lack of an organizing skill which it is the province of the Western peoples to supply.[38]

In a brilliant public relations coup, Yuan Shih-kai requested America to pray for China as its new National Assembly convened in Peking in April 1913. President Woodrow Wilson was 'stirred and cheered', while *The Christian Herald* compared Yuan's initiative to Constantine's and Charlemagne's 'in subjecting pagan nations to the yoke of Christ'.[39]

But Yuan's 'democracy' was a farce from the start and republican dreams of transforming China into a modern nation-state soon turned to night-mare. Like some Chinese 'Macbeth', Yuan embarked on a tyrannical course that effectively strangled the republic at birth and led ultimately to his own downfall. First, he arranged the murder of the man responsible for transform-ing the Revolutionary Alliance into the Nationalist Party, the Kuomintang (KMT). Sung Chiao-jen had been on his way to take up his seat in the National

Assembly where he would have almost certainly been elected Premier, had he not been shot at Shanghai station. Following this assassination, Yuan went on to intimidate and bribe the parliamentary delegates before unleashing a full-scale purge of the KMT (just after the powers had formally recognised his government), finally dissolving the National Assembly in November 1913. Once again Sun Yat-sen fled to Japan.

Morrison was not the only foreign adviser employed by Yuan. Ariga Nagao (nicknamed 'Methuselah') was a Japanese law professor taken on to help draft a new constitution. A monarchist by instinct, he did little to dissuade Yuan from dictatorship, although he did try to modify Japan's increasingly strident demands on China. Frank Goodnow, also recruited to assist with the constitution, was a distinguished American political scientist (he left China in 1914 to become the president of Johns Hopkins University), but demonstrated little interest in defending republican principles. So much so, that shortly after his arrival in 1913, he actively began to support Yuan's moves towards dictatorship. These two advisers, like most foreigners (and many Chinese), would have agreed with Abrikosov's comment: 'A nation cannot with impunity break with its old tradition and embark on experiences absolutely alien to its history and character.'[40]

Morrison, meanwhile, continued to work diligently for Yuan, largely turning a blind eye to his employer's more unpalatable behaviour. But although he stoutly defended both President and republic to the West, he was far from content. Before resigning from *The Times* he had been able to boast (despite being Australian): 'I am the best known Englishman at present east of India, and I am often told the best known correspondent in the world.'[41] Two and a half years later he was writing to a fellow veteran of the Boxer siege: 'The most satisfactory part of the appointment, next to the salary, is the title. Occasionally I have, I think, some influence with the President but I have many disappointments and I cannot see that the Chinese of the Republic are very different from the Chinese we knew 15 years ago.'[42]

Despite its shakiness, the new republican government was determined to take a firmer hand with the foreign diplomats who, according to W.W. Yen, sometimes 'abused their privileges and held extraordinary ideas of their quality'. No longer, he added with evident satisfaction, were they after the revolution able to presume instant access to the President. There was 'no more pounding of tables or discourteous language and getting red in the face on the part of the foreign visitor'. In short, he noted, that although they were 'always treated with respect and courtesy there was an end of catering to them or pampering them. "Yes" was "Yes", and "No" was "No".[43] To the Chinese authorities, Sir Francis Aglen (who had formally succeeded Hart as Inspector General of Customs in 1911) was typical of the kind of foreigner that they found so offensive. According to Yen,

> the exceptional prestige he enjoyed for looking after the foreign indebtedness and the domestic loans gave him exaggerated notions of his personal importance…he treated the Chinese Government in the same lofty manner that Sir Robert Hart was reported to do in the olden days, minus his *savoir faire* and astuteness.[44]

Although so vital to its existence, the Maritime Customs Service was a constant reminder to the government of its humiliating dependence on foreigners like Aglen. Yen expressed his frustration when he wrote:

> China has been unfortunate in that her foreign employees have not rendered loyal services in a constructive spirit. Take for instance the Customs Service, wherein every nationality, except our own people, enjoyed huge salaries and favourable treatment not to be found anywhere else in the world. For decades our young men were admitted after examination into the service at 16 taels per month, while foreign beginners received ten times as much…The policy of Sir Robert Hart and his successors was to perpetuate the foreign character of the Service, and not to build up a Chinese organization, which they would have done, if they had any sense of loyalty and genuine gratefulness to their benevolent master.[45]

Yet from the perspective of most foreigners trying to live and work in China, the British-run multinational Customs seemed the one thread of stability in an otherwise disintegrating country.

Yen maintained that the more authoritative attitude his government took towards the diplomats after the revolution led to them treating Chinese officials with greater respect. Cosmetically, this may have been so but the fragility of China's new democracy became all too obvious when five of the powers (Britain, France, Germany, Japan and Russia) agreed to lend 25 million pounds to Yuan despite protests that the loan was illegal since it had not been approved by the National Assembly. Having tightened its fiscal grip on China, the foreign consortium then attached a humiliating condition to the loan by insisting that another foreigner, Sir Richard Dane, be put in control of the salt *gabelle* (tax) whose revenues secured it. To make matters even worse in the eyes of Chinese nationalists, the 'Reorganization Loan' was signed on 26 April 1913, the very day that evidence was published linking Yuan to Sung Chiao-jen's murder. But, with his coffers replenished and his authority increasingly centralised, Yuan was now able to retain power on his own terms and ignore the revolution.

Guy Hillier, the Hong Kong and Shanghai Bank's permanent agent in Peking since 1891, was a central figure in the negotiations. He had been involved in many important loans to China, on one occasion personally signing a cheque for 16 million pounds. He was the only qualified banker among his foreign colleagues, the others having all been seconded from their respective diplomatic services. He was widely admired for his political acumen and mastery of intricate detail and his achievements were all the more remarkable, given that since 1900, he had been totally blind. His son, sent back to England as a small child, remembered his father arriving home in 1911 on one of his rare visits:

> There was a general upheaval in arranging...accommodation for the Chinese servants without whom he never moved...I was allowed to accompany the luggage cart to the station, where we collected quantities of tin trunks, folding chairs, beds, tables and all the other paraphernalia with which a journey from the East was in those days undertaken. Later in the evening he arrived by another train, accompanied by his secretary and his two Chinese 'Boys'. He stood by the open French window of his study, very straight and slim, with a brown face smiling over a clipped grey beard...and he turned upon me a pair of eyes so bright and intelligent that it seemed to me...impossible that he should be quite blind.[46]

During the immediate post-revolutionary period, the diplomats found themselves professionally in a curious position. They were accredited to a redundant court that continued to exist within a republic as yet unrecognised by most of their governments – a situation which, many of them pointed out, could only happen in China. The oddness of the arrangement was brought home to Daniele Varè on the death of Empress Dowager, Lung-yu, who (Countess Ahlefeldt-Laurvig was informed by her amah) had committed suicide in the aristocratic manner by swallowing gold leaf. Whatever the cause of her death might have been, the republican authorities saw fit to invite foreigners to her official mourning ceremonies at the Forbidden City. These impressed Varè by both their splendour and tawdriness – a mix reflected in the crowds he watched thronging the great marble courtyards. Some of the

Chinese were shoddily dressed, others 'ridiculously Europeanised'. There were Mongols in orange and red silk robes, priests in strawberry red, imperial staff wearing white (the colour of mourning), tall Manchu soldiers, Europeans in silk top hats, casually dressed tourists and uniformed schoolteachers carrying swords and singing strident patriotic songs with their students. Suspended over an altar was a coloured photograph of the dead empress to which the Chinese bowed three times, while priests prayed and a local band played alternately Viennese waltzes and Chopin's *March of the Dead*.[47] The revolution, it seemed, had confused everyone.

Despite all the political excitement, Europe showed as little interest in China as ever. Only one month after the revolution, D.D. Braham (shortly to be foreign editor of *The Times*) wrote to Morrison: 'Although from your point of view – and mine – China is easily the most important thing in the world at present, it is for many reasons not so interesting to our average reader as the choice of a successor to Mr Balfour or even the antics of the latest Russian dancer.'[48] Two years later Reuters' managing director, Baron Herbert de Reuter, made it quite clear that 'whereas the British public was eager for exciting news of war or revolution in China and of violence involving Westerners, its interest in more prosaic developments, however important was small'.[49] Certainly it was a common complaint among diplomats that except when matters concerning commerce and concessions arose, their governments barely recognised their existence. It was therefore hardly surprising that after the murder of Archduke Franz Ferdinand in Sarajevo on 28 June 1914, China was to sink yet further down the West's list of priorities.

7
WAR

For Peking's foreign residents, the summer of 1914 began little differently from any other. As usual, most of them planned to spend the hottest weeks at the seaside town of Peitaiho, about 180 miles due east of the capital (a few miles south of Shanhaiguan). Although the village itself did not amount to much, the resort had become so popular with foreigners from all over north China that several Peking and Tientsin shops opened branches there during the season to provide necessities such as medicines and buttons that even the most resourceful number one boy would otherwise have been unable to find.

The foreigners may have been on holiday but social distinctions were still strictly observed. The sharpest divide lay between 'society' and the missionaries. The latter's bungalows were set in dusty fields unprotected from the sun's glare, while in the 'West End', the smartest part of the resort, stood large villas in shady gardens, their verandas cluttered with bicycles, tennis racquets, rush-chairs and bridge-tables. Strung along the bluffs above the beach, were more modest dwellings half hidden by stunted pine trees, thorn bushes and mimosa, each with its own sandy path leading down to the sea. But for every expatriate, wherever they ranked in the pecking order, Peitaiho offered a welcome respite: 'I haven't read much down here,' wrote one woman, 'as I find it such joy just to see distance after the walls of Peking.'[1]

Peitaiho had first become popular with Peking's foreigners during the early 1900s when the spectacle of Madame Pokotilov's daily bath had been a highlight. The capacious wife of the former Russian Minister (whose arias had aroused the Boxers to such frenzy) was carried down to the sea, 'attired in her most chic costume' in a sedan chair supported by four coolies. An advance party cleared the way, while more coolies formed an escort to the rear.[2] In later years, the French Minister, Alexandre Conty, provided similar entertainment by leading his household each evening into the sea for its ritual dip. According to Bettina Varè, this had something of the biblical about it: 'He, his wife, his children, his servants, his cattle, and the stranger within his gates.'[3] Conduct of a rather less moral character was noted by Jack Garnett: 'Everyone is still away at the seaside where it is rumoured they are having a very skittish time; mixed bathing apparently leads to a great deal in China waters according to gossip.'[4] Sexual peccadilloes may have been acceptable but the community was outraged when Prince Borghese allowed his nine-year-old son to roam around wearing nothing but a helmet and sandals.[5]

Some Westerners preferred Shanhaiguan, a few miles to the north-east, where the Great Wall descends dramatically from the mountains to meet the sea. As it was a politically sensitive area (the Wall marked the boundary with Manchuria), foreign troops had been stationed there each summer since the Boxer troubles. French, Italian, Japanese and Indian soldiers (the latter under the command of British officers) established their encampments along the beach. An English artist visiting Shanhaiguan in 1908 had been shocked to find Japanese soldiers dismantling the Great Wall and using it for target practice.[6] More pleasing was the picturesque ritual, recorded by Varè, that took place each evening when the tall, bearded Pathans turned to the west to pray, their turbans briefly silhouetted against the setting sun before they knelt to touch the ground with their foreheads.[7]

Peitaiho and Shanhaiguan were not the expatriates' only means of escape from the heat of Peking. Since the 1860s, many of them had found refuge in the Western Hills just a few miles beyond the Summer Palace. Scattered among these wooded hills were scores of Buddhist temples, which the foreigners discovered could be rented for a modest sum. Here, generations of them spent summer days walking and reading in the cool air, and at night sleeping under the stars in a temple courtyard, lulled by tinkling bells and Buddhist chanting. Jordan's temple, lying among oaks, maples and pines, was reached by a path that wound its way up the mountain beside a stream. Varè occupied one further down the hill:

Sir John and I used to meet on the stone-flagged path. It was he who pointed out to me a Chinese poem sculptured on a smooth rounded rock that the stream flowed over. We could read the characters through the running water…One evening they brought me a telegram, with a piece of news at the time thought to be important. I thought I would show it to Sir John. It was then about half-past seven, but still light. I started off up the path and, when I reached Sir John's temple, I walked in unannounced. He was dining in one of the courtyards. And though he was all alone, on a hot summer evening in a Chinese temple, he was correctly dressed in a dinner jacket with a black tie. There is something typical of the English character in that scene: the background of lacquered columns and curved roofs; the warm air scented with lotus…the Chinese servants, in their blue cotton coats and red satin waistcoats, moving about to serve the white-haired gentleman who dined in the open, at a little table with a fine table-cloth and glass and silver. He was dressed for dinner – because one *does* dress for dinner when one is the British Minister, even alone in far-off temples in the hills.[8]

Shortly after this encounter, on 4 August 1914, Britain declared war on Germany. Two days later, the ministers met round the large dining table in Jordan's residence. Dominating the room was the life-size portrait of Queen Victoria still bearing the marks of Boxer bullets. Through the window could be seen blossoming lotus flowers in the Chinese courtyard, while Jordan's Chinese-speaking parrots chattered away in their cages. But inside the atmosphere was sombre, as Varè recorded:

Sir John Jordan presided as doyen. He was nervous…Everyone was very constrained deciding only to elect a new member of the administrative committee…After that we adjourned. All the Ministers shook hands. I think it will be the last time for some while.[9]

For the latter, the war had changed everything and nothing. The Italian Minister, Count Sforza, forecast that the war would probably last 30 years and that none of them would be able to leave Peking until it was over.[10] There was frustratingly little they could do except play tennis, walk on the wall and read depressing telegrams from their respective capitals. 'It seems mean to live when so many men are going to death fearlessly,' wrote Jordan to the Foreign Office in London, 'Why should I write about our petty doings here when such momentous events are passing in Europe?'[11] Hundreds of young men agreed, at once applying to be released from their jobs to join up. Sir Francis

Aglen was among many employers faced with the problem of how to replace them. Anticipating the risk to foreign authority, Jordan noted: 'It is a difficult and somewhat risky experiment as the Chinese will want to fill vacancies with their own people.'[12]

Returning from their holidays in Peitaiho that September, the foreigners soon realised that life in the legation quarter was going to be very different. Until war broke out, they had formed a close-knit society, bound together by the shared experience of living in a fundamentally alien society. Many of the diplomats were from Europe's old aristocratic families – Prince Borghese, Count Sforza, Count Limburg-Stirum, Count Kroupensky and Count Ahlefeldt-Laurvig, to name but a few. Now, although they still lived alongside one another, the old European order in which they were so rooted was being torn apart on the other side of the world. As the Danish Minister rather fancifully lamented in December 1914:

> I suppose Peking was the most international spot on the earth and all the nationalities got on together as in the Garden of Eden. Today it is more like a social hell, people who fought together as brothers on the barricades in 1900 are now cutting each other in the streets.[13]

One of the 'brothers' was the Frenchman Paul Pelliot. He had been only 22 at the time of the Boxer siege when on his own initiative he had risked his life by crossing the lines and entering the Chinese general Jung-lu's headquarters. Once inside, he had convinced them that both the besieged and their defences were in such splendid condition they could last out indefinitely. Although none of his comrades had expected him to reappear alive, Pelliot not only survived the siege, but within a few years had also become a famous sinologist and explorer. In 1910, at a time when it was still possible for a Western scholar-adventurer to roam around China and Central Asia at will, he had removed a large number of manuscripts from the Cave of a Thousand Buddhas at Dunhuang and taken them back to France.[14] His flair for languages (he allegedly picked up a working knowledge of Turkish at Tashkent while waiting for his luggage) and particularly his mastery of Chinese made him an invaluable member of the French legation during the war, where he served as military attaché. With his particular talents, Pelliot was well equipped to monitor the conspiracies and rumours, now more rampant than ever, circulating in the legation quarter. The North China Herald (the 'eyes, ears and voice of China's foreign community') described 'the high secretive walls of Legation Street, the suggestion of great events taking place behind closed doors, the rapidity with which one rumour follows another and the whispered confidences, assurances and guesses exchanged in odd corners of the club'.[15]

In this atmosphere, thick with intrigue, it was up to the British Minister, as dean of the diplomatic corps, to find an acceptable *modus vivendi*. Jordan did so with his usual pragmatism, as he explained in a letter to London:

> You ask me how Diplomatic meetings are carried on these days. The answer is simple. They are not carried on at all. I do everything by circular, propose a certain course of action which is sometimes accepted in its entirety sometimes with modification... Fortunately there have not been many controversial questions and the French Minister, who used to be in opposition, is now arrayed on our side. So far the system has worked wonderfully well as I can always command a good majority composed of the Japanese, Russian, French, Belgian American and some other Representatives. I meet Maltzan [German *chargé d'affaires*] and Rosthorn [Austro-Hungarian Minister] occasionally on the wall and the exchange of bows is the only form of relation that exists between us.[16]

Yet only six months earlier he had written to a colleague: 'It may be heresy to say so but I prefer the Germans a thousand times to the French in practical questions.'[17] It was a remark that underlines the abruptness with which everything had changed in the foreigners' small world. Social life – so central to their existence – waned but was by no means abandoned. With the belligerents avoiding each other, the neutrals now found themselves twice as busy hosting dinners in pairs – one for the allies, another for the central powers.[18]

The German Minister, Admiral von Hintze, described by *The New York Times* as a man with 'a genius for intrigue and adventure',[19] only managed to reach China late in 1914 by travelling incognito as supercargo aboard a Norwegian ship and at one point hiding in a coal chute to escape Japanese detection. At odds with his ally, the Austro-Hungarian Minister, Arthur von Rosthorn, and convinced that his servants were all spies, von Hintze turned to the neutral United States for friendship. This did little to dispel allied suspicion surrounding the American Minister, Dr Paul Reinsch – a second-generation immigrant of German stock – who, it was whispered in legation circles, spoke Yiddish at home.

'Japan is now taking a leading part in the game,' Jordan wrote to London shortly after the outbreak of war, 'it was her opportunity and she was bound to seize it.'[20] Following its rejection of feudalism in favour of modernisation in 1868, Japan's territorial gains had been extensive. Victory in wars with China (1895) and Russia (1905) had won Formosa, the Pescadores and Southern Manchuria, including Port Arthur. Furthermore, it had successfully annexed Korea in 1910. Now the European war, coupled with China's continuing weakness, gave Japan the perfect opening to expand its boundaries yet further. As its minister, Hioki Eki, put it, 'when there is a fire in a jeweller's shop, the neighbours cannot be expected to refrain from helping themselves'.[21]

So, while China remained neutral, on 23 August 1914 Japan declared war on Germany. Within three months (using the pretext of her 1902 alliance with Britain) Japanese troops had captured the port of Tsingtao – since 1897 the jewel of Germany's Eastern possessions. China, naturally wanting to restore the concession to its own sovereignty, had asked whether it could join the British in ousting the Germans but its offer had been rejected. As a result, it had been forced to watch impotently from the sidelines while Britain uneasily supported the Japanese coup. Morrison fumed at both Japan's blatant opportunism and Britain's reluctance to acknowledge it, describing Jordan as a 'crushed worm'.[22] But the British Minister, recognising the allies' needs in the wider context, bowed to the inevitable:

> The foreign policy of Japan is now in the hands of the military party and I know from Corean experience what that means. Hioki, the new Japanese Minister, is perfectly friendly and conciliatory and... speaks quite frankly. He is treated as a mere cypher and is overruled when he makes any suggestion that conflicts with military ideas. It would be folly to kick against the pricks when we are dependent upon Japanese assistance and one must subordinate local interest to the wider and graver issues at stake.[23]

France's former Foreign Minister and Boxer siege veteran, Stéphen Pichon, agreed. In an article published in *The New York Times*, he recalled Japanese valour during the Boxer uprising and pressed for Japan to take a full part in the European war, though he did admit 'that the official participation of the yellow world in the solution of problems which for a hundred years have tormented Europe would be somewhat of an event'.[24]

Maintaining momentum, on 18 January 1915, the Japanese government presented Yuan Shih-kai with a list of 21 demands, threatening war if they were not fully complied with or if their details were made public. The 'demands' were grouped in five sections, each reflecting a specific Japanese ambition: to succeed Germany permanently in the Shantung Peninsula; to consolidate the Manchurian territory it had won in the war against Russia and add to it parts of Mongolia; to gain a controlling share of China's iron industry; to underpin Japan's security through a monopoly on the leasing of all eastern ports and coastal islands; and finally – and most controversially – to impose such tight economic, military and political controls on China as to make it virtually a Japanese colony. Hioki, who like his immediate predecessors, had little sympathy for his military masters, was the reluctant messenger, confessing to Jordan that he had endured much 'moral suffering' in being obliged to carry out instructions that he considered unjust. Even the caustic Morrison wrote sympathetically of Hioki, noting that he was a reasonable man of great ability who (unlike most of his Japanese colleagues) spoke very good English.[25]

Faced with such a devastating document Yuan Shih-kai played for time. Jordan, whom he frequently consulted, could offer nothing but sympathy, since the British Foreign Secretary, Sir Edward Grey,

> …held a very decided opinion that we should not intervene in any way in regard to [the demands]…as it would be madness to quarrel with the Japanese while this war lasts…Of course he has been disappointed with the Japanese and does not conceal his opinion that the Alliance has had a shake…At the same time he recognises that as the Japanese are excluded from our Colonies and from the United States and can get a footing nowhere in Europe they have a right to claim a special position in the Far East and room for expansion there, and if they had at a less critical moment appealed to him frankly on that subject, I believe that they would have had a sympathetic hearing.[26]

It was clear that London was distressed not so much by Japan's imperial ambitions as by its crude diplomacy. Four months later, China agreed to the demands but only after international pressure had forced Japan to drop the most contentious of them.

***

Japan's tightening grip on China was not the only subject preoccupying Jordan in the spring of 1915. By then two things were clear: that the European war was going to last much longer than anyone had at first thought and that Britain was woefully short of arms. It was this latter problem that brought Peking to the attention of Lord Kitchener since the War Office was convinced that large numbers of weapons were readily available in China. Jordan was sceptical but in the face of overwhelming pressure from London had little choice but to put forward a plan of action. As China was neutral, any purchase of arms would have to be negotiated in utmost secrecy and certainly not by a diplomat. Only one man was known to the British legation whose knowledge of Chinese, both language and officials, – was thought sufficient for such a delicate mission – Edmund Backhouse.

Backhouse's career had not stood still in the interval between his forging of the Ching-shan diary and the spring of 1915. Shortly after the publication in 1910 of *China under the Empress Dowager*, he was in England hoping to persuade his father to provide him with enough money to live on. Instead, Sir Jonathan had found his wayward son a 'proper' job with John Brown & Co. The firm, impressed by the extent of Backhouse's contacts, employed him to extract orders from the Chinese government for battleships to be built on the Clyde. J.O.P. Bland, Backhouse's co-author was quick to point out that given the uncertain state of China's finances there were unlikely to be any funds available for buying fleets of ships, but by then Backhouse was already dreaming of the vast fortune he would earn on commission.

Although by the early summer of 1915 Backhouse had failed to procure a single order for John Brown & Co., he had not been idle. In 1913, he and Bland had published a second book, *Annals and Memoirs of the Court of Peking*, and, by donating an extraordinary collection of rare Chinese books and scrolls to the Bodleian Library, he had, at a stroke, made Oxford University pre-eminent in the field in Europe. Furthermore, his scholarly reputation together with this generous gift made it almost certain that he would be offered the professorship of Chinese at Oxford that he so coveted. Meanwhile, Backhouse's fantasy world was given a new lease when in the summer of 1915 he was appointed a secret agent for His Majesty's Government. Working under the cover of his job with John Brown & Co., his assignment was to purchase 200,000 rifles. Within weeks, as Trevor-Roper writes, Backhouse

> …was in his element, negotiating in profoundest secrecy, with mysterious Chinese officials, giving orders to distant Chinese generals, providing the Legation with lists of guns, calibres, manufactures, organizing transport, discovering, explaining and surmounting a continuing series of elaborate oriental obstructions…Telegrams became longer and more frequent as Backhouse announced coup after coup.[27]

By late September, plans were in place to ship the massive consignment of arms Backhouse had so ingeniously acquired – Skoda quick-firing field guns, Krupp machine-guns and field-guns, Mauser and Männlicher rifles, not to mention gun-carriages and thousands of rounds of ammunition – down the Yangtze to Hong Kong where British warships would lie waiting to receive it. Guy Hillier was brought into the secret so that the British government could deposit two million pounds with his bank in readiness to make the payment. Thus, the War Office, the Foreign Office, the British Legation in Peking, the Hong Kong & Shanghai Bank and the General Officer Commanding troops in China, all stood by on tenterhooks for news of the Chinese convoy. Sir Edward Grey even considered asking the Japanese to send a cruiser to escort it. They waited in vain. The guns never arrived, for the simple reason that they never existed – except, that is, in Backhouse's imagination. Because of the legation's need to distance itself from the whole operation, Backhouse had been given *carte blanche*. No one had ever thought of questioning his version of events which (as with the Ching-shan diary) was always made plausible by a wealth of convincing detail. In a last-ditch attempt to find out what had happened to the missing guns, Jordan, abandoning secrecy, went direct to the president, Yuan Shih-kai, who denied all knowledge of any arms transaction. Even then it did not occur to anyone in London that they might have been duped by Backhouse. Instead, they were convinced that a dastardly mix of German bribery and oriental deception had derailed the deal. Only Jordan suspected the truth:

> By the way, I see you think our deal for rifles was squashed by German money. That is Backhouse's yarn, but it is not the case. If it had been a question of money we could and would have outbidden the Germans…The truth is that Backhouse's arrangements rested upon the most flimsy foundations and fell to pieces the moment they came to be tested in practice. Sometimes I wonder if the whole thing was not a creation of his own fancy![28]

***

Backhouse was not the only individual nurturing extravagant fantasies in Peking that summer. On 14 August 1915, the President's bid to become emperor was formally launched. The sceptics were not surprised. Yuan's intentions, long since suspected, had been confirmed when he had earlier reinstated the rituals that for generations had been performed by emperors at the winter solstice. In parody of this sacred imperial tradition, Yuan, accompanied by his ministers, had in the small hours of 23 December 1913 been taken to the Temple of Heaven – not in a palanquin, but in a tank. Hidden from view by his personal bodyguard, he was driven along streets covered with sand (the colour of imperial yellow) and lined with frozen soldiers three rows deep. At the Temple of Heaven, he exchanged his western-style uniform for traditional sacrificial robes. Then, on the Altar of Heaven, to the sound of chanted invocations, he presented ceremonial offerings of meat, jade and silk.

For Morrison, already discontented with his job, this imperial folly was just one more reason for disillusion:

> Here am I political adviser kept in entire ignorance until the campaign has started of the intentions of the President to break all his promises and cast to the winds all his declarations, and engineer himself on to the throne. Never would he accept the Imperial Yellow and yet...he is manoeuvring himself to the throne. This in accordance with the prophecy of the Japanese and of Sun Yat-sen. He makes himself, his country, and his advisers a byword and a derision.[29]

France, Russia and Britain took every opportunity to throw cold water on the monarchical movement, while by 1915 Japan was also utterly opposed to Yuan's dynastic schemes. It had no wish to see a resurgent China united under a military monarch and, as one British diplomat remarked, 'the idea that an upstart murderer should aspire to monarchy and place himself on a level with the Emperor of Japan was the last straw'.[30] Ignoring all the warning signals, Yuan nevertheless forged ahead and, after twice refusing the entreaties of the several thousand members of his puppet National Congress, 'reluctantly' accepted the throne on 11 December. Rehearsals for his enthronement came as a welcome distraction from more pressing problems, although even these did not run smoothly, as Morrison reported:

> Yuan Shih-kai sitting with his Crown; 3 thrones at his side for the 1st 2nd and 3rd wives on descending levels. First wife came in arrayed; kowtowed; took her proper seat. Long delay and 2nd wife the Korean wife, failed to come. Sent for peremptorily. She came in but refused to take her seat, saying Yuan had promised her a throne on the same level as the No. 1. Hearing this, No 1 jumped down from the Throne and went for No. 2 with her fingers. The Master of the Ceremonies...was supervising the Enthronement, but he could not lay

impious hands on the struggling Empresses, where upon Yuan waddled down from the Throne and tried to separate the two combatants. Order was finally restored but the rehearsal was postponed.[31]

In the event, it was not just the rehearsal that was postponed. Having mis-read foreign opinion, Yuan had also badly over estimated his domestic support. Rebellion broke out in Yunnan and quickly spread. The 'emperor', at last seeing the writing on the wall, first postponed then, on 22 March, cancelled the enthronement. His Hung-hsien Dynasty or 'Era of the Grand Constitution' had lasted 83 days. He did not long outlive his reign, dying a broken man of uraemia on 6 June 1916. Yuan had for many years been the leader on whom foreigners had pinned their hopes to deliver a strong resurgent China but when he died, there was only widespread relief.

Morrison, like many other foreigners, had admired Yuan's generosity and kindness, his loyalty to his friends, courage and good humour. But he could not hide his professional frustration:

> The most striking characteristics…of [Yuan's] relations with the foreigner were his caution, his unwillingness ever to give full confidence, his invariable withholding of the essential fact. Thus he could never be given a well-balanced judgement, because he never submitted the full facts of the case.[32]

Jordan, who also had a soft spot for the dead president, paid tribute to his achievements:

> With all its faults, and they were legion, I am afraid it will be some time before we get an Administration which will be an improvement upon that of Yuan Shih-kai. For the last two years foreign trade has flourished and foreign obligations have been punctually paid. Any government that does better than this in China should be warmly welcomed.[33]

Reinsch detected no sign of grief among the thousands who lined the streets for Yuan's funeral procession, only mute indifference.

> The tragedy of the great man who had died as a consequence of his ambition made this occasion impressive to the foreigners present, even the most cynical. It was the last act in one of the most striking dramas of intrigue, achievement and defeat.

***

A few weeks after Yuan's death, Reinsch hosted a dinner party. As usual, the German Minister was there as well as his neutral but pro-German, Dutch colleague, Frans Beelaerts van Blokland. Also present were two American women, one of whom, Ellen La Motte, made a striking contrast to the normal Western globetrotter. She had arrived in Peking with her companion, Emily Crane Chadbourne,[34] fresh from the war where she had worked at the front in a field hospital. By nature a rebel, her withering comments on the foreign powers' treatment of China were unlikely to have found much sympathy among her fellow guests:

> I grow tired of all this talk about the corruptness of the Chinese! They are corrupt, all the officials, or the greater part of them. But you don't hear much about those who corrupt them. Why? Because it suits the great Western nations to keep this government in a state of weakness, of indecision, of susceptibility to bribes and threats; it makes China easier to control...It is a tremendous game, each foreign power striving to cut the ground from under the next foreign power and to gain the ascendancy for itself. Diplomatic Peking is a great, silent battle-ground; on the surface Oriental politeness and suave political courtesies but underneath a seething sea of strife.[35]

However, disapproval of foreign conduct in China did not prevent Ellen and Emily from throwing themselves into the social whirl. Like so many others, they quickly discovered that the best place to feel the pulse of Peking was the 'dark shabby' lounge of the 'Hotel des Wagon-Lits', nicknamed 'Wagon Slits' by American marines.

> Over in a corner sits a so-called princess, a Chinese lady, very modern, very chic, very European as to clothes, who was formerly one of the ladies-in-waiting to the old empress dowager [Princess Der Ling]...next to her sits a young Chinese gentleman, said to be the grandson of one of the old prime ministers...I may say that the lady is almost completely surrounded by the young man, but no one gives them more than a passing glance...The British adviser to the Chinese Government [G.E. Morrison] is talking with a burly Englishman, hunter of big game, but now, according to rumor, a member of the secret service. Concession-hunters and business men sit about in groups, representatives of great commercial and banking firms from all over the world. A minister from some legation drops in; there are curio-buyers from Europe, with a sprinkling of tourists, and a tired-looking, sallow group of anaemic men and women who have just come up from Manila on an army transport.[36]

La Motte soon realised that if the Chinese had little sympathy with the allies they were equally unmoved by the Germans. Their chief reaction to the European war was one of complete indifference. To them it was, as she pointed out, merely a 'struggle between a nation who is mistress of the world (and the world's markets) and a nation who wishes to become mistress of the world (and the world's markets)',[37] an analysis borne out by Jordan's remark: 'Personally, I had only one policy and that was to try and keep China intact as a commercial asset during the War.'[38]

La Motte's account of a day spent at the races in the spring of 1917, is a telling snapshot. Caught up in a dust storm, she sought refuge in the club house, where 'tiffin' was served on trestle tables in a large, bare room:

> Everyone was dust-grimed, wind-blown and bedraggled, and it was a gay noisy meal, with laughter and cigarette smoke and dust all through it. In spite of the noise, however, there seemed little real merriment. One became conscious of the atmosphere, of the forced, rather strained…hostile atmosphere. Every nation as if by prearrangement withdrew to itself…There was no real intermingling, no camaraderie…There was much hand-shaking of course, and greetings and perfunctory politeness, but no genuine friendliness. Over all there was a feeling of constraint, distrust, national antipathies but thinly veiled, with but the merest superficial pretence of disguising intense dislikes and jealousies.[39]

Shortly after this race meeting, the USA entered the war on 6 April 1917, urging China to do the same. China trusted America – the only power not to have deprived it of territory – and so four months later, on 14 August, China also declared war on Germany and Austria-Hungary. It was a momentous step. For the first time in its history, China had entered a global conflict.

PEKING JOINS UP

On Sunday 1 July 1917, just six weeks before China entered the war, a startling event took place in Peking. The British *'chargé d'affaires'* Beilby Alston, at once telegraphed London: 'Young Manchu Emperor was restored to the Throne this morning at 2 a.m. by Chang Hsun.'[1] A few hours later, a medical missionary, Dr Margaret Phillips, on her way to church, was astonished to see the imperial flag (a black dragon on a yellow ground) flying over all the shops.[2] The American Minister, having slept late, was awoken by the excited cries of his number one boy: 'Emperor come back again.'[3] Reinsch and Alston were not the only diplomats to be caught off guard. After Yuan Shih-kai's failure to found a new dynasty, few in Peking had expected an attempt to restore the old one.

Chang Hsun, the man behind the coup, was an illiterate warlord devoted to the monarchy. In deference to the emperor, he and his soldiers (of whom some 5,000 were encamped in the Temple of Heaven) continued to wear queues, thus earning their nickname 'pigtail warriors'. According to Cecil Bowra, Chief Secretary of the Customs, they also carried fans and umbrellas, had tigers painted on their coats, pulled horrible faces and gave alarming roars to terrify the enemy.[4] In the early hours of 1 July, Chang decided that the moment had come to restore the 11-year-old emperor, Puyi, to his throne. The general and his entourage changed into court robes before driving by motor car to the Forbidden City, where their appearance caused panic among the eunuchs. Chang persuaded the equally flustered Lustrous Concubine and Grand Guardian to fetch the emperor and, as soon as the boy was seated on his throne,

> flopped on his knees in a kowtow, imitated by his followers, some of whom seemed a little out of practice. There was a chorus of "may he live for ten thousand years!" and then, when silence had returned, Chang presented to the throne the documents to be promulgated as the first decrees of the restored monarchy.[5]

In fact, Puyi's reign lasted not 10,000 years but little more than ten days. Morrison remained sanguine, writing shortly after the restoration to his young wife: 'Everything is very quiet here...I should think the monarchy is already trembling, in a week it will totter and in a fortnight fall.'[6] He was right. Fall it did on 12 July but not before a fierce battle had taken place between the pigtail and republican armies. Given that the legation quarter lay directly in their line of fire, it was with relief that Alston was able to report to London that there had been no casualties, though bullets and shells had fallen within the legation walls. A decisive factor was the dropping of three bombs on the Forbidden City from an aeroplane – the first aerial attack to take place in China. Only one exploded causing little damage but, as Henry McAleavy writes in *A Dream of Tartary*, 'the Lustrous Concubine and her companions were nearly out of their wits with fright crawling under the tables and shouting for the bamboo curtains to be lowered in front of the windows'.[7]

No one captured the comic opera aspect of the whole affair better than the young French diplomat, Alexis Leger, also known as the poet (and later Nobel laureate) Saint-John Perse. Given the task of escorting the president's family to the safety of the diplomatic quarter (the president himself had already fled to the Japanese legation), Leger waited in the Hall of Honour for his charges to appear. The room was dominated by a larger-than-life portrait of the president, which suddenly swung open to reveal a courtyard where the whole household had assembled: Madame Li, her daughters, numerous concubines dressed in plum-coloured silk, stable boys, ancient retainers, chambermaids, stewards, roast-cooks, confectioners, healers, policemen and porters. Towering over them all stood a giant in a beige bowler hat carrying the president's latest son dressed only in silver bracelets. Leger described the chaotic scene: 'The clamour of crickets, jackdaws, guinea-fowl, and magpies, the cawing of crows, the barking of thoroughbred dogs, the murmur of neighbours perched in trees and the sobbing of numerous clientele...'.[8] As he struggled to dislodge the 'clusters of humanity' clinging to the car reserved for Mrs Li and her children, the concubines stormed two purple automobiles that had appeared from nowhere, and they were whisked off to the sanctuary of the British hotel, the Wagons-Lits.

Margaret Phillips, living outside the legation quarter, witnessed a darker side of the restoration attempt. On 12 July, Bishop Norris (one of the dwindling number of Boxer siege veterans still in Peking) summoned her to the mission hospital where she treated several seriously wounded women hit by stray bullets. In addition to running her medical practice, Margaret also taught physics and chemistry at Miss Bowden-Smith's now well-established school for upper-class Chinese girls, the Peihua, whose pupils not infrequently won scholarships to America. The admiral's daughter reacted to her second dose of Peking insurrection with impeccable *sang-froid*, but in any case it was all soon over. Walking back from the hospital the next morning, Dr Phillips watched the shopkeepers packing up their imperial flags. By the time she reached home, a large republican flag was flying once more over the Forbidden City.

The defeated Chang fled to the Dutch legation while his soldiers, having chopped off their pigtails (leaving 'a trail of severed plaits which in places covered the ground like matting'[9]), melted into the crowd. Later, they were allowed to march back to their quarters in the Temple of Heaven where Bowra went to meet them and have a 'friendly chat'. In excellent spirits, they were eventually put on a train and sent home – well content with their expedition. As for their general, a telegram from Alston to London made it clear why Chang had sought refuge with the Dutch:

> Rumours regarding Chang's connections with Germans are increasing both in Chinese and foreign circles. Former German Legation guard had been recalled to Peking on the 10th instant from their place of internment outside city and supplied with arms by Dutch Minister, and it is alleged that Chang and his family were brought into legation quarters by German officers.[10]

Although his country was neutral, the Dutch Minister, van Beelaerts, was intensely pro-German and as such did everything possible to support what was, as it soon became clear, a restoration attempt backed by the Germans. The *quid pro quo* was that, once back in power, the Manchus would ensure China did not enter the war on the side of the allies. Van Beelaerts was not the only neutral working actively for the Germans. The sympathies of the Swedish Minister, Gustav Wallenberg,[11] lay so obviously with the Kaiser that in 1918, the Chinese requested his recall. Amid these complex affiliations, the diplomats continued to live cheek by jowl alongside one another, so that as the war dragged on the atmosphere in the legation quarter became increasingly surreal.

Germany had failed to stop China from entering the war but it was not sympathy with its enemies that motivated the Peking government to join up. Rather it was the glittering prize of a seat at the eventual peace conference. The pro-war faction argued that a place among the great nations of the world would win China international respect, enabling it to resist Japanese aggression and to re-establish sovereignty over Shantung – a view to which Morrison passionately subscribed. Other foreigners, like Varè, thought that from the allied perspective it was a great mistake: 'The war in Europe was a civil war among white peoples. It destroyed the common front which they had maintained till then at Peking. When we started fighting one another in China itself (at Tsingtao) our prestige in the Far East suffered a blow from which it never recovered.'[12]

Apart from a seat at the peace conference, China had another good reason for joining the fray. Anyone reading Varè's diaries might well assume that the diplomats' only function in Peking was to extract as much money as possible from the Chinese government. Claims poured in from everywhere and everyone. Longstanding claims concerning the Boxer siege and the 1911 Revolution, claims from missionaries in remote provinces, claims from outraged businessmen, claims from distressed globetrotters right down to the most trivial claims from any Tom, Dick or Harry who happened to have washed up in China. All of these, channelled through the respective legations, had to be properly examined, negotiated and settled. 'It's so annoying,' wrote Varè, 'that all the barbers here are Italian. I cannot put my nose in one of their shops without them wanting to discuss their claims with me.'[13] But, by declaring war on Germany and Austria-Hungary, the Chinese government at one stroke was able to cancel two Boxer indemnities. Furthermore, it hoped that its new allies would not only defer their own indemnities, but also provide the loans it so badly needed – not least to fight the continuing insurrection in the South.

China's two most lucrative sources of revenue were still the Customs and the salt gabelle – both run by Britons. Sir Francis Aglen remained in charge of the former, while Sir Richard Dane (a retired Indian civil servant) had been drafted in to reorganise 'the Salt' in 1913. Dane, displaying the same enthusiasm for his new job that he once had for hunting game in Africa and India, in 1915 produced a massive six million pounds in salt revenue for the Chinese government. Because he 'talked salt morning noon and night', he was affectionately known around Peking as the 'salt gabbler'.[14] Jordan admired the 'impetuous Irishman…literally saturated with brine', reporting to London in September 1914: 'The Salt has proved the salvation of China. The Chinese may curse us for opium but if they have any gratitude they will bless us for salt.'[15]

Once China was definitively at war, the entente powers had to find some way of deploying their new ally. There was little enthusiasm for using Chinese troops in Europe or indeed anywhere else. If, it was argued in London, they were sent to Egypt, the Japanese would want to follow suit and that might threaten the *status quo* in India. This was no idle concern, since as far back as 1903 a Chinese correspondent had informed Morrison that prominent Japanese were telling Indian students in Tokyo that as soon as Japan was strong enough India would be cleared of all Englishmen.[16]

Alston, with an eye to Britain's post-war commercial interests, was quite clear: 'We consider the complete liquidation of enemy businesses to be one of the most important results which should accrue from China's entry into the war.'[17] But even that was a more awkward matter than at first sight for, as Jordan had noted some months earlier, British firms, after clamouring for the expulsion of German employees and businesses, soon discovered that the enemy's skills were indispensable in such areas as hotel management, accountancy and the brewing of beer. Consequently, Jordan was continually being asked to issue licences enabling 'amenable enemies' to remain.[18] A case in point was the Wagons-Lits Hotel in the legation quarter which, although British-owned, was almost entirely run and managed by Germans. Further objections to the wholesale expulsion of Germans came from the Belgian Minister who feared that it would trigger reprisals in Belgium. But even though the Germans escaped eviction, life was hardly a bed of roses, as one businessman complained:

> The crusade against the Germans and everything German is getting more and more accentuated…you can have no conception of the bitter and hateful feeling that exists and for which the dreadful lies and accusations in the English Press are responsible…Most of our former acquaintances do not bow any more, and…most of the neutrals are sticking to the English side, lest they are otherwise put on the British black list and thus precluded from doing business.[19]

Its soldiers may have been found wanting but China had one resource that the allies did value – labour. Between 1916 and 1921, Britain and France employed an estimated 140,000 Chinese coolies in the war zone. The novelty of their presence was recorded in a *North China Herald* article describing how an entire French village 'agog with excitement' turned out to watch a batch of coolies in their smart new uniforms march from the station to their depot.[20] Several thousand Chinese were to lose their lives in the conflict, many after the armistice while clearing mines.

Few in Peking would have linked the tough, resilient peasants who made up the coolie corps with Edmund Backhouse. But on 15 September 1917, just one month after China's declaration of war, Backhouse telegraphed John Brown & Co.: 'I presume you approve my taking up the post with Chinese labour in France to which I have been gazetted.'[21] He had (or so he claimed) been offered the job of censoring Chinese mail in France and, as he had just been exposed as perpetrator of yet another astonishing fraud, involving the American Bank Note Company, he may well have decided that even the Western Front was preferable to remaining in Peking. But it was not to be. An exasperated Jordan, having just returned from leave, telegraphed London, cataloguing Backhouse's crimes and concluding, 'in view of the above I regret I can no long regard Backhouse as a trustworthy person and must recommend that he be given no Government employment of any kind'.[22] Jordan had left Peking on leave in the wake of one Backhouse debacle, only to return months later to find himself in the middle of yet another. To his relief, Backhouse chose to spend the rest of the war a long way from Peking, dreaming up new frauds and fantasies at a hotel in Victoria on Vancouver Island.

***

Among the many issues facing Jordan on his return in 1917 was the deterioration of relations between the British and American communities. To counter the problem, a number of Anglo-American social gatherings were organised to which Chinese were also occasionally invited. At one of these, held in the YMCA hall, a young man fresh out from Wisconsin

>...hoisted himself on a chair in the centre of the room. He proceeded to give directions for the systematic promotion of sociability and conversation. The Chinese guests were to join hands and form a circle around the room, facing inward; within that circle the British and American guests were to join hands, forming a circle facing outward. At the given word the outer circle was

to revolve to the right, the inner circle to the left. At the word 'halt,' everyone was to engage his or her vis-à-vis in conversation. To eliminate every risk of stalemate, the topics for conversation were given out, one for each stop of the revolving line, the last being: 'My Greatest Secret.'

Reinsch recorded that although the British initially 'seemed somewhat aghast at the prospect of this rotary and perambulatory conversation', Jordan rose to the occasion by making lively conversation with the 'simpering little Chinese girl' opposite him.[23] At any rate, these parties were deemed so successful that an Anglo-American club was formed – the beginning, so Reinsch claimed, of the closest relationship that had ever existed between the Americans and British in the Far East. Certainly this club, together with the newly formed choral society and the lectures organised at the Peking Language School, offered a welcome addition to the moribund social life of the legations. Introducing one of the lectures, Jordan even suggested that the time had come when foreigners might begin to take a deeper interest in Chinese civilisation than they had before.[24]

When Alston arrived in Peking in 1916 to relieve Jordan, he had found him 'much aged and depressed but as vigorous as ever with his pen'.[25] In an effort to persuade the Foreign Office to pay for a second typist, Jordan's first secretary, Miles Lampson (later Lord Killearn and himself minister in Peking, 1926–33), wrote to London describing his 'preternaturally active' chief:

> Every spasm of activity on his part entails increased effort all the way down so that when he presses the button and our large staff all get to work the output of brainwaves is truly staggering and the consequent amount of ink-slinging commensurately large.

Lampson found it hard to believe that 'good old sleepy Madrid with their *four* stenographers' had a fraction of the work of Peking. 'They have no extraterritoriality, no Decanat of the Diplomatic Body, No Chinese Government to ballyrag, no nice little Manchurian-Siberian imbroglio to get busy about as we do for our sins.' But his argument fell on deaf ears, leaving him to reflect that:

> It is really rather exasperating that we should be cut down in this respect when, on the other hand, you see the truly wicked waste of good money on absolutely footling telegrams that is going on at home. However that is our way of doing things. I have heard it called muddling through. But there is more muddling than getting through about it.[26]

Although the legation failed to get a new typist, Jordan had more success with transport. In a dispatch to London he described the elaborate network of broad macadamised streets in Peking that had replaced the primitive cart tracks, while the old *yamens* had given way to modern public buildings. New government offices and official residences were springing up everywhere and had become scattered over so wide an area that it was quite impossible, Jordan argued, to cover the ground in an old-fashioned carriage.

> The moment has in fact now arrived when the increased facilities of the motor-car have become indispensable and the Minister has therefore been obliged to follow the example of the other foreign representatives in Peking and employ a motor.

With no further need for a mounted escort, Jordan suggested another radical proposal to London – that the legation messengers' ponies be replaced with bicycles.[27]

Indeed, *The North China Morning Herald* maintained that Peking was developing so rapidly into a modern city that motor cars had become a serious problem. The eight mph speed limit inside the legation quarter had not prevented the Portuguese Minister (who Morrison claimed not only dyed his hair but also lived off his wife's immoral earnings[28]) from being crushed between a tree and an automobile. The real trouble, fumed the newspaper, was the 50,000 rickshaws in Peking:

> Whenever a potential fare heaves into sight half a dozen of the rickshaws rush toward them regardless of other traffic. The prospect of earning a few coppers obliterates all thought of death…At railway stations scandalous confusion is the order of the day…The motor-car danger and the rickshaw nuisance are closely related and it is time something was done in relation to both.[29]

In March 1917 (two months before the air raid on the Forbidden City), Dr Margaret Phillips was among the large crowd of foreigners on the wall craning their necks to watch the 25-year-old American, Katherine Stinson, looping-the-loop in her small bi-plane. The twentieth century had arrived.

***

Of all the ministers present in Peking during the Great War, Jordan arguably carried the heaviest burden. But at least by the end of 1917 he still had a government – unlike his colleague, the Russian Minister, Prince Nicholas Koudachev. The abdication of Tsar Nicholas II in March followed by the Bolshevik Revolution in October left the Russian legation in a precarious position. In December, it put out a defiant press announcement renouncing the 'Maximalist' government in Petrograd and insisting that they would continue to represent the true interests of the Russian people. Jordan was sympathetic:

> The position of the Russian Legation and of Russia generally in China is pathetic... Prince Koudacheff has been an excellent colleague and I feel keenly for him. The other day he received instruction to hand over charge to the next senior member of the Legation who sympathised with their political views. The offer was made successively to every member of the staff, from the Counsellor down to the latest student interpreter. All declined the honour and dissociated themselves from the Maximalists, the only exception being the student interpreter, who confessed to socialist leanings but was not prepared to accept the offer.[30]

Money soon became a pressing problem, especially after China stopped remitting the Boxer indemnity. But despite having no visible means of support, Koudachev continued to keep up a brave appearance until the Chinese government finally withdrew his credentials in 1920. Meanwhile his colleague, Dmitri Abrikosov, produced a novel theory that the Russian Revolution was in part caused by the trans-Siberian express.

> After you leave European Russia, you pass hours and hours without seeing any village or habitation. Near the stations are a few houses. Usually, when the express train arrives at the station, the entire local population comes to stare at the travellers. Especially in the evenings, when the train is brilliantly illuminated by electricity and the elegant figures of the inhabitants of Shanghai or other Far Eastern ports are visible inside, the travellers must appear to the local residents like men from another planet. What envy and dissatisfaction the exotic creatures in furs must provoke in the hearts of those doomed to spend their entire life in some miserable station!... The train stops for five minutes. The passengers, looking like people from a fairyland, jump on the platform; they laugh and joke. There is a whistle, the train with its passengers disappears, and darkness, emptiness, and dullness reign again... It is unjust that some should move from place to place in luxury, while others must remain in some forsaken place in

misery...I am convinced that the Siberian express played an important part in the awakening of the population of Siberia and thereby hastened the coming of the Revolution.[31]

Varè (travelling with his wife, two small daughters and a nanny) also remembered the huge figures 'dressed like Mongols' that congregated at each station to watch the Westerners pass through. Impressed by the sheer bleakness of the landscape, he commented that it was only when a man or a horse came into view – 'no bigger than flies' – that it was possible to get some sense of scale in the vast plain through which the train travelled for days on end.

> At 5 pm we passed Omsk and the frozen river Irtysh. What desolation! The roads are half snow and half mud. Wooden cabins, Russian churches with dead coloured green roofs and small domes. The odd sleigh crossing the river on frozen roads seemed only to add further melancholy to the scene.

Varè's fellow passengers were typical of the mix that travelled regularly between North China and Europe:

> Various unappealing globetrotters (with the exception of a six foot tall Englishwoman wearing snakeskin shoes and a monocle), a little Dutch boy called George, a real pest. His mother seems to hate him as much as all the other passengers, two lovely English girls with huge feet and no corsets who spend their time amusing other peoples' children, a Russian general in full uniform whose hidden liqueur chocolates were discovered and consumed by George...[32]

Jordan recalled bumping into Hayashi Gonsuke – 'The best Japanese I ever met'[33] – at a wayside railway station in Siberia in the middle of the night. Having served together in Korea, the two men were old friends but had only time to exchange a few words before departing in different directions. When in 1916 Hayashi arrived in Peking as Japanese Minister, the appointment was widely welcomed. Many hoped that his integrity and humanity would prove an effective counterbalance to Tokyo's more excessive demands on China. Jordan and Hayashi spent long hours together trying to make sense of the disintegrating world around them: 'Just as in India,' wrote Jordan,

> ...the revolution in Russia has given rise to political aspirations in China, and if we are going to concede the right of self-determination to India, I do not see how we can deny the Chinese people the right to rule their own destinies.

Jordan added that Hayashi privately endorsed this judgement but was not free to express his own opinions publicly. 'If Japan would only model her China policy upon the views of moderate men like Hayashi,' Jordan continued, 'the future of China need give no undue anxiety.'[34]

***

The inevitable rupture of communications during the war left the foreign community in Peking feeling deeply isolated. Even when letters did get through, their news was several months old. Only the telegraph could be relied on and for most individuals that was prohibitively expensive. In January 1918, Jordan received a telegram informing him – not of the death of either of his two sons or of his son-in-law, all of whom were fighting on the Western front – but of his 29-year-old daughter, Edith. Jordan, always the exemplary public servant, refused to let grief interfere with work, although in a letter to a colleague he briefly allowed his emotions to surface:

> You will not expect a long letter from me at present. I have received a stunning blow and am heartbroken at the loss of my dear Daughter who was all in all to me…I have only one consolation – she and I had never a shade of difference and our relations were as nearly perfect as perhaps the most delightful of all human relations – those between a Father and Daughter – can be in this imperfect world. I feel terribly for my wife who will never recover from this blow.[35]

When Jordan received the news of his daughter's death, the armistice was only a few months away. Reports of it first reached Peking's foreign community at a theatre – the Peking Pavilion – where Varè was entertaining guests (Jordan among them) at a variety performance. A telegram was brought to their box during a comic turn. Interrupting the clowns, Varè stepped on to the stage to announce that the war was over. The Belgian Minister was only prevented from falling out of the box in his excitement by an American hanging on to his tails while, as Varè recalled, 'There were shouts and clapping and songs. Newspaper reporters ran out to telephone Tientsin and Shanghai. Naval officers hurried off to communicate by wireless with ships at sea. Thus the news of peace came to China.'[36] As everyone began to leave the theatre, Hayashi asked Varè if he would care to accompany him to the Great Wall. Varè thought it an odd moment for the Japanese Minister to be planning an excursion but nevertheless asked him which day he would like to go. 'Now,' answered Hayashi. Varè pointed out that it was 11 o'clock and they were in evening dress. 'We have time to put on a sweater and to catch the night train to Kalgan. It is a goods train but they will let us travel on it, you and me.' Varè was tempted but it was cold, he was tired and he did not relish a night journey on an unheated train. So Hayashi went alone. One senses that Varè always regretted he did not go with the Japanese Minister that night, for as he himself put it:

> I had spoken of 'peace' and at that word the theatre had been in an uproar, men shouting and stamping women waving handkerchiefs and flags. But that was victory, not peace. There is no peace and can never be, where there are men. Baron Hayashi had gone to seek for it where he knew it could be found. At dawn, in the winter hills.[37]

9
PROFESSORS AND PROPHETS

As soon as news of the armistice reached Peking officially on 11 November 1918, the government declared a three-day public holiday. Jubilant crowds poured on to the streets waving placards and shouting 'long live justice, long live national independence'. The large stone lions that stood outside the German legation were toppled and *Der Tag* scrawled over the entrance gates. An attempt to burn down the German bank failed but Baron von Ketteler's memorial – hated symbol of Chinese humiliation – was rapidly dismantled and recycled in a nearby park as a monument to 'Right over Might'. Swept up in all the excitement, Dr Margaret Phillips led her female students through the streets, waving the Union Jack she had bought in an Indian silk shop. On 28 November, she was among thousands of people invited into the Forbidden City to watch the formal victory celebration which, with its marching bands and multiple national flags, must have reminded the Boxer siege veterans of a similar parade in 1900. But this time there was a notable difference. Ten thousand smartly turned-out Chinese troops were also present.

Many foreigners were astonished by Peking's enthusiastic response to the armistice. After all, the war had not touched the city and most of its citizens had been quite indifferent to its outcome. They missed the point. The cause of celebration was not the allied victory but the forthcoming peace conference. For out of this (or so 'Young China' had been convinced by men like Reinsch and Morrison), a New World Order would emerge – one that under American leadership would reject imperialism and restore China's national pride. Expectations rose even higher when it was learned that President Wilson would personally attend the peace conference due to open in Paris in January 1919. To many Chinese, Wilson was the world leader of 'spiritual democracy',[1] a hero whose country, unlike Japan or the European powers, wanted a modern, more equal dialogue with China. Excited students gathered outside the American legation chanting 'Long Live President Wilson'.

With so much riding on the peace conference, China sent a big delegation to Paris – so big that it raised some eyebrows. Colonel Bruce, who before the war had been adviser to the Peking police, wrote to Morrison: 'Addis says China has sent a large staff over to Paris, why he could not say, except that it was like them. Over 200 altogether, which seems extraordinary considering they do not represent any of the great five, nor even of the lesser ten, nations who count.'[2] Bruce's scepticism reflected a widespread conviction among foreigners that China was now in such rapid political, moral and cultural decline it was even less capable of managing its own affairs than usual. Sir Alexander Hosie,[3] another old China hand, expressed the opinion of many colleagues when he wrote in 1920:

> In spite of many years residence in China, I have never been able to bridge the gulf which separates white & yellow. I am told that within late years much progress has been made in this direction; but I may still be allowed my doubts as to the sincerity of this movement. A few educated and English-speaking Chinese do not make a nation.[4]

Despite such views and China's deplorable state there were some foreigners in Peking who looked beyond the political chaos to a brighter future. Jordan thought that the country's commercial development would be one of the wonders of the twentieth century, while Alexis Leger believed that its vast natural resources and, as yet unrecognised, ability to assimilate new technologies could soon make it an industrial nation on par with America.[5] But although such men recognised that in the post-war world the old diplomacy of grab and exploitation was bankrupt, few had much idea what would replace it. Meanwhile corruption was rife. Throughout the war the Peking government had played into Japan's hands by mortgaging China's resources for ready cash – money that had been quickly squandered. Jordan was one of a number of influential foreigners in Peking who thought the only way to protect China from Japan was to put the country's finances under the control of a foreign consortium. 'It will be a glaring moral delinquency on the part of America and Great Britain,' he wrote to the Foreign Office in London in 1918, 'if they do not proceed to rectify the situation which the war has produced in China more specially because it has been very largely the direct consequence of the action of one of our allies – Japan.'[6]

On 19 February 1919, Morrison arrived in Paris as an accredited member of the Chinese delegation. He was already ill with the pancreatitis that would soon kill him, so his appearance at Versailles was to be his last on the public stage. He may have been ailing but – as a diary entry illustrates – his ambition remained undimmed: 'I pray that I be given the K.C.M.G for it was promised me and that the Lord will set me on high and make me the British Minister to Peking.'[7]

Despite his poor health, Morrison worked vigorously with the Chinese delegation to present its case in the best possible light. But from the start there was disappointment for, while other countries were allowed five seats at the proceedings, China's enormous delegation was allotted only two. By far the most important issue on China's agenda was the return over its own sovereignty of Shantung province (regarded by the Chinese as the cradle of their civilization), which Japan had snatched from Germany in 1915. But even Morrison's drafting skills failed to prevent disaster. For it emerged that during the war, Tokyo had signed secret deals guaranteeing Japan's right to hold on to Shantung, not only with Great Britain, France and Italy, but also with the Peking government, thus providing Japan with the legal (if not moral) basis on which to retain the province. And, despite President Wilson's fine words regarding the rights of weak nations, it was ultimately Japan's support for the League of Nations that mattered more than any claim China had over its own territory. 'Everything I feared for poor unhappy China has now come to pass,' wrote Leger from Peking, 'Her humiliation at the Peace Conference is complete and entering the war on the side of the Allied Powers has been of no benefit whatever to her … Worse – it is a political blunder whose consequences we shall pay for dearly.'[8]

The Paris decision allowing Japan to keep the Shantung concessions was announced on 4 May 1919 – a date that resounds in Chinese history. For it was the 'May Fourth Movement', as it came to be known, that marked the country's modern political awakening. On hearing the news, some 3,000 students demonstrated in Tiananmen Square (then a much smaller space) before marching towards the foreign legations, chanting 'down with the traitors, return Shantung, boycott Japanese goods'. The next day they protested outside the American legation where only six months earlier they had gathered in celebration. Dr Reinsch, who within weeks of the announcement resigned as American Minister, felt the 'stunning, paralyzing blow' of the decision as keenly as the students:

> Probably nowhere else in the world had expectations of America's leadership at Paris been raised so high as in China. The Chinese trusted America, they trusted the frequent declarations of principle uttered by President Wilson, whose words had reached China in the remotest parts. The more intense was their disappointment and disillusionment due to the decisions of the old men that controlled the Peace Conference. It sickened and disheartened me to think how the Chinese people would receive this blow which meant the blasting of their hopes and the destruction of their confidence in the equity of nations.[9]

Morrison left the peace conference for London ill and depressed. Despite his international fame as an authority, he knew that his influence on the Chinese government had been negligible. Nor, for that matter, had he made a lasting impact on British policy. He had little money, had not been appointed British Minister nor had he received the coveted knighthood. Even his last ambition – to die in his own house in Peking – was thwarted when his life ended in a Sidmouth nursing home on 20 May 1920. He was 58. Although Morrison was a man of great courage, his caustic commentary on his contemporaries and inflated ego made him difficult to like. But whatever his failings he had worked tirelessly to further what he had genuinely believed to be China's best interests and to maintain the country's profile in Britain at a time when few there were interested in its affairs.

Shortly before Morrison's death, John Jordan retired as British Minister – a post he had held since 1906. Morrison, despite having lobbied for his appointment, poured scorn on his record claiming he had achieved nothing of value. It is true that Jordan, the quintessential public servant, had put his own country's interests first – especially during the war: 'I have acted upon the plain assumption that China had to be subordinated and, if necessary, sacrificed to the main object of winning the war.'[10] But once that constraint had been lifted, he had not hesitated to warn his government in the bluntest terms of the Japanese threat to China and of its responsibility to do something about it. He himself took most pride in having ended (officially at least) the opium trade – a scar on British honour that he felt deeply. 'It was the first question I had to deal with on my arrival here in 1906 and for twelve years it has been my constant companion. The final act was rather dramatic. Opium worth £4 million in China was publicly burnt a month ago at Shanghai.'[11] Jordan's modest background – he never lost his Belfast accent – was always an issue in an expatriate community keenly sensitive in such matters. That he should have retired to East Putney ('of all places!')[12] and preferred to travel on public transport ('I fancy at his age this is somewhat risky'[13]) were traits considered unacceptably bourgeois for a man in his position.

A few days before Jordan left Peking for the last time, he paid a farewell visit to his temple in the Western Hills with Sir Alexander Hosie (they had been fellow student interpreters in the 1870s). Hosie recorded the moment:

> With sad hearts we wended our way down the hill talking of the old days…a foreign hotel now lies at the foot of these hills – vandalism we call it. We entered our cars after saying goodbye to the temple priests and others who had descended the hill with us and drove back to Peking in well under a hour. In the old days we had to ride there – 13 miles. The car and the new motor road, if very convenient, appeared to us at that moment as much vandalism as the European built hotel at the foot of the Western Hills.[14]

***

Although disillusioned with the outcome of the peace treaty, most Chinese intellectuals still looked to Western-style democracy for China's salvation. Yet it was impossible to ignore the growing, and to foreign eyes disturbing, number of young people drawn to a rival ideology – Marxism. 'Bolshevik propaganda is unsettling Chinese minds and adding to the general dislocation,'[15] commented Francis Aglen.

Few men at the time could have put the case for democracy more convincingly than the American philosopher and educationalist John Dewey. In 1919, the China Lecture Association (formed to bring great minds to China) invited him to give a series of talks in Peking. Dewey reached China expecting to stay only a few months but, having arrived in the middle of the May Fourth protests, found the situation so gripping that he and his wife remained for two years. Watching the demonstrations at first hand, he was impressed by the students' commitment and mature conduct. 'To think of kids in our country from fourteen on, taking the lead in starting a big cleanup in reform politics movement and shaming merchants and professional men into joining them. This is sure some country.'[16] Dewey was delighted by China's dignified refusal to sign the Versailles peace treaty on 28 June. He delivered his lectures at Peking University, the heart of the city's intellectual life, where even before the war a dozen or more foreign professors had been employed. Eager to find an alternative to Confucianism (widely blamed for China's woes) many intellectuals responded warmly to Dewey's pragmatic philosophy – 'learning by doing'. But his message urging the importance of rationality, reflection and, above all, education rooted in science and democracy was not radical enough for those on the left. They looked for inspiration to another intellectual giant – Bertrand Russell.

Russell, a more outspoken critic of Western imperialism than Dewey and recently back from the Soviet Union, arrived in China with his lover, Dora Black (later his second wife), on 13 October 1919. On the voyage out he had given a pro-Bolshevik talk that so incensed the rubber-planters and businessmen on board that they had sent a telegram to the British authorities in Peking urging them to prevent Russell from disembarking. In fact Russell had disliked Bolshevik Russia but had no intention of giving his reactionary shipboard audience the satisfaction of knowing this. Once safely ashore he received a rapturous welcome particularly from 'Young China' who even produced a magazine – the *Russell Monthly*. 'The eagerness for knowledge on the part of the students is quite extraordinary,' Russell observed, 'when one begins to speak, their eyes have the look of starving men beginning a feast.'[17] Dora Black found all the attention 'terribly fatiguing. Everywhere we are treated like an Emperor and Empress. The Chinese papers report and describe us every day, what we look like and what we wear and so on... B is represented even on a cigarette advertisement, with his finger held up as in benediction, looking like an Ancient Sage.'[18] Russell took a strong liking to the Chinese, writing to Ottoline Morrell that he would do anything in the world to help them, but adding, '...it is difficult. They are like a nation of artists, with all their good and bad points. Imagine Mark Gertler, Augustus John and Lytton Stratchey set to govern the British Empire and you will have some idea of how China has been governed for 2,000 years.'[19]

Russell's interpreter (a distinguished mathematician and translator of *Alice's Adventures in Wonderland*[20]) helped to settle the couple into their Peking house where, Dora confessed, they lived in disgraceful luxury with a cook, two rickshaw boys, head boy and maid. They did not think much of their fellow expatriates: 'We hardly ever see Europeans and when we do, we are glad we don't meet them often because the kind you meet out here all seem villainous or frivolous or both, barring the missionaries who are good but dull.'[21] The fact that Russell and Black lived together so openly produced a frisson of excitement in the foreign community. Although professing outrage at their shocking morals and left-wing politics, everyone wanted to meet them except possibly those missionaries attempting to convert the Chinese to monogamy. For them it was galling to be reminded by smirking mandarins that the West's most famous philosopher was living in sin with his favourite concubine. In fact, Russell and Black provided a welcome role model for many young Chinese trying to escape the rigid system of arranged marriages and family control at a time when a parent could still legally authorise the execution of a trying offspring.

One bitterly cold day in March 1921, Russell lectured (as usual without his overcoat) in an unheated hall. Three days later he was dangerously ill with double pneumonia and for the next two weeks lay in the German hospital – his life hanging in the balance. The English newspapers (having picked up a Japanese report of his death) delighted Russell by publishing obituaries. One in a missionary journal gave particular pleasure: 'Missionaries may be pardoned for heaving a sigh of relief at the news of Mr Bertrand Russell's death.'[22]

Russell owed his recovery to a serum provided by doctors working at the brand new Peking Union Medical College (the PUMC). Dubbed 'The Oil Prince's Palace', the College was funded by the Rockefeller Foundation whose philanthropic mission – the well-being of mankind – was nothing if not ambitious. After long deliberation its board of trustees had concluded that given the backwardness, poverty and ignorance of the Chinese, there could be no better place to start healing humanity than China. As a result, in 1914 the Foundation's China Medical Board sent out a commission to explore the best way of teaching Western medicine to Chinese doctors. The nucleus of the project was a medical training college in Peking (jointly run by six different Protestant denominations) that had been in operation since 1906 under the direction of a British medical missionary, Tom Cochrane. Cochrane had nearly lost his life in the Boxer uprising but had later become a regular visitor to the Forbidden City where he had not only won the Empress Dowager's support for his medical college but also successfully treated her chief eunuch, Li Lienying, for a delicate condition common among eunuchs.[23] With money no object (the PUMC cost eight million dollars to build and equip), Cochrane's modest enterprise had, by 1920, been transformed into a medical college equal to the best anywhere in the West and what was to become arguably the most enduring of all foreign enterprises in Peking.

The faculty and equipment may have been on par with the most up-to-date schools in America (it was modelled on Johns Hopkins), but outwardly the PUMC was quite unlike any medical college in the West. In a conscious effort to reflect Peking's historic palaces and temples, its curvy green glazed roofs soared above the elegant courtyards and grey walls of the 59 buildings that made up the college. Finding craftsmen capable of carrying out such traditional work was not an easy task, since Peking's finest buildings had for so long been allowed to decay, that many of the old skills were on the point of extinction. Undaunted, the PUMC agents combed local villages in search of elderly artisans who could be persuaded to return to Peking to work on this, its newest 'palace'.[24] In September 1921, John D. Rockefeller Jr arrived in China at the head of an enormous entourage for the formal opening. It was, as the wife of the Harvard Professor of Medicine, Mrs Peabody, recorded, a splendid occasion:

> The colour of the academic dress was stunning, and the ladies paled beside it. Dr. Tuffier of Paris was unquestionably the most brilliant, for he wore a veritable crown, and his hat was trimmed with ermine with red about it, and crossing his breast were innumerable medals... Sir William Smyly wore a gown of scarlet and a scarlet hood. Even those with black gowns had them so covered with bands of red or green velvet that they were scarcely less brilliant. A sprinkling of bishops added another touch, and the British and American ministers were the only ones who brought us down to earth by their sombre cutaways.[25]

Not everyone admired American benevolence on this grand scale. Russell, while grateful to the PUMC for saving his life, was highly critical of such institutions believing that as long as foreigners were in charge of them they would never answer China's needs. The young English novelist Stella Benson arrived in Peking in May 1920 to work in the PUMC's X-ray department. She too viewed such American largesse with cynicism: 'Mrs Hillier & her sister brought me round to my new home & job. The Rockefeller is a great imitative Chinese erection – still building. Its use seems to be ostensibly the training of Chinese in medicine & sanitation, actually it is US propaganda I should say... My fellow workers or rather fellow boarders are all American and female, very brisk, efficient with piercing voices.'[26] Her cool response was not untypical of British attitudes to American efforts in China. Despite Jordan and Reinsch's attempts to bring the two communities closer together, there was still a good deal of tension. For, while the British accused the Americans of hypocrisy, believing them, despite their 'open door policy',[27] to be as much interested in commercial advantage in China as any other foreign power, the Americans were convinced that the British remained rooted in outdated imperialism. The British were still the biggest foreign presence in China, but American prodding put them on the defensive, sparking reactions that often reflected jealousy and snobbery.

But whatever the initial failings of the PUMC – no Chinese were appointed to its board; policy was dictated from New York and no attempt was made to recognise the merits of traditional Chinese medicine – it lured a stream of able Westerners to Peking, whose energy and achievements made a very real contribution to the city's intellectual life. And, as far as foreign representation in Peking was concerned, the PUMC community provided a welcome alternative to the curiously detached world of the legation quarter.

***

In her autobiography, Dora Black recalled her amusement at the sight of the emperor's tutor, Reginald Johnston, being carried in a sedan chair with great pomp and ceremony through the gates and courtyards of the Forbidden City. As a Bolshevik sympathiser it is not surprising that she found the scene absurd, but for Johnston, devoted student of Chinese imperial history, the ceremonial aspect of his role held deep significance. A perfect example of the colonial official 'gone native', he had long considered China his home and for many years had planned to live in retirement a quiet scholarly life in the Western Hills. But when in 1918 he was offered the job of tutor to the emperor he needed no persuading. For Johnston this was a fantasy come true and a position for which he believed he was uniquely fitted.

Certainly, few foreigners in Peking at the time could rival his knowledge of China – its language, geography, traditions and religions. But in the eyes of most of his fellow countrymen, such expertise only labelled him a maverick. As Bertrand Russell noted:

> The Englishman in the East … is a man completely out of touch with his environment. He plays polo and goes to the club. He derives his ideas of native culture from the works of 18th century missionaries and he regards intelligence in the East with the same contempt which he feels for intelligence in his own country'[28]

Johnston was different. Having begun his career in Hong Kong he then spent 14 years in the small treaty port of Weihaiwei (leased by the British in 1898) on the north shore of the Shantung peninsula. Professionally it was a backwater (its chief purpose being to provide a summer base for the Royal Navy's China fleet and holiday resort for the British), but it had allowed Johnston to live – as he had wished – simply among the Chinese, and to write esoteric books about their religions, folklore and customs. But he was no recluse. He loved the company of clever women, was himself a lively conversationalist and at various times in his career nurtured ambitions to be Governor of Hong Kong and Vice-Chancellor of Hong Kong University.

Any prospects of promotion, however, were thwarted by his own eccentricity. His imaginary friends – the outspoken Quork, Mrs Walkinshaw and the Baron – popped in and out of his conversation even at official gatherings. And, rather than return on leave to England like any normal expatriate, he chose to spend months walking across little known parts of China, sometimes accompanied only by his bull-terrier, Jim. His colleagues found such conduct unsettling but it was his hatred of Christianity that caused them most alarm. Johnston particularly disliked protestant missionaries (whom he attacked in several publications[29]), claiming that their activities were as immoral as the opium trade. He described himself a Buddhist but was more Confucian in outlook, even carrying out his duties more in the manner of a traditional Chinese magistrate than a modern British official.

It was against this background that on the afternoon of 3 March 1919, the 47-year-old Scot first went to the Forbidden City to meet his imperial pupil. In contrast to Johnston's austerely formal top hat and tails, the emperor was dressed in sumptuous court robes and was carried to the audience chamber in a yellow silk palanquin by 16 eunuchs. Attendants wearing queues and richly embroidered imperial uniforms crowded the room, the whole scene forming a brilliant tableau. This, in Johnston's view, was the real China – an infinitely superior model to the drab, struggling republic he had left behind at the palace gates. The fact that he himself now had such privileged access to 'The Great Within' only strengthened his longing to see the Manchu Dynasty fully restored to its former glory. After Johnston had bowed three times to the emperor they shook hands and made polite conversation. Then, with all the ceremonies auspiciously completed (and having changed his clothes), the emperor was ready to begin his first lesson with his new tutor.

The two got on well from the start. Johnston, always blind to Puyi's faults, thought the 13-year-old vivacious, intelligent and humorous, while the boy, at last able to learn something of the world beyond his gilded prison, admired his tutor's patience and imagination. Although slow to learn English, he eagerly absorbed all he could of the West from the newspapers and magazines Johnston brought him, and, to the despair of his Chinese tutors, became besotted with everything foreign. The fact that Johnston was himself something of a social outsider did not prevent him from doing his best to teach the emperor how to behave like an English gentleman:

> If Your Majesty ever appears in London you are bound to be invited to tea very often. Tea parties are informal but important occasions that usually take place on Wednesdays. At them one can meet peers, scholars, celebrities and all sorts of people Your Majesty will need to meet. There is no need to be too dressed up but manners are most important. It is very bad to drink tea as if it were water, to eat cakes as if they were a real meal, or make too much noise with your fork or teaspoon. In England tea and cakes are *refreshment*...not a meal.[30]

The more Puyi learned of the West, the more he longed to escape the Forbidden City – an ambition that Johnston did nothing to discourage. There was even a suggestion that he might go to Oxford University, to Magdalen College where Johnston had himself been an undergraduate. But while England remained a distant dream, Johnston could see no reason why the boy should not in the more immediate future be allowed to live in the relative freedom of the Summer Palace.

> Although the emperor does not appear to have been spoiled, as yet, by the follies and futilities of his surroundings, I am afraid there is no hope that he will come unscathed through the moral dangers of the next few years of his life unless he can be withdrawn from the influence of the hordes of eunuchs and other useless functionaries who are now almost his only associates.[31]

In the end, it was the vested interests of the 'useless functionaries' that won the day in preventing Puyi from ever enjoying a more normal existence. The Imperial Household Department controlled every aspect of the Forbidden City, the emperor's life and the eunuchs that served him. In republican China, the lucrative livelihood that these thousand or so people derived from the emperor's presence was already fragile enough, but should he ever be allowed to leave the Palace, the whole corrupt structure would collapse. Johnston loathed the Imperial Household Department and all it stood for. From the moment he took up his post it was open warfare between 'canny Scot' and 'wily oriental'.

Their battles were fought over issues such as the presence of eunuchs during lessons, whether or not the emperor should be allowed a telephone or a car and, more seriously, the disappearance of countless imperial treasures. Some Johnston won, others he lost. One victory was especially sweet. He had noticed the emperor was short-sighted and reported the fact to the household officials, none of whom responded with the slightest interest until Johnston recommended that a foreign oculist be consulted. This suggestion was met with outrage especially from one of the ancient dowager consorts still living in the palace. Her objection was that a foreign doctor would prescribe glasses and 'the wearing of spectacles by emperors is a thing that is not done'. Furthermore, if such a blasphemy were allowed to pass, she would commit suicide by opium. Ignoring this, Johnston in turn threatened to resign (an act the eunuchs would have greeted with joy) if the matter was not immediately addressed. Eventually an American professor from the PUMC was allowed to examine the emperor and spectacles were duly prescribed. The old lady did not commit suicide (Mongolian bandits later kidnapped the professor) and Puyi became so devoted to his glasses that he refused ever to be parted from them.

Despite his problems with the eunuchs, Johnston revelled in his new job. As the hours were not arduous he had plenty of time to enjoy the fine courtyard house near the Drum Tower in which he lived rent-free. Not only did he have a wide range of Chinese friends but was also lionised by foreigners eager to learn the secrets of the Forbidden City from the one Westerner who had an intimate knowledge of them. Inordinately proud of the honours he received from the emperor, Johnston had them inscribed on red tablets and placed inside the gates of his house for all his visitors to admire:

Companion of the Yu Ching Palace
Privileged to be carried in a sedan chair with two bearers
Awarded the hat button and robes of the first rank
Endowed with the right to wear a sable jacket

On 26 June 1920, Stella Benson wrote in her diary:

Mr Johnston came to dinner. I have been dreading meeting him in a way because ever since I arrived in Peking I have been told incessantly how much we should like each other. But as a matter of fact we did...he is alive in every corner of his mind…suffering from not being able to talk quickly enough to say everything he wants to say. He is entirely self-confident and it would seem never could have a doubt of himself and never have time between thoughts to hate himself. Has more than his fair share of life really.

She also noted how his 'funny secret friends come in and out of the burble very graciously, a Baron & also one Mrs Walkinshaw'. A few days later she dined at his house observing that most of it seemed to be a library 'and most of the books were books that one terribly wanted to read'. After dinner everyone lay down outside and listened to the great bell: 'It is the most exotic and dramatic voice a bell ever had,' she wrote, 'it is a growl rather than a resonance, almost too deep to be understood…you feel at once put in your place. If it could, it would ring you dead and that, one suddenly sees, would not matter at all.'[32]

Of all the perks Johnston received, none gave him more pleasure than the house the government built for him in the Western Hills. Here, in a remote valley, he created a haven complete with shrines to long-forgotten gods, a temple, an exotic garden and even a statue of Buddha borrowed from a nearby village. A stream of visitors – academics, poets and Manchu princes among them – flocked to this rural idyll where culturally the only jarring note was his choice of name – 'Cherry Glen'. In 1921 the mediaeval historian Eileen Power spent a weekend at Cherry Glen and was captivated by both the beauty of the place and the erudition of her host. '…it was when I was on a walking tour with Miss Harding…I remember him with pleasure because he was soaked in Chinese things & because he was so amusing & because he lent me a horse.'[33] Theirs was a lasting friendship, renewed seven years later in Weihaiwei, where Johnston had been appointed Commissioner. 'I have a charming person staying with me just now,' he wrote to a friend, 'namely Miss (!!!) Eileen Power…she is spending a fortnight with me – Mrs Walkinshaw being the only chaperone.'[34] They planned to marry but once back in England where Johnston was appointed Professor of Chinese at the School of Oriental Studies in 1931, and too far perhaps from the magic of China, the engagement petered out.

In April 1924, Johnston organised a meeting between the emperor and the Indian poet Rabindranath Tagore, regarded in China with deep respect not just as a poet but also as a great oriental prophet and philosopher. Following in the footsteps of Dewey and Russell, Tagore was invited to China to give a series of lectures. In the event, his visit to the Forbidden City was the one happy memory of his stay in Peking, which in every other respect proved a disaster. For, despite his saintly appearance enhanced by long beard and flowing garments, he managed to upset everyone – Chinese and foreigner alike. At first sight his mission seemed innocent enough. His aim was to inspire a renewal of the spiritual relationship between India and China by encouraging a return to the values of their ancient civilizations. Such a renaissance, he hoped, would lead to a united oriental culture free from Western materialism. This, however, was the last thing 'Young China' wanted to hear. Nor was it only the students who objected. Every Chinese who longed for his country to escape poverty and subservience interpreted Tagore's message as dangerously reactionary. The Westerners in their turn did not appreciate being cast in the role of wicked materialists, while the Japanese were furious at Tagore's reference to their 'barbaric' nationalism based on 'pride, greed and lust for power'.[35]

Yet it had all begun so well. When the great Indian sage arrived at Peking station on 23 April 1924, a huge crowd had cheered him and showered him with flowers. The *North China Standard* even claimed that:

> No event in recent years has aroused so much interest in Chinese intellectual circles as the visit of Rabindranath Tagore. Many men have come to China and gone yet none of them has been so enthusiastically received. What is the explanation? It is because Dr. Tagore belongs to the East and in honouring him the Chinese intellectuals are honouring the civilisation of the East.

After such a warm welcome and given his own high expectations of China, Tagore was understandably embittered by the hostile reception to his lectures. Johnston, naturally sympathetic to Tagore's call for a return to traditional values, and anxious that the poet should not leave Peking without having some sense of 'the courteous and dignified China that has never failed to rouse the homage of foreign visitors',[36] worked hard to make a success of Tagore's audience with the emperor. At 10 am on 27 April, the poet and his party arrived at the Forbidden City to be greeted by Johnston and dozens of court officials. As they were conducted through one courtyard after another, the artist Nandalal Bose noticed how the number of accompanying courtiers steadily diminished since only the most senior was allowed to be anywhere near the now heavily bespectacled Son of Heaven. At last they reached the pavilion where the emperor and his two wives (he had been married off in 1922 at the age of 16) waited to receive them. Puyi himself guided the Indians through the Palace, showing them so many exquisite works of art that Bose felt depressed by (as he saw it) the huge cultural gulf between China and India. Though he also noted that 'alongside an old carpet wonderfully soft and beautiful, is an ugly modern rug with cheap designs of gaudy coloured wall-flowers'.[37]

It is unlikely that on this pleasant occasion – enjoyed by Puyi and Johnston every bit as much as by their Indian guests – it crossed anyone's mind that within a few months the emperor would have been expelled from the Forbidden City for good and that, paraphrasing Johnston's words, the lingering twilight of the Manchu court would have deepened into night.

1. Sir Claude MacDonald, British Minister in Peking 1896–1900 in his elaborate diplomatic uniform. After commanding the defence of the legations during the Boxer siege he was appointed Britain's first ambassador to Japan.

2. Emperor Street, 1901. Foreigners loved the colour and life of Peking's streets but not the lack of sanitation. This photograph is one of a collection taken by Alfons Mumm von Schwarzenstein who in 1901 succeeded the murdered Baron von Ketteler as German Minister.

3. The 9th US Infantry Regiment lining the way to the Forbidden City where the foreign armies held a victory parade after the relief of the Boxer siege. In the foreground can be seen the American Minister, Edwin H. Conger and his family.

4. Strings of camels, characterised in winter by their thick woolly coats, were a familiar sight. They were used to transport coal to Peking from the mines at Mentoukou, close to where Peking Man was discovered at Choukoutien.

5. The first steam engine to arrive at the newly built railway station close to Peking's main gate, Chien-men, on 1 November 1901.

6. Mrs Cecil Carnegie entertaining court ladies at the British Legation, 6 June 1906. They were fascinated by this rare encounter with the West, especially with their upside down reflection in Mrs Carnegie's silver spoons. Manchu women were distinguished from Chinese women by their elaborate headdresses and unbound feet.

7. The Allies' victory parade held in the Forbidden City on 18 November 1918. China entered the war hoping to regain its lost territory and to establish a new dialogue with the West. The students' bitter disappointment at the outcome of the 1919 Versailles Peace Treaty led to the May the Fourth Movement, and the country's political awakening.

8. Cecil Lewis and Doushka Horvath 'flying' on the Altar of Heaven. It was here that each December the emperor performed sacred rituals to ensure a good harvest. The couple were married in 1920 at the chapel of the Russian Ecclesiastical Mission.

9. The White Russian leader, General Dmitri Horvath in his study, c.1920. Behind him hangs a picture of the Temple of Heaven. After losing to the Bolsheviks in Siberia, Horvath took his large family to live in the abandoned Austro-Hungarian legation. He died in Peking in 1937.

10. Bertrand Russell and Dora Black, 1920. Although they disparaged Peking's expatriates they were much impressed by the Chinese students they encountered. Dora became Russell's second wife in 1921.

11.   Patriotic children on holiday at Peitaihe under the watchful eye of nurse, *c.*1925.

12.   One of Peking's neglected gate towers, probably on the northwest of the Tartar City as the Western Hills can just be glimpsed to the left of the photograph.

13. The entrance to the British Legation. The gate still exists.

14. Dining room at the British Minister's residence. The portrait of Queen Victoria was damaged by Boxer bullets during the siege. It was in this room that all the foreign ministers gathered in 1914 at the outset of the First World War. They did not meet again as a group until after the armistice four years later.

15. Six servants, commonly referred to as 'boys', standing on the steps of the British Minister's residence, *c.*1930. As it was vital never to lose 'face', legation servants always helped each other out when in need. Consequently foreigners became used to seeing their own dinner services, and sometimes even their clothes, appear at other people's parties.

16. In 1929 the embalmed body of Sun Yat-sen, was interred, four years after his death, in a specially built mausoleum just outside Nanking. Although the foreign diplomats had travelled all the way from Peking for the occasion, most of them missed the final ceremony due to an administrative muddle.

17. American marines exercising on the Tartar wall close to the Chien-men gate, *c.*1930. They are looking into the legation quarter.

18. Foreigners on a camel at the Ming Tombs, 1932.

19. An American diplomat in his private rickshaw, *c*.1935.

20. Carrying chair for sightseeing, 1933.

21. 'Lunch en route to the station.' Lady Lampson, seated on the left, died suddenly in 1930 at the age of 44.

22. An expedition to Pao Chu Tung Temple, 4 September 1932. Nelson T. Johnson, American Ambassador to China 1929–41, is standing on the right. The Western Hills were close enough to Peking for a day's excursion although foreigners often stayed in rented temples for much longer periods.

23. Pierre Teilhard de Chardin with the sculptor, Lucile Swan, at her courtyard house. Her struggle to reconcile love and celibacy is revealed in their long correspondence.

24. House guests of the British Minister, Sir Miles Lampson, in Mongolian dress, 1931.

25. The Rt. Hon. Sir Alexander Cadogan and Lady Theodosia. Cadogan was
Britain's first ambassador to China where he served 1934–36. Their dog 'Joseph'
is as perfectly groomed as his owners.

26. Sir Edmund Backhouse, Bt. His
fraudulent escapades remained
largely hidden from Peking's
foreigners who regarded him
benignly as a scholarly eccentric.
This photograph was taken on
one of his rare public appearances
c.1935. He died in Peking in 1944.

27. A New Year's Eve party hosted in 1930 by the American entrepreneur, Helen Burton, two of her adopted Chinese daughters can be seen standing. Fancy-dress parties were a much-loved tradition in Peking's foreign community up to the Communist victory.

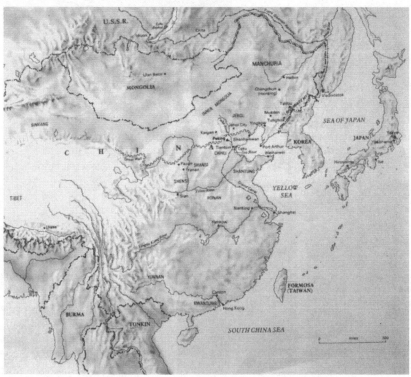

28. Map of China.

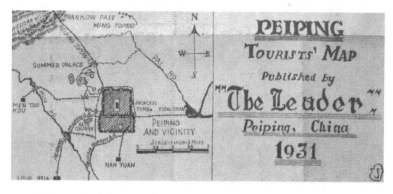

29.   Peking and its vicinity.

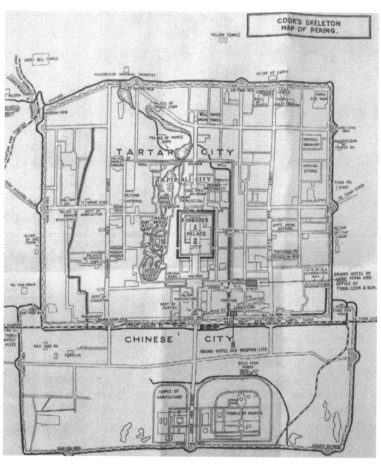

30.   Plan of Peking.

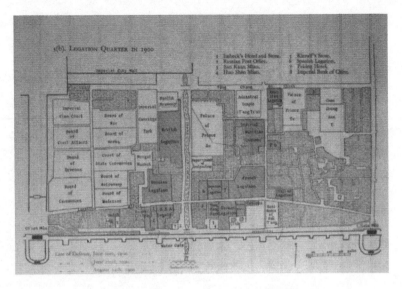

31.   Plan of the legation quarter as it was at the time of the Boxer siege in 1900.

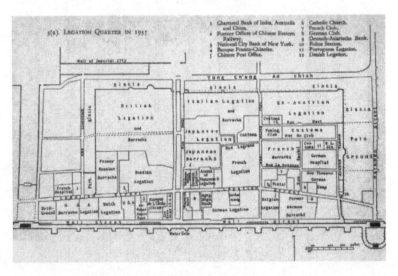

32.   Plan of the legation quarter, 1935.

10
PICNICS AND PONIES

'My clothes are a screaming success and I am cutting a spectacular dash,' wrote Alice Green Hoffman from Peking in January 1925. Mrs Hoffman, a wealthy American matron related to the Roosevelts, was a guest of the British Minister and his wife, Sir Ronald and Lady Macleay. Entranced with Peking (where there was no prohibition) she expected it soon to become the social centre of the world – not least because a case of champagne cost only 30 dollars.[1] By 'Peking' she was of course referring only to its foreign residents and more especially to those living within the legation quarter where life still went on much as before. To the likes of Mrs Hoffman this was the real world while the Peking that existed beyond its walls was little more than a grubby inconvenience.

In fact, it seemed that nothing, not war, revolution, famine or Bolshevism, could be allowed to interrupt the flow of social life. 'So, while outside the legation quarter Reginald Johnston yearned for the restoration of empire and the Communists for social revolution; while John Dewey preached democracy and the missionaries repentance, inside the newly arrived wife of the British military attaché Molly Orpen-Palmer was struggling to make up her mind on what to wear at the fancy dress ball on 16 January 1921. It was a difficult decision, but in the end she decided to go as Pierrette:

> I called in the legation tailor four days before the Ball and asked him to make me a Pierrette dress. He made me such a sweet one, masses of skirts, the top one

being in three flounces with the edges *raw*. It was all pale pink with touches of black. Rather dainty I think. Everyone thought I had brought my dress out from home. No one could believe the legation tailor had made it in four days. It was very simple once he seized the idea. I would place the stuff at a certain angle and say 'Can do?' and he would say 'can do'. Then I would say 'I no like this tailor', pointing to a part of the dress. 'Can do like this?' And he would say 'can do, can do'. Once he had said 'can do' all was well.[2]

Molly, in common with most foreigners, admired her Chinese servants and with good reason. For it was their ingenuity, humour and cheerful acceptance of their employers' idiosyncrasies that not only made life possible for them in Peking but, as the century progressed, increasingly desirable. But while the Westerners were pleased to sing their praises (too often like the proud owner of a clever pet), few were prepared to admit that without their boys, amahs, cooks and rickshaw coolies they could barely have survived one day in China. Sir Alexander Hosie's conviction that as a white foreigner (and especially as an Englishman) he was innately superior to all Chinese was hardly unique. After seven years away, he returned to Peking in 1920, delighted to find 'Jumbo', the British Minister's number one boy, still in charge and the servants as resplendent as ever in their silk scarlet and blue livery, though he was saddened to find that they no longer wore pigtails.[3]

Over the years, Chinese servants had become so adept at handling foreigners that once the newcomer had understood the complexities of 'squeeze' he could safely leave all his domestic arrangements – from the mixing of Manhattans to the elimination of bed bugs – in the hands of his number one boy. In one of Ann Bridge's three Peking novels (she was married to Owen O'Malley, counsellor at the British legation, 1925–7), the newly arrived Mrs Grant-Howard is initiated into the system:

It was ruled by the strictest of conventions. The cost of any given article bore an exact relation to the official rank of the household consuming it. Whereas a chicken in the market cost some thirty cents, the moment it entered the Legation Gate it cost thirty-five – the five cents being the legitimate 'squeeze' or rake-off of the gate porter. But the further possibilities of the chicken in the matter of price were endless. If it went to the students' mess, it would figure on the bill at a paltry thirty-eight cents; if to Mrs Hugo, who was only a consul's wife, at about forty-one; and so up through every grade of diplomatic rank till it reached the Leroys' kitchen at fifty-four, while the Ministerial chickens cost Sir James Boggit sixty-three or thereabouts.

Although the diplomatic wife had to absorb many alien conventions before she could run her household satisfactorily, it was, in the words of Bridge's heroine, 'all immense fun...much more so than keeping house in any European country'. And the beauty of it was that 'it was all so wildly cheap'.[4]

The resourcefulness of Chinese servants was never more apparent than during the numerous expeditions so beloved by the foreigners to the Western Hills, the Great Wall or the Ming tombs. Everything – canteens of silver, beds, food, champagne and fuel – had to be transported by train or motor-car and then, when the rails and roads ran out, by mule to the ultimate destination. Whatever the season, a party of foreigners would arrive after a long dusty journey at some isolated temple or dilapidated village to find ample hot water, the table immaculately laid for dinner and beds made up with their own spotless linen. On one such occasion when Daniel Varè was hosting a lunch party at the Ming tombs, the party entered the temple (next to the Yung-lo emperor's tomb) to find a table laden with steaming pasta, chicken cutlets, galantine, salads, puddings, stewed fruit, coffee and wines. The food had been cooked in an oven built on the spot out of bricks and ornamental tiles.

The more adventurous went on longer expeditions, sometimes trekking far into the Western Hills. Ann Bridge was away for over two weeks with three friends from the British legation. They did not travel alone. Accompanying them were a dozen servants, a cook, two butlers and a head donkey boy. Four more coolies walked behind each member of the party all day, carrying, rucksack, camera, coat, walking stick, Burberry, fly switch, umbrella, fan, topi and any other oddments that might be needed. Apart from the party's five personal donkeys, there was a further train of 16 to carry all the camping equipment and food. The large Union Jacks, sticking out at intervals from the pack loads, were considered adequate protection against attack by bandits.

The Orpen-Palmers arrived in Peking in 1920 during one of the worst famines ever to hit North China. In her letters home Molly never refers to this disaster – terrible even by China's standards – but she does give a full account of their first Christmas:

> Cook gave us a topside tiffin of creamed soup (most delicious), fish soufflé, goose in aspic, turkey stuffed with chestnuts, potatoes, steamed celery, bread, mince, blazing plum pudding and mince pies, two delicious cream puddings one filled with chestnuts then savoury, dessert, coffee and liqueurs. We all felt stuffed!

Not that she was unappreciative: 'The Chinese out here work like old Harry for the English Christmas & do anything rather than let you down in anyway as it would mean losing face for them if anything went wrong.'[5]

Even summer holidays at Peitaiho would have been unthinkable without servants, sent on ahead with the silver, linen, glass and china to prepare the bungalows. As in Peking, life at the seaside had its established rhythm:

> No one dresses till after tea. We breakfast on the verandah in a kimono then at 11 a.m. get into bathing dresses with a kimono on top & a big sun shade & stroll down to the beach. We have boat (with a man) and a raft to bathe from which makes it all heaps of fun. Then cocktails, ginger snaps & cherry brandy are brought down to us on the rocks where we sit in our bathing things. At 1 p.m. we lunch in kimonos, hair screwed up just as it was under our bathing caps then we slumber in long chairs & only dress for tea at 4.30.

After siesta, there was tennis or a stroll along the bluffs followed by a moonlit picnic on the rocks:

> Such an attractive scene with the cloth spread & dark red lights (which we all have down here) and standing on the cloth, bowls of flowers, cut glass & china. These Chinese boys do everything *de rigueur*. It's all so comfortable & from a little hole in the rock in the distance emerges course after course. How the cooks do it is a marvel.[6]

Of course such an existence so far from home did not suit everyone, and homesickness, especially for those with children away at school, was rife. But for the Mollies of the world, Peking's social whirl offered a temporary escape from the ordinariness of life back home and Molly, for one, was determined to make the most of it:

> We are having our usual bewildering time. I shall soon want new clothes – one is out so much you don't give them much chance of a rest! It's nothing but a succession of lunches, afternoon dances, dinner & evening dances. Last Monday I was lunching with some people, came home & slinked off on a few calls, at a big reception at 5 p.m. with dancing, got home at 7 p.m., dressed and dined at the Japanese Legation at 8.30 & when we left there at 10.45 we went to another house for a dance & got home at 3 a.m.! & that's not an exceptional day. I go often to afternoon dances which are always from 5-7 & then dine out & go on to another dance.

Not every foreigner in Peking shared Molly's enthusiasm for social life. Although Stella Benson fell in love with the city, believing that Peking had the stuff from which enough beautiful dreams could be made for a lifetime, she soon became depressed by what she saw as a 'vulgar and repressive society'. There were however moments to treasure – even at uncongenial parties:

> I fled to the best of my power by sitting behind a rock and running the Victrola for Miss Gillpillen to dance to. She danced in the pools of moonlight in wispy white clothes and bare feet. It was really lovely, so prancy and dancy and full of happiness and yet so dim and quiet.[7]

Arguably, the foreigners had evolved this frenetic lifestyle to mask the chronic boredom suffered by so many of them in Peking. Apart from a handful of ministers and the professional sinologists the average diplomat had little work of real substance to fill his day. Unable to speak Chinese, fearful of disease and denied the distractions of a more cosmopolitan capital (there was one cinema), Peking's diplomatic community relied on two pursuits to give their life meaning – sex and horses.

The riding, racing and polo were genuine enough but the sex often more imagined than real. As Alexis Leger noted:

> A delightful immorality reigns here, and nothing comes of it; whereas everywhere else, especially in Europe it is so amusing to see people struggling desperately against their fundamental morality in order to live a little. It's even more amusing to see people here with all their basic lack of morality make nothing of it.[8]

Laura Leroy, the heroine in Ann Bridge's best-known book, *Peking Picnic*, agreed, remarking that half the people in Peking are always having liaisons and half pretending that they have them. The chronic shortage of young women meant that those adventurous enough to come out from Europe and stay with relatives often found themselves a husband: 'Most girls who come to Peking leave it engaged, generally to the wrong man,' remarks Mrs Leicester, another of Ann Bridge's characters, 'and nearly all women leave Peking with a broken heart.'[9]

While most legation affairs were little more than bedroom farce, one at least turned to tragedy. The Italian Minister, the Marchese Durazzo (whom Stella Benson thought too pleasant and polite to be very interesting), had a beautiful but neurotic wife. Having formed a passionate attachment to the legation's assistant commercial attaché, she was less than delighted when her lover's former mistress turned up in Peking. Late one night, the Marchesa went to the Wagons-Lits hotel to confront her rival. Once inside her bedroom, she hit her over the head with a decanter and then tried to polish her off by slicing her wrists. This episode did little for her husband's career but even less for the attaché's who shortly afterwards committed suicide. The Marchesa herself was put on trial in Italy for attempted murder. Cecil Bowra, the very English Secretary of Customs, found the whole saga mystifying:

> Captain Pitri was an uninteresting individual of commonplace type; and why two women, one at any rate of unusual charm and attractiveness, with a delightful husband and nice children, should have cared sufficiently about him to go to these extraordinary lengths is a mystery buried in the dark depths of Latin femininity.[10]

The scandal kept tongues wagging at the club for many weeks as did, a few years later, the *ménage à trois* involving Mrs Wallis Spencer (as she was then, later Mrs Simpson, and later still the Duchess of Windsor). There are lurid rumours surrounding Wallis's time in Shanghai, the most persistent of which centres on a dossier allegedly compiled for the British Prime Minister Stanley Baldwin in an attempt to discredit her in the eyes of the besotted Prince of Wales. Having finally parted from her abusive and alcoholic husband (then serving in Hong Kong as an American naval officer) Wallis arrived in Peking in 1924 intending to stay only a couple of weeks. But after meeting up with an old friend and her husband she moved in with them and remained for what she described as her 'Lotus Year'. The three Americans epitomised the sybaritic lifestyle enjoyed by an increasing number of rich expatriates living in Peking during the 1920s. Money went a long way and they knew how to spend it.

They certainly spent a great deal of both money and time on horses, even though by Western standards the creatures were considered ridiculously small and ugly. The ponies ran wild on the Mongolian grasslands until they were six years old when they were lassoed and brought down to Peking. Such was their dislike of the smell of foreigners that the *mafoos* habitually hung a piece of their employer's old clothing in the stables to get them used to it. While almost everyone rode, the cost of keeping a horse in Peking was relatively expensive – double that of a servant. But those who could afford to also kept a string of racing ponies out at the racecourse at Paomachang, several miles to the west of Peking. Many people had weekend houses near the racecourse where, as described by Ann Bridge, they provided lavish entertainment before the paper hunts and race meetings that regularly took place in the winter months:

On Sundays, a general exodus takes place to Paomachang by car; lunches are consumed in the villas and temples, and then the paper-hunt is witnessed by a large crowd. The onlookers stand and shiver in a cruel wind, up to their ankles in sand, watching a cloud of dust disappear; after a prolonged interval the cloud of dust reappears, and they have the fun of seeing whether their husbands, sweethearts or jockeys will fall or be rolled on at the last two jumps or not. After which everyone drinks cherry brandy, the two cups are handed out by some woman, the lottery tickets are drawn and the proceedings close till next Sunday when they begin all over again.[11]

Riding gave foreigners the freedom to explore Peking in a way that would have been impossible on foot. Occasionally these outings led to unpleasant experiences. On 12 August 1920 Stella Benson was riding towards the Temple of Heaven on her horse, Woodrow:

It was lovely until we got to the great space outside the gate...which was full of an excited crowd of thousands & thousands all the way down the wide street to Chienmen...coming to see the show. I made the mafoo ask what the show was & after enquiring he said 'five men makee dead'. Then I could see the little ominous crowd of soldiers & over their shoulders craned a large group of American soldiers eager for the show. I felt very sick & wanted to go away, the crowd was so thick & all pressing from all sides against us so we moved about a yard at a spurt, very slowly. It was a rough crowd & men kept on hitting Woodrow so that he plunged a bit now & then...a lot of very angry soldiers besides the driver all with their bayonets pointing at the condemned men. The first man was either quite drunk or in an ecstasy of bravado, he was shrieking & singing, & his head was right back & his eyes shut. All the prisoners had their elbows tied very tightly behind them, the other four were not making a sound & had their heads crouched so far forward as to hide their faces...After the last cart had passed the crowd tried to rush the carts from behind & the soldiers walked backwards hitting so violently with the flat of their bayonets that you could hear the clankings of metal against the men's heads. Behind the cars came another cart full of soldiers & with something so suggestive it made me sicker than ever – a great domestic zinc bath...I cannot forget that first yelling man's face, fat & upturned & with terrified closed eyes & a grin.

But worse was to come. Following the carts she saw 'four automobiles, one flying the Union Jack, one the Stars & Stripes & two un-flagged full of foreigners, men & women, the latter in pretty fluffy clothes, all eager and greedy for the show'.[12] Beheadings, it seemed, along with temples, tombs, picnics and ponies, were an essential part of the foreigner's Peking experience.

***

At 9 o'clock on the morning of 5 November 1924, soldiers serving the warlord Feng Yu-hsiang had entered the Forbidden City demanding to see 'Mr' Puyi. Confronting the emperor, they ordered him to sign a revision of the abdication agreement and, with his wife and the two surviving dowager consorts, quit the palace within three hours. The old ladies refused to go, threatening, as usual, to kill themselves with opium. But the emperor and empress had no choice. After collecting a few personal possessions, they were escorted by armed guards to the imperial garden where cars waited to take them to Puyi's father's house in the northern part of Peking. Thus for the last time, the last Chinese emperor left the Forbidden City – heart of the Ch'ing Dynasty for nearly 300 years. That so few were present to witness his departure only added to its poignancy.

Ignorant of Puyi's fate and fearful for his safety, Reginald Johnston had driven that morning straight to the legation quarter to inform Sir Ronald Macleay and the Dutch Minister William Oudendyk of the emperor's plight. But there was little the diplomats could do except seek assurances from the new Chinese authorities that no harm would come to him. Alice Hoffman revelled in all the excitement: 'One is constantly reminded of the *Mikado* with the fear that one may wake up some day and find that he has been beheaded in the night.'[13] Just over three weeks later, on 29 November, Johnston took matters into his own hands. By means of a clever subterfuge, he extracted the emperor from his father's closely guarded house and drove him to the legation quarter. There he left him in the German hospital while he tried to persuade Macleay or Oudendyk to offer Puyi asylum. Neither minister was prepared to involve his government in such murky waters, but for the Japanese diplomats it was a different story. Seizing their opportunity to gain control of the emperor, by nightfall they had him safely installed in their legation. Then, three months later, on 24 February 1925, in great secrecy and without even informing his tutor, Puyi, under the protection of his new 'friends', took the train to Tientsin where he and his retinue were housed in the Japanese concession. He was to remain there for seven years. Johnston, deeply hurt by this, did eventually visit Puyi in Tientsin, and technically remained on his staff for some months. But after a year of unemployment in Peking he needed a job. When the British government offered him the post of Secretary to the Boxer Indemnity Committee, he accepted and by February 1926 had left Peking.

Feng Yu-hsiang, responsible for ousting the emperor, was among the most prominent of the bevy of warlords whose armies ebbed and flowed across China, bringing untold misery and chaos to the country. Frances Butcher, a missionary writing in 1923, paints a dismal picture:

> The whole country appears to be seething with unrest, from North to South, and one wonders what will be the outcome of it all. The forces of evil seem to be overwhelming at present, and the will of the people so impotent. The government consists chiefly of rapacious officials whose one aim is to serve self...the constant change in the ministry is positively bewildering, and one cannot keep count of those in power for almost every week there is deposition and fresh appointment to office...The country is virtually without a head as the President has been driven from office in Peking and had to flee to Tientsin where he is living in one of the foreign concessions...Bands of looters are a menace. Besides spoiling homes, acts of violence to women and children, they take many captives for ransom and keep them in custody sometimes for months, treating them abominably, and there is little done to repress them. One hopeful sign is the rising of the students in the large cities and though many of their demands are preposterous, they are a sign of growing national conscience. Just now there is a general boycott of Japanese articles both in the North and the South, and feeling is very high between the two peoples...The Chinese would greatly oppose intervention by foreigners and yet China seems unable herself to control her national affairs satisfactorily.

However gloomy the outlook, missionaries instinctively searched for a silver lining and Frances Butcher found one: 'Looking at things from merely a political point of view the aspect is hopeless,' she wrote, 'but on turning to the Christian Church out here one is filled with hope. She is going to be the leaven that will leaven the whole lump.'[14] So when Feng Yu-hsiang (nicknamed the 'Christian General') decided to have his entire army of some quarter of a million men baptised, many a missionary heart beat a little faster.

But others interpreted the Christian General's actions more cynically. As Brigadier Leonard Field (a language student in the British military attaché's office, 1922–5) pointed out, China was very fashionable in the United States and American dollars flowed in a steady stream to any cause which smacked of converting, healing or otherwise doing good to the 'heathen Chinese'. When Feng became a Christian, a great many dollars flowed in his direction. Field recounts how one day Feng sent for the missionary who had converted him, informing him that he wanted his entire army baptised. The missionary, delighted, if daunted, by the sheer magnitude of the task, explained to the General that it would take a long time to instruct so many men. Waving aside such trivial concerns, Feng ordered him to be ready the following Tuesday armed with his Bible:

> A large car with four very large toughs, all armed to the teeth, standing on the running boards, presented itself at the missionary's house. He got in and the car set off for the great barracks outside of Peking where Feng's soldiers were concentrated. When the missionary got there he was greeted with the sight of Feng's army – every man jack of them – jammed like sardines into the fortunately very large barrack square. Through this mass of humanity a narrow lane led to a raised platform in the middle. Feng led the missionary up on to the platform, then said, 'Well, go on start reading.' The missionary began the service of baptism, Feng gave a signal, and powerful, fire hoses, which had been strategically placed around the perimeter of the assembled army, opened up and began to shower water over everybody and everything within reach. Feng informed the troops that they were now Christians and that they had better learn to behave themselves as such. The ceremony then concluded, the missionary was returned to Peking, and Feng sat back to await the flow of dollars which he confidently expected as soon as the news of this most gratifying event had time to soak through to the great American public.[15]

Although the warlords' skirmishes around Peking caused intense suffering to the Chinese, they made little impact on the lives of the foreigners even if the sound of distant gunfire did become a regular part of daily life. Whenever possible, the generals avoided direct fighting, preferring to win their battles by bribery. A better cash offer was often all that was needed to persuade the opposition's troops to defect. The foreigners knew that the city was about to change hands when they saw long lines of carts pour into the legation quarter piled high with the possessions of rich Pekingese. It was a frequent occurrence. Field recalled that even in the three years he lived there, Peking was captured four or five times by different armies. Ever since the Boxer siege, Chinese troops had been forbidden to enter the quarter, so that ousted Chinese politicians – together with their concubines, strong-boxes and spittoons – would make a rapid retreat to the legation quarter's only hotel – the Wagon-Lits. In a letter to Ann Bridge, Eric Teichman (Chinese secretary to the British legation) neatly summed up the foreigners' attitude to the warlords: 'Ching Chung Cheng is attacking Chang Ching Chung, while Cheng Chung Chang is manoeuvring to oust Chung Cheng Ching, who in turn is threatened by Chang Chung Ching.'[16]

Occasionally, foreigners found themselves caught up more directly in the fighting. Stella Benson was staying at a temple in the Western Hills with friends when she was woken in the middle of the night by Teichman. He had come out from the legation to warn them that unruly troops were heading their way and that they should return immediately to Peking:

> With one stroke of the hand we dressed and squeezed into the car, a four-seater Ford, but now holding eight including a Chinese exquisite creature from the legation with a red plume on his hat. I sat on the hood at the back and had a swift and exhilarating drive the only drawback being that we ran over a dog. At the gate they seemed to have forgotten us. Somebody made a loud cry through the crack...finally they opened and we squeezed into alarmed Peking.[17]

But Benson's sense of it all being little more than a light-hearted adventure was soon dispelled when she went into the PUMC the next morning:

> Work is rather hectic now as the wounded come in in such large groups and lie groaning...some of them cry like little boys but most have a perfectly indifferent look on their faces. One cannot understand them except by thinking they do not much mind pain or that they can tolerate the risk of death without thinking it matters.[18]

For most foreigners though, the actions of the warlords mattered only inasmuch as they affected their own plans. It was, as Molly Orpen-Palmer discovered, very irritating not to be able to go to the seaside.

The Chinese war has been going on near Peitaiho and Shanhaiguan, so none of us have been able to get away. Now it's over the troops are clearing & we hope to get down to Peitaiho next month. The railway carriages are in such a filthy state because of the Chinese soldiers that they have to be disinfected before we can use them. The first class, I hear, are the worst![19]

When in *Peking Picnic*, news of a warlord's approaching army reaches the legation quarter, the only really important issue at stake was that 'Nina's picnic was, for the second time, quite disastrously off.'[20]

No-one has penned a better portrait of Peking's foreign community in the 1920s than Lady (Mary Anne) O'Malley alias Ann Bridge. In those days, the idea of a diplomat's wife publishing under her own name was frowned upon by the Foreign Office so she confected a pseudonym by adding 'Ann' to the name of the house where she and her family lived in England – Bridge End. From then on even her own family called her 'Bridge'. She wrote three novels based on her time in China[21] but it is the first, *Peking Picnic*, that is best remembered (reviewers compared it with *Passage to India*) and which, when it was published in 1932, brought her instant fame. In the days before mass travel, her gift was her ability to transport her readers to remote parts of the world where she let them see and feel for themselves the places she described. She soon fell in love with the Peking plain: 'Altogether it is rather beautiful, this immense expanse of landscape in two colours only, pale brown and pale blue, with its extreme simplicity of design.'[22] Unlike many foreigners, she also loved the bleak winter landscape of 'buff on buff', especially when 'a line of camels stretches across it like a colonnade'.[23]

Ann Bridge's books (she wrote 26) are rooted in real places and real people. In particular, her own emotional life and unhappy marriage are clearly charted through the experiences of her fictional characters. One reason why *Peking Picnic* was such a success (it beat 750 entries to win the *Atlantic Monthly* prize of 10,000 dollars) was because so many readers – male and female – fell in love with its heroine. Laura Leroy is recognisably Ann Bridge herself – if an idealised version. Yet, while she empathised with China more than many of her contemporaries (she learned enough of the language 'to hobble along with the natives') and developed a keen political sense, Bridge made no serious attempt to analyse the country or its problems other than in the context of British interests or by using familiar clichés. Chinese peasants, for instance, are always 'rational' and 'content'. And she responded to China's appalling poverty either by romanticising it: 'They saw the coolie stretch his superb limbs...his hairless polished torso was modelled with the perfection of a god's; his movements were full of grace and natural dignity...,' or by ignoring it, 'a rickshaw is the most delightfully civilised form of locomotion.'[24] Yet in most other respects Bridge's still highly readable books are full of acute observation and insight.

Although she was so clearly stimulated by foreign travel and was herself half American, Bridge confessed that she could never forget

> ...how English I am, the whole of me that matters is English through and through and these strange sights that I see pass like movies over a screen leaving the screen the same. It is very sure that whatever corner of the world we are in will be England till we leave it.[25]

It was a sentiment shared by many of her fellow countrymen and by extension the characters in her books. No matter how beautiful the temple or unspeakable the bandit atrocity, it is only their own culture that holds their lasting interest. China's role is little more than an exotic backdrop to their musings on how to love and live within the confusing social parameters of their times.

If the various armies posed little threat to the foreigners, sickness did. Even though Peking's climate, despite its extremes, was considered healthy, deaths in the expatriate community occurred frequently and often at great speed. 'I was at a party with charming Madame Sabine last Friday,' Bridge wrote to a friend in May 1926, 'and yesterday I went to her funeral.'[26] Disease lurked everywhere and no-one could afford to be complacent. Draining into the filthy canal that flowed parallel to the Tartar city wall were a criminal graveyard, a slaughterhouse and a manure processing plant. When the canal froze in winter, blocks of ice were cut from it and carried to waste ground next to the graveyard. Here, alongside the criminals, it lay buried until summer when it was dug up and sold to the foreign legation. 'Do you wonder,' Bridge wrote to friends, 'that I keep a lynx-like eye upon my ice-chest?'[27] The source of the scarlet fever her children contracted (and from which her seven-year-old son nearly died) was traced to contaminated toys from a Chinese market and shortly after that crisis the family went down with dysentery. Others in the legation were similarly afflicted, so when a young consul died and the minister became seriously ill, Bridge commented: 'Peking begins to seem hideous –everyone is dying here.'[28]

Others in the legation agreed and in their search for the cause lit upon Bridge's 'bong' – a yellow glazed pottery hen that normally sat with dogs and dragons on the upturned eaves of Chinese buildings repelling evil spirits. Bridge, having discovered one in the Forbidden City, fallen from its perch on the Temple of Ancestors, had boldly secreted it in her coat under the noses of a large crowd. Only later did she discover that bongs were considered hideously unlucky. Her legation friends, initially amused, now wanted the bong to go. And, as at the time the Bolsheviks were stirring up anti-British feeling in China, they urged Bridge to toss it over her garden wall into the Russian compound where it might usefully do its worst. Whether or not the bong influenced events is a matter of conjecture. But one fact is certain. The Soviet presence in Peking unsettled the entire foreign community.

11
RUSSIANS RED AND WHITE

On 9 August 1924, as reported by *Time* magazine, Soviet Russia's first ambassador to China, 'clad in immaculate evening clothes, shod in shining leather, gloved in white kid, and wearing a glossy silk hat', was taken in a gilded state coach drawn by six ebony horses and escorted by 24 cavalrymen, to present his credentials to the President.[1] Ever since 1918, the new Soviet regime had courted the Chinese government with promises of equality – annulment of unfavourable treaties, liquidation of the Boxer debt and surrender of extraterritorial rights. But Peking had played hard to get, so it was not until May 1924 that agreement was finally reached and China was prepared to give Soviet Russia *de jure* recognition. At last, the new ambassador Lev Karakhan was able to take possession of the former Russian legation – empty since the departure of the last Tsarist envoy, Prince Kudachev, in September 1920.

Although formally dismissed from his post in 1917, Kudachev had survived a further three years in his legation before the Peking government finally withdrew recognition and he was forced to leave. Stella Benson met the Prince and his sister shortly before their departure. She found the Prince's 'old gallantry manner' charming enough but it was the Princess, 'with her harsh voice and constant cigarette', who really caught her attention:

> A woman must have something about her to allow her to sit dominating
> and dignified among beautifully clothed guests, herself wearing a white shirt

without a hint of womanliness and a child's cotton hat worn back to front on the back of her head.[2]

Benson also admired Princess Kudachev's sharp mind and uncompromising views:

She is the only person I know who is admittedly anti-democratic & really hates the worker, a necessary but odious animal. When she argues against the encouragement of uniformity and the average she is, of course, on my road. That to her is the only result of democracy.[3]

For the legation quarter residents, the arrival of Karakhan and his team was a bitter pill. It was bad enough having Bolsheviks as neighbours but even worse was the fact that Karakhan, as an ambassador (the other heads of mission were mere ministers), outranked everyone and was thus automatically dean of the diplomatic corps. So it was on 7 November 1924 (according to the Gregorian calendar) that Sir Ronald Macleay and his staff presented themselves at the Soviet Embassy dressed in full diplomatic uniform to offer their congratulations to the Soviet ambassador on the seventh anniversary of the Russian Revolution.

But no diplomatic niceties could disguise the fact that the low wall separating the British and Soviet compounds had now acquired a sinister significance – and not just for the British. 'The Legation Quarter made a painful impression,' wrote Vera Vishnyakova-Akimova, then a 20-year-old language student,

...everywhere were walls piled upon walls behind which the imperialists carried on their base and bloody affairs. From here they exerted pressure on the Chinese government. Here their henchmen confidently hid from the judgment and anger of the Chinese people...such were the neighbours with whom we had somehow to coexist.[4]

Arriving in Peking from Vladivostok in 1925, Vera was shocked to see Russian embassy officials riding around in rickshaws, just like the imperialists, and was only slightly mollified when she learned why. The rickshaw coolies – furious at the Russian embargo – had officially complained to the embassy. After that, the Soviets agreed to ride in them but insisted on paying five times the usual fare and using them only for short distances. One military adviser was honest enough to confess that despite the 'absurdity, archaism and abasement of this means of locomotion' he found the experience 'altogether delightful'.[5] For the idealistic Vera, it was an uncomfortable lesson in pragmatism and one, she noted, that 'the imperialists observed with delight'.[6]

The Bolsheviks were not the only Russians in town. After the revolution, around a quarter of a million refugees had flooded into China and, while most settled in Harbin or Tientsin, a good many found their way to Peking. There the nucleus of their existence was the Russian Spiritual Mission tucked into the north-eastern corner of the Tartar City and only a short rickshaw ride from the Soviet embassy. The mission's origins went back to the late seventeenth century when 100 or so Albazinians, captured in border skirmishes by the Chinese, had been allowed to settle there and pursue their orthodox religion. For more than a century, the mission had performed a quasi-diplomatic role, but once the Russian legation was established in 1861 it concentrated its efforts on publishing a wide range of texts from its own press. After 1917, the mission's chief task was to care for white Russians by providing them with a place to stay and, when possible, jobs. This was not as hard as might have been expected since the mission was largely self-sufficient, maintaining considerable holdings of land and property, a flour-mill, bee-hives and a dairy.[7] Nevertheless, the refugees' existence – as described by the American traveller Harry Franck – was far from luxurious:

> They live thick as prisoners in the stone-walled cells of the old monastery where once only Orthodox monks recited their prayers – frail women and underfed children as well as men bearing a whole library of strange stories on their gaunt faces. Groups of refugees who came too late or have not influence enough to find room in the cells live packed together in stone cellars, some still wearing the remnants of tzarist uniforms, or of various 'White' armies that have gone to pieces before the advancing 'Reds', some still not recovered from war-time wounds and sundry hardships.[8]

On 28 December 1920, Ivan Serebrennikov and his wife Aleksandra, Siberian refugees from Irkutsk, arrived at the mission where they had been promised employment at the press – by now one of the oldest businesses in Peking. The day after she arrived, Aleksandra wrote in her diary:

> I set about cleaning our room. The bedsteads were full of bedbugs so I poured pure spirit on them, let it soak through then scalded them. It took me about two hours. By evening it was a little more like home: I hung a tulle blind on the window, I put a lace mat on the chest of drawers and a mirror on that, then laid

out my toilet things. My husband had bought a comfortable wicker chair, two mats for the floor and a large standard lamp with a green shade. On the wall we fixed up two strips of bright calico. It is now so cosy that I really look forward to the long hours I will be working there.[9]

But no amount of calico – however bright – could stem the homesickness, especially on Russian Christmas Eve.

In the evening my husband went to the Christmas service. I stayed at home on my own – I felt very low. I thought about my near ones left in Siberia: how were they spending this evening? Are they remembering us, as I remember them now, with love and sadness? I miss so much my native Irkutsk and the people I have left there that it's sometimes unbearable. Shall I ever return? And if I do, will I find any of them still alive?[10]

Sometimes to comfort herself, Aleksandra would wrap up in her fur coat and sit out on their small veranda to stare up at the night sky as she used to in Siberia:

I was amazed by the stars here: they are huge, incredibly bright, they flicker, burn, change colour – beautiful! One star by the dome of the Mission's church did not twinkle and was so big that it even lit the ground like a new moon.[11]

The Serebrennikovs were among the lucky ones – they had jobs and somewhere to live. Many other white Russians were forced into prostitution or begging. 'The prestige of the white race fell precipitously,' commented Daniele Varè, 'when Chinese could possess a white woman for a dollar or less, and Russian officers in tattered uniforms begged at the doors of Chinese theatres.'[12] Nor, as Franck pointed out, did the other foreign residents in Peking much care for them:

One's sympathy for the dispossessed Russians in China always soon comes to a frayed edge. Their scorn of manual labor even as an alternative to starva-tion, the unregenerate selfishness of their exiled fellow-countrymen in more fortunate circumstances, their lack of practicality, of plain common sense from the Western point of view, in a word their Orientalism, so out of keeping with their Caucasian exterior, tend to turn compassion to mere condolences which in time fade out to indifference.[13]

Despite their poverty and reliance on Chinese goodwill, many refugees continued to behave as if they were citizens of an imperial power living in a colony. Consequently, the majority made little effort to understand the society in which they found themselves or to build friendships with their hosts. But, in a city devoid of Western theatre and music, the émigrés did make one welcome contribution. Twice a week in the Peking Hotel, Russian musicians gave a concert of classical music. Presiding over them all was Metropolitan Innokenty Figurovsky who, according to Franck, not only behaved as if the north-eastern corner of Peking was his personal domain but expected a mediaeval servility from his flock.

After Kudachev's departure from Peking, the most prominent secular white Russian was General Dmitri Horvath. Immensely tall, his bald pate offset by a patriarchal beard, he was tsarist to the core. Not only was he related to Nicholas II but also directly descended from Prince Kutuzov – victor over Napoleon at Borodino. Furthermore, his wife, Camille Benois, had taught music and art to the Tsar's children. Since 1903, Horvath had been in charge of the Chinese Eastern Railway (CER) – a line of great strategic importance running south from the main trans-Siberian railway through Manchuria to Vladivostok. As the Bolshevik revolution rolled over Siberia, Horvath had been at the heart of the complex political situation, even at one point seizing control of the CER zone and declaring himself head of a new 'All-Russia Provisional Government' based in Harbin. But in 1920, having lost all support, he was forced to abandon his large estate and retreat to Peking.

There, the still wealthy Horvath family moved into the abandoned Austro-Hungarian legation where a young English pilot, Cecil Lewis, was invited one evening to sing Russian songs with the General's three beautiful daughters. 'It was the first day of my new life,' he later wrote.[14] On 19 October 1920, he married Doushka Horvath in the little Russian church attached to the mission. Their backgrounds could hardly have been more different. While Lewis from the age of 16 had been a fighter pilot in the thick of the First World War, Doushka had grown up cocooned in the wealth and security of her large family. Each summer the General's private train took them to the Crimea where he had bought six estates – one for each of his children. 'Lights were always green for this train,' Doushka recalled, and, 'since there was only one track, there were few opportunities to pass so that other trains often had to wait for hours or even days.'[15]

Lewis was one of a number of pilots recruited after the war by Vickers Ltd., who planned to launch commercial services in various parts of the world. Although this had never been tried before and there were as yet no suitable aircraft, early in 1920 Lewis found himself on his way to China with a team of pilots and mechanics – their mission to teach the Chinese to fly and to set up an air service between Peking and Shanghai. Vickers promised not only to supply more than 100 commercial and training aeroplanes but to invest half a million pounds in getting the service up and running. Given China's chaotic state, it was a wildly optimistic venture – doomed to failure. Although the Vickers team reached China that spring, the aircraft did not. For Lewis, this was a godsend, leaving him free to explore Peking on a good salary and with no responsibilities. He would have liked to do so alone with Doushka but this was not the Russian way. Wherever the young couple went, Madame Horvath and her other children went too. After they were married, Lewis attended the Easter service with his new family and was astonished by the large congregation of White Russians. There, crowded into the small church, surrounded by the familiar chanting, icons and candlelight, the refugees were for a short while able to forget the realities of the revolution that had beached them in such an alien city.

Finally, after nine months, the aircraft arrived in boxes. Once they had been unpacked and assembled, Lewis was able to start training. He described meeting the pilots for the first time:

> A group of young men, whose long silk coats swept in unbroken line from shoulder to ankle…Clasped hands hidden in their sleeves, they bowed, timid and smiling, the little red buttons in the centre of their black skull caps nodding brightly at us. They were introduced…each proffering a delicate hand which emerged magically from the long sleeves and then, clasping the other, disappeared again.[16]

When at last they took to the air, Lewis faced challenges as exacting as any he had confronted in wartime. There was no communication between the cockpits, so he was forced to shout his instructions in rudimentary Chinese with no way of knowing if they had been heard, let alone understood. The only solution was to land the aircraft, instruct his pupil through an interpreter (who had not the slightest concept of flight) take off again and hope for the best.

Despite all these difficulties, the freezing temperatures and the death of Lewis's only able trainee in a crash, China's first commercial air service was inaugurated with great fanfare in the spring of 1921. It lasted two days. Heavy rain turned the Tsinan airfield (the first stop on the 800-mile journey to Shanghai) into a quagmire embedding Lewis's aeroplane in mud.

Fifty coolies were placed under the leading spar of each lower wing. They crouched and raised the spar with their shoulders, then, with both engines at full throttle, foot by foot, the aeroplane moved slowly forward on to the higher ground.[17]

This was hardly the modern air service envisaged by Vickers and, for the time being at least, the experiment was abandoned.

From the moment Lewis arrived in Peking he had been intoxicated by its novelty and beauty. But he had a job, a car and a girlfriend. He also lived in a charming courtyard house where servants cared for his every need. For his exact contemporary, 23-year-old Harold Fleming, life was not so sweet. 'Peking continues to be a very dull place,' he wrote on 10 August 1923, 'my income isn't very large and I haven't any friends... I'm a small frog in a big community of famous men, ought-to-be-infamous diplomats, wicked newspaper correspondents and businessmen and the like.' Fleming, a Harvard graduate, had just lost his job with an American relief organisation in Russia where he yearned to return. Despite his loneliness, he met a number of interesting women. One in particular – beautiful, cosmopolitan and highly educated – attracted him, but she was of mixed race. 'The colour line is drawn pretty sharp here,' he wrote to his family,

> ... and even sharper against half-breeds than against full-blooded Chinese. I am going to consult a good friend of mine who has been here seven years and can give me the dope on where I can take her and where I can't.[18]

Prejudice towards people of mixed race was deeply rooted in Peking. As a teenager living there in the late twenties and early thirties, the author Han Suyin was made well aware of the fact that Eurasians 'were *expected* to be just for sleeping with. If a Eurasian was seen out once with a boy, everybody assumed she slept with him and immediately that she was available for anyone and everyone.'[19] With such views rampant during the 1920s, it is easier to understand Molly Orpen-Palmer's panicked reaction to her mother's suggestion that she should visit Peking bringing with her Molly's Anglo-Burmese half-sister: '*Don't encourage Emily to come,*' Molly wrote back immediately,

> I don't want to be unkind but I know she wouldn't go down out here and I don't think the Legation crowd would care to have her at their big shows. The diplomatic crowd here are very fussy about *Easterns* and with Japs and Chinese about I think it would be rather tactless to bring Emily.[20]

But racial prejudice was by no means a one-way street. George Barbour and his wife Dorothy, both teachers at Yenching University, were invited to a party given by the university's 'inter-racial' group on the grounds that she was American and her husband Scottish. There they met Chinese academics whose European wives, Dorothy reported, were regarded by their Chinese in-laws with the same bigotry that American southerners would a black son or daughter-in-law. [21] Only the Russians, according to Fleming, were more liberal in such matters (one of General Horvath's sons married a Chinese-Belgian girl). But then – whether red or white – they were themselves despised by almost everyone.

***

A surprising chink in the Soviet ambassador's Bolshevism was his passion for tennis. But this bourgeois pastime did little to reassure his diplomatic neighbours, who were well aware that off the tennis-court he spent his time at Peking University or at large public gatherings addressing anyone who would listen on the evils of imperialism. As Vera Vishnyakova noted,

> ... it was impossible to ignore his speeches; they were printed in all the enemy
> and friendly newspapers; people became engrossed by them, marvelling at the
> iron logic of the Soviet diplomat, his bold polemics against the colonialists, his
> ability to use any situation to bolster his position.[22]

While Karakhan stirred up revolution in the North, his comrade Mikhail Borodin was making great strides in the South. A professional revolutionary (whom the British had once imprisoned for six months in Glasgow), Borodin arrived in Sun Yat-sen's stronghold, Canton, in October 1923. His mission was to inject new life into the stalled 1911 revolution by reorganising Dr Sun's Nationalist party (the Kuomintang or KMT) into an instrument capable of defeating both the northern warlords and foreign imperialism. And, according to Stalin's hidden agenda, once that had been achieved, any surviving non-Communist elements could be eliminated and China re-built on the Soviet model.

The Chinese Communist Party (CCP) was founded in Shanghai in 1921 but made little initial impact. Borodin, Karakhan and a multitude of Russian advisers soon changed that. In return for Soviet aid, Sun Yat-sen agreed to accept Communists into the KMT and appointed Borodin as his senior adviser. Soon the Russians, so Owen O'Malley (Ann Bridge's husband) reported to London, 'were supplying everything that the Chinese lacked, brains, money, persistence and method'.[23] He might also have added large quantities of arms. The year 1924 saw the establishment of a crucial component in the Nationalists' resurgence – the military academy, Whampoa, whose commandant, Chiang Kai-shek, had only recently returned from studying the Soviet military machine in Moscow. Before long, the Academy was turning out the thousands of high-calibre officers so vital to securing the KMT's immediate objective – Peking. 'Now that we have Whampoa,' Sun declared shortly before his death, 'I may die peacefully.'[24]

In fact, he died of liver cancer on 12 March 1925 in Peking where, accompanied by Borodin and other Russian advisers, he had arrived six months earlier on an implausible mission to discuss national reconstruction with the prevailing warlord. Already seriously ill, Dr Sun was also there to seek treatment at China's best hospital, the PUMC. According to an English nurse who looked after him, he was a difficult patient, and his wife Ching-ling even worse. Nor was the nurse's task made any easier by the knowledge that she was under constant Russian surveillance.[25] Intent on promoting Sun as 'the Lenin of China' the Soviets found themselves facing an unexpected problem. Sun, a practising Christian, had tactlessly requested a Christian funeral service. So little did this chime with either Soviet propaganda or the anti-foreign mood sweeping China that those taking part in the funeral did so in fear of their lives. Ignoring warnings that the chapel had been mined, George Barbour and his wife Dorothy (both missionaries) joined a handful of other foreigners who, despite the danger, were determined to be present. Barbour recorded the occasion in a letter home:

> Thousands of people filled the open court and the narrow unpaved street that separated the chapel from the hospital where he died. Then, at ten o'clock, 500 students from the Christian University marched down the street, four abreast. Opposite the Chapel entrance they turned left and right in pairs and pressed back against the crowd, thus forming a double cordon, shoulder to shoulder, between the hospital and its chapel. Twenty theological students marched rapidly along passage they had opened up, singing 'For all the Saints' followed by the theological professors who carried the coffin at a run – across the narrow street and into the chapel. Once inside, the door was swiftly bolted behind them. Faces pressed against the windows which we expected at any moment to

be smashed in…the Lord's Prayer was repeated at breakneck speed, then, the professors picked up the coffin and ran back to the door just as it was battered down by the mob. By the time we got to the door, all we could see was the coffin carried away down the hutung – swaying above the heads of crowd.

'The Communists may have got Sun's body,' Barbour added, 'but they could not claim his soul.'[26] A week later thousands gathered in the street to watch his coffin process from the PUMC to the central park where it lay in state for three weeks. Dr Margaret Phillips (as usual in the crowd) noticed that at the head of the long line of mourners walked the Soviet ambassador Lev Karakhan.[27]

Throughout his career, Sun had struggled in vain to persuade the foreign powers to underwrite his revolution. Now that he was dead, embalmed and in a (Russian-made) glass coffin, he basked in a fame that had eluded him when alive. Soon the temple in the Western Hills where his coffin was to rest until a suitably magnificent mausoleum could be built became a place of pilgrimage where even hardened generals like Chiang Kai-shek or Feng Yu-hsiang were said to have wept with emotion. The new Sun cult also permeated the Western-run PUMC where, Margaret Phillips noted, the graduation ceremony now started with three bows to his portrait and a two-minute silence.

By the summer of 1926 Chiang Kai-shek (now commander-in-chief of the KMT National Revolutionary Army) felt strong enough to launch the Northern Expedition of which Sun had so long dreamed. Ahead of his soldiers went the propaganda cadres (many of them enthusiastic young women in blue uniforms) whose job it was to convert workers and peasants to the cause. Their success greatly contributed to Chiang Kaishek's rapid progress, which, to everyone's surprise, had by the end of the year put him firmly in control of the Yangtze valley. In Peking, the foreigners watched events unfold with mounting anxiety. They had never taken much notice of Sun's attempts to spread revolution from the South, but this young general, operating hand in glove with the Bolsheviks, was something quite new. He threatened not only their financial interests but their personal safety.

The British in particular had cause to be apprehensive. As the biggest foreign power in China, they were the chief focus of the Nationalists' anti-imperialist campaign even before 30 May 1925, when British police in Shanghai had fired on Chinese demonstrators, killing 11. This tragedy provoked a deeply damaging boycott of British goods and a strike in Hong Kong that lasted over a year, bringing the colony to the point of collapse. But that was not all. On 3 January

1927 an angry local mob overran the British concession in Hankow, sending a shock wave through the whole of China's expatriate community. Old China hands (especially those in Shanghai), convinced that gunboat diplomacy was the only way to deal with the Chinese, were outraged by the British government's refusal to respond with force. And when a few weeks later an agreement was signed by the Nationalist foreign minister, Eugene Chen, and Owen O'Malley formally conceded the Hankow concession to the Chinese, the *North China Herald* described it as 'the most disastrous document in the files of British Far East diplomacy'.[28]

In Peking, Sir Miles Lampson (recently returned to China as British Minister) was more pragmatic. In a letter to Ramsay MacDonald he wrote:

I am continually dinning it in here that our sole permanent interest is trade and that you can't do real trade for very long at the point of the bayonet. You must be in friendly relations with your customer *but equally on terms of mutual respect.*

In the same letter, he implicitly acknowledged that the treaty port system had had its day:

…the best way to safeguard British interests is to get an ultimate and permanently friendly settlement with China which will put our relations with her on as modern and as normal a footing as the state of her institutions allows.[29]

To the more perceptive foreigners and to those aware of Eugene Chen's declaration – 'We are no longer the sick man of the East, we do not want you to give us independence, we are independent'[30] – came the realisation that the loss of Hankow foreshadowed the end of foreign domination in China.

Two months later came a further shock. After taking Nanking on 21 March, Nationalist forces looted the British, Japanese and American consulates, killing a number of foreigners. This violence (later blamed on the Communists within the KMT) did little to soothe nerves in Peking. A stream of telegrams passed between London and Lampson who, fearing an imminent repeat of the Boxer uprising, urgently requested his government for more troops. But in Whitehall, although there too the spectre of the Boxers hung over all discussion on China, there was unanimous agreement that Britain had neither the resources nor the will to protect the Peking legations. It was concluded (in Washington as well as London) that it was up to Japan to defend North China from Chiang Kai-shek and his Russian allies. And if Japan failed to do so, then, in the worst case, there was just one option open to Peking's foreign community – evacuation. 'There is one place and one place only in China which we are in a position to defend at any cost,' wrote a Foreign Office official, 'and that is Shanghai.'[31]

For his fellow countrymen 8,000 miles away in Peking, particularly those living outside the legation quarter, this was not a welcome message. 'Peking is like an enormous powder keg, just waiting for something to set it off,' wrote the Chinese scholar Liang Qichao.[32] The foreigners agreed. Feeling abandoned by their respective governments, they watched and waited, expecting the worst. A letter written by an English teacher to her solicitor – forwarded to the Prime Minister Stanley Baldwin – in April 1927 set the scene:

> You have never lived in a panic-stricken town so you do not know how insidiously unnerving it is. New rumours every day, stories of plots and now, to make it worse, we have got all the details of Nanking. Not even here did we realise how ghastly it was…Nearly all the women were raped and most finally arrived at the gunboats without one single article of clothing. One case was a lady still in bed, her baby was 8 days old, she was raped by six soldiers and was found raving mad…another is alive but only just, as because she resisted they afterwards cut her open from breast to stomach. On top of all this Mit and I have lost most of our pupils. I haven't enough to pay expenses…we shall have to stay till the bitter end and lose everything. The silver is all packed and sent to the Italian Guard, most of our clothes also. I have rented a room in the Chinese city for the old amah where she will retire with six of the dogs. At the last moment we shall empty books, china etc. into a cellar place, the trap door is concealed in the floor under a bed and hope that a few things will be saved and I have told the servants to leave at once, directly we go they must go, for their own safety and that we shall come back as soon as it is possible to do so. There are over 600 servants of foreigners out of work just now…At the auctions held now, the prices are awful, things are going for nothing…Wealthy Americans who had glorious collections of carved black-wood are selling up in a hurry…I do hope you will hear soon that everything is all right in China and that the nations have agreed to give China the good licking she deserves. I should like a general massacre of Chinese. That would 'larn 'em'![33]

Even the normally sanguine president of Yenching University, John Leighton Stuart, suggested setting up a secret committee that *in extremis* would issue women students with phials of poison gas to fling in the faces of would-be rapists.[34]

Despite the approaching threat, most long-term foreign residents did not want to leave Peking. With their prestige in China already so weakened, they knew that if they fled now they would be unlikely to return. On the other hand, the Boxer siege was an all too vivid reminder of what could happen should they leave departure too late. During the spring of 1927, the British legation made detailed plans for evacuation. If the worst came to the worst, the 300 or so British subjects living outside the legation quarter were instructed to make their way there on foot (a sore point since other countries planned to send cars), bringing towels, soap, four days worth of rations and a 'camp bed clearly marked with their name'.[35] Some expatriates rose to the challenge better than others: 'I should not abandon this house until the last possible moment,' wrote Arthur Moore Bennett, an explorer who had spent years under canvas in Mongolia in search of Kublai Khan,

> but I have my wife and another lady resident here to prepare for. If we were allowed to erect a tent on any spare space we should be entirely self-contained requiring nothing except water as I have lived in camp most of my life and have gear, food and all necessities.[36]

Ann Bridge found the whole situation rather entertaining. With her husband, Owen O'Malley, away in Hankow negotiating the handover of the British concession, she wrote home:

> Things are getting very exciting with plots and counter plots, alliances and counter-alliances and rumours of all sorts…we hear of Russian mobilisations on the North, of Feng Yu-hsiang bearing down on us from the West, of a Cantonese 'drive' to Shanghai, and of Chang letting loose the mob here. All these rumours are contradicted as soon as they arise, and then crop up again. We are becoming artists at believing nothing, disbelieving nothing, and sleeping sound at night as a result.[37]

But in the summer of 1927, despite their earlier reluctance, both the American and the British governments sent additional troops to Tientsin ready to defend Peking should the need arise. In fact it never did because two crucial events had occurred in April that dramatically altered the situation. Chang Tso-lin, the powerful Manchurian warlord backed by the Japanese, had installed himself in Peking in 1926. He was a diminutive figure with large boots and black moustaches and his hatred of Bolshevism was made plain to all from the slogan he had plastered over his Peking headquarters: 'Absolutely

Destroy Communism'.[38] The fact that (in the imperial tradition) he had yellow earth scattered over the roads he travelled on and made personal sacrifices to Confucius hinted heavily at his ultimate ambition. Ann Bridge, who met him at the British legation, described his car – a vast black saloon with machine gun on the windscreen, rapid-release bullet-proof shutters (worked by a handle in the roof) and a silver spittoon on the floor. 'Two or three revolvers,' she also noted, 'lay among the priceless sable rugs on the seat.'[39] But whatever Chang's more disagreeable features (Lev Karakhan had wisely left Peking before he could be assassinated) his implacable opposition to Communism coupled with his strong military record led the foreigners to regard him as the best hope of halting the KMT-Communist advance. For this reason, at a meeting on 4 April 1927, the Western ministers made an extraordinary decision. Breaching all rules of diplomatic immunity, they agreed to admit Chang's police into the legation quarter in order to search premises attached to the Russian embassy. That the ministers were prepared even to consider such a risky precedent shows how badly the Communists had rattled them.

The raid on the Russian embassy took place on 6 April. In a letter home, Ann Bridge described what happened:

> We have had a most exciting day. This morning at about 11.20 Chinese police and troops raided the military side of the Soviet Embassy and pinched as follows: 30 Chinese Communists, 16 Russian agitators, and masses of literature, Cantonese flags, and some arms and ammunition. A woman we know was in the Chartered Bank close by, changing a cheque and 'happened along' just as the first lot were being dragged out, green with terror. She saw the flags and hampers of pamphlets. Our garden was full of soldiers all day, as our wall gives on to the Soviet premises, and in China you never know when an enterprise of this sort will not turn into a first-class row. But it was smartly done and only one shot was fired. My friend took photos which I will send in due course. The 'Resolute Trippers', 400 world tourists, happened to be in Peking and had a wonderful time – they sent for their private movie-man and he 'shot' the whole show.

The foreign community was delighted: 'I do hope this will choke off Mr [Charles] Trevelyan and Mr [George] Lansbury and the rest who talk about the "fantastic superstitions" of Bolshevik activity in China,'[40] wrote Ann Bridge. Within a few days Chang, who had a particular fondness for the garrotte, dispatched 20 Chinese Communists seized from the Soviet embassy including the co-founder of the CCP, Li Dazhao.

The raid dealt a heavy blow to the Soviets but only six days later they suffered one even worse. Instead of heading north from the Yangtze as Borodin had hoped, Chiang Kai-shek turned east, his sights set on the great prize of Shanghai. There the workers, having already rid the city of its warlord, welcomed him as their ally, little suspecting what lay in store. A rift between the left wing of the KMT and Chiang Kai-shek had, in fact, been growing steadily since Sun's death though Stalin remained confident that he still held the upper hand, remarking: 'we shall squeeze him like a lemon and then be rid of him'.[41] But Chiang had other ideas. On 12 April, with complete ruthlessness, he ordered his troops to round up all the Communists and union leaders and shoot them. Three months later, Borodin and his staff packed their bags and, in a fleet of specially equipped cars, headed back to Moscow across the Gobi desert. The Nationalists' love affair with Bolshevik Russia was over and, as one British official put it, 'Our prayers for a Russian downfall in China have been answered beyond our wildest expectations.'[42]

12
NANKING INTERLUDE

By the early summer of 1928, Nationalist forces were so close to Peking that Chang Tso-lin had no option but to retreat. On 1 June he invited the foreign ministers to his residence where he bid them a dignified farewell before boarding a train for Manchuria laden with his treasures and concubines the next day. Just outside Mukden a bomb planted by the Japanese blew up the train killing him, Despite Chang's more questionable qualities, Lampson had liked him, commenting:

> Although he represents an order of ideas which is incompatible with modern developments in China, I certainly greatly regret his failure...I have little doubt that when Chang has gone and we find ourselves up against the Nationalists in earnest in our daily routine we shall look back with regret to the peaceful days when Chang was here. Of course I know that he was an anachronism and was bound sooner or later to go; yet he represents a type which is easier to deal with – I would almost say more honest – than the new brand of Chinese with whom we are now confronted. I never knew him not to keep his word, and that is distinctly unusual in China today.[1]

The Netherlands' Minister William Oudendyk agreed, describing the ruthless warlord as an 'outstanding and sympathetic personality, courageous and sincere'.[2] The nostalgia felt by old China hands for the passing order is not surprising. Doing business with the likes of Chang Tso-lin, whatever his faults, was a good deal more entertaining than with the aggressive Nationalists who wanted only to tear up the foreigners' treaties and deprive them of their privileges. After his own experience, Owen O'Malley expressed a view shared by many of his diplomatic colleagues when he wrote that, as not even the Chinese themselves could understand Chinese politics, the only prudent course was to have as little to do with them as possible.[3]

This, though, was not an option for Sir Miles Lampson who during his seven years as British Minister (1926–33) had to deal with one crisis after another. Not that he minded. Nearly six and a half feet tall and weighing 18 stone, he was a large man in every sense. He relished being in the thick of things whether at the negotiating table or shooting duck. And if on occasion 'the battle with the wind was rather difficult', the solution was straightforward: 'One simply had to steel oneself against all criticism and just go ahead.' His diary is endearingly honest:

> My trouble is that when I am faced with a problem I sit down and write first one reply then another on totally different lines; and by the end of a little time I succeed in completely befogging my mind. Also I am always tempted to sauce the [Foreign] Office and that really does not pay.[4]

When the Nationalists finally entered Peking on 8 June 1928, China was (theoretically at least) united under one government for the first time since the emperor's abdication. *Time* magazine was ecstatic:

> So dry and full of cogent wisdom were President Chiang Kai-shek's remarks, that only persons of lively imagination realized that in the precise little man before them they beheld the greatest and most romantic conqueror of today. All of vast China has been his battlefield, and from South to North he has conquered or reduced all to submission.[5]

In light of the foreigners' earlier panic, the peaceful occupation of the city by a mere 5,000 troops was a welcome anti-climax. Certainly there was nothing in the British Minister's programme that day to suggest that the foreigners were under threat. Having hosted a lunch for the Commissioner of the Salvation Army, Lampson played tennis with the Inspector General of Customs. True his game was interrupted by a telephone call with an update on the situation, but nothing else occurred to interfere with bridge that evening or the dance hosted later by the Varès at the Italian legation.

Although physically Peking had survived this latest occupation, its status suffered a severe blow when the Nationalists confirmed that Nanking (on the Yangtze 700 miles to the south and 190 miles up river from Shanghai) would be China's new capital. Peking (northern capital) now became 'Peiping' (northern peace). And, as if this was not humiliating enough, the city's familiar red walls were daubed Nationalist blue. Demoted to a provincial town, Peking came to resemble, in the words of one writer, 'a deposed empress, still clad in the remains of her imperial wardrobe, making ineffectual attempts to pose as an ordinary housewife'.[6] Six weeks later, Chiang Kai-shek, his glamorous new wife, Mei-ling at his side, made his first formal contact with the diplomats at a reception. Lampson thought that he seemed 'distinctly intelligent' but, having heard so much about his wife's beauty was disappointed that she was not better looking.[7] Varè, Italian Minister since 1927, was also impressed describing the Generalissimo as realistic, stubborn, long-sighted and supremely cautious – a man caught 'between the devil and the deep blue sea'.[8]

Treaty revision, extraterritoriality and tariff autonomy were all problems needing urgent resolution but the issue closest to the ministers' hearts was whether or not they would have to move their legations to Nanking. The problem, as Varè was quick to point out, was that the new capital of China had for decades been little more than the empty husk of a dead city. Now it had all the unpleasant characteristics of a pioneering town in the middle of nowhere. 'There were no Chinese luxuries and no foreign comforts,' lamented Varè, 'what *can* you do where there is no water supply?'[9] Compared with the delights of Peking, China's new capital certainly had little to offer. Within its extensive wall, there were only fields of millet, reed marshes, stagnant water and wallowing buffalo – in fact, just like anywhere else along the Yangtze. Furthermore, the foreign quarter had only three good houses – the Customs, the Standard Oil and the British Consulate. The rest, according to Varè, consisted of nothing but a few jerry-built villas. By persuading their respective governments that the new leadership was too fragile to justify the high cost of moving their operations to Nanking, the diplomats averted the immediate threat but there was a price to pay. Now when they did business with the Chinese government it was necessary to travel for days, either by rail, subject to endless delay and bandit attack, or by sea via Tientsin and Shanghai. It proved a cumbersome arrangement that did little to ease dialogue between China's new government and the three big powers – Great Britain, America and Japan. As Varè remarked, it was as if a foreign diplomat accredited to Washington were to live in London.[10]

Lampson, who during his years in China had to spend many weeks in Nanking was equally unimpressed:

> The worst of these visits to Nanking is that one alternates between spurts of intense activity and spells of almost complete idleness. One fires in a broadside to the Chinese and then has to wait for days and days until either they reply or one gets fresh instructions from London. No one leaves the Compound if they can possibly avoid it so one moons about either entirely idly or sits and reads more or less indefinitely to kill time. All of which is intensely monotonous and boring.[11]

The Japanese Minister, Yoshizawa, solved the problem by spending most of his time in Shanghai while his American colleague, Nelson Johnson, amused himself listening to his gramophone and playing 'dark southern ditties' on his guitar. Lampson's own method of dealing with boredom was to shoot game at every possible opportunity – often from a Royal Navy gunboat:

> Began shooting reed beds where there was quite a good show of pheasants. We had fifteen sailors on shore from *HMS Cockchafer* to beat. One of them unfortunately touched off the cut reeds with a match and before we knew where we were the blaze had taken charge. A vain attempt to put it out, then fearing trouble from irate villagers, we skidaddled trying to look as though we were not responsible! Not a very glorious proceeding but no doubt the best way to handle the thing. Oddly enough the Chinese did not seem to connect our presence with the fire. We all got on board without any hindrance and soon after we shoved off and moved up ten miles or so. Landed and did some flighting. Bag for today thirteen pheasants and eleven duck, one of which was shot by Teichman from the bows of *The Lois*.[12]

But for all his sporting pleasures, Lampson was an energetic and effective diplomat. And although in a memo to London he had only recently written of Chiang Kai-shek: 'Please don't, please *don't* bank too much on the new star at Nanking that has arisen; leopards do not readily change their spots in China; and the new star was a very spotty creature in his previous incarnation,'[13] he was soon on excellent terms with the Generalissimo:

> From there went on to a big lunch given by Chiang Kai-shek. Terribly hot. After we had talked a bit Mrs Chiang came in and carried us all off to tea and mango ices. During this time Chiang became extremely friendly. Mrs Chiang

told me that last time I was down here he had said to her 'I like that man: he is loveable (!). If he was not British Minister I should like to engage him as a Chinese government adviser, This Chiang repeated at the tea table – rather to my embarrassment. Altogether it was a remarkable demonstration, the more so since he has not sent for any other foreign representative, and has certainly not talked like that to any of them.[14]

By the spring of 1929, Sun Yat-sen's mausoleum (built into the flank of Purple Mountain a few miles outside Nanking) was at last ready to receive his embalmed body – still recognisable but by now quite black. Naturally such a momentous occasion required that all the foreign ministers be present, so a special train was arranged to carry them with their staff from Peking to Nanking – a three-day journey. Several military bands, each playing a different funeral march, were on the platform to see them off, a performance that was repeated at every stop. Despite the intense heat, the threat of bandit attacks, and the Spanish Minister's volubility (after downing three bottles of warm champagne) the ministers plenipotentiary arrived in good spirits. Those representing the most important powers were installed in gunboats anchored on the Yangtze. Lesser diplomats were lodged in the new government guesthouse, while yet smaller fry – with no influence and no gunboats – had to be content with the Yangtze Hotel, famous only for its bed bugs.

The funeral cortège began its ten-mile journey from KMT headquarters to the tomb in the small hours of 1 June so that long before dawn Varè found himself in full diplomatic uniform and decorations, being rowed ashore in a small boat: 'Oars creaked in the rowlocks, a waning moon shed a feeble light over the broad waters – we all, I think, felt extremely foolish.'[15] The diplomats walked on one side of the hearse, the Chinese mourners, wearing simple blue cotton gowns, on the other. The procession was directed by Sun Yat-sen's brother-in-law, Dr Kung, waving a flywhisk over his head, whose own outfit was anything but simple. Lampson did not approve: 'He was garbed in baggy white duck breeches with high black thigh boots. On his head a "gent's boater" held on by a thick elastic chinstrap. This plus large goggles made him look indescribably hideous.'[16] Thousands of spectators lined the route, held back by a thin line of policemen, their fingers on the triggers of their Mausers ready to shoot any lurking Communists.

Having accompanied the coffin for several miles, the diplomats retreated for breakfast intending to rejoin the mourners later for the interment. But as

Lampson recorded, 'there was a bit of a hitch, for nearly everyone got lost and by the time I myself had reached the foot of the steps leading to the tomb, the funeral procession was already halfway up'. Undaunted, and despite the blazing sun, and his thick blue uniform, Lampson doubled up the long stairway of 392 steps, reaching the top just in time to join Oudendyck and Yoshizawa (the only other ministers there) for the ceremony. They made a striking trio: Lampson, six and a half feet tall in a sun helmet with a six-inch spike, towered over the diminutive Dutchman and even tinier Japanese who, in a rare attempt at humour, was heard to whisper, 'Sir Miles looks like a pagoda.'[17]

Despite such Gilbert and Sullivan moments, the foreigners all agreed that the Nationalists had put on an impressive show worthy of a past when emperors were buried like emperors. Nevertheless, it was with profound relief that they returned to 'dear old Peking' – no longer China's capital but so infinitely preferable to the new one.

13
DRAGON BONE HUNTERS

On 25 April 1927, three weeks after Chang Tso-lin's raid on the Russian embassy, 11 men met for dinner at the Hotel du Nord. Even by Peking's exotic standards the menu was unusual, as each course was named after a creature such as *Chilotherium anderssoni* (rhinoceros) or *Struthiolitus juvenelis* (giant ostrich) that had been extinct for millennia.[1] The joke was well targeted since the diners were all palaeontologists, geologists or anthropologists. Despite counting six different nationalities between them, they were a close-knit group, their two most celebrated members being the Swedish explorer Sven Hedin and the Jesuit priest Pierre Teilhard de Chardin – the latter exiled to China by the Vatican for his attempts to reconcile God and evolution. But all those present that night were distinguished in their field and all were involved in exploring China's vast interior, much of which even in the late 1920s was little known and unmapped. For such men, it was an exciting time to be in China. The fossils they brought back to Peking from their field trips were transforming understanding not only of China's geological and evolutionary record but that of the whole of Asia.[2]

Since the late nineteenth century, European collectors had known that fossils of animals like the three-toed horse or sabre-tooth tiger could be found in Peking's apothecary shops, labelled as 'dragon bones'. Because such bones were believed to have magic healing properties they fetched high prices, providing the peasants who collected them from quarries and mines with a valuable income. Having no concept of the fossils' true worth, the peasants often smashed up the bones or removed teeth from the animal skulls in order to increase their earnings. This crude method began to change in 1914 when the Swedish geologist, Johann Gunnar Andersson (in whose honour the dinner was held) arrived in China to work for the Chinese government as a mining consultant. He was also a keen fossil collector who, spurred on by two prehistoric human teeth that had emerged from a Peking medicine shop in 1903, set about tracking the 'dragon bones' to their original sources. Enlisting the help of missionaries living in central China, Andersson not only identified promising sites but also began to organise systematic excavations – thus for the first time revealing the country's great treasure trove of vertebrate fossils.

Andersson's fellow geologist (and another of the diners) Amadeus Grabau had arrived a few years later, in 1920, to take up a teaching post at Peking University. Sacked from the geology department of Columbia University in New York after the war for his pro-German sympathies, he was delighted to find himself in a city where he was not only surrounded by eager students but fed a constant supply of interesting fossils. In fact Peking suited him so well that despite offers to return to New York he was to remain there, at the heart of the scientific community, until his death in 1946. Shortly after reaching Peking he wrote to an American colleague describing a typical fossil expedition:

> The fieldwork here is wonderful. You can judge the richness when I tell you that as the result of a nine-day expedition which I led to the Kaiping basin we brought back forty boxes of fossils... Geological work in China is difficult... on account of the lack of good maps, the time consuming and fatiguing journeys before you reach the field – much of the area can only be reached on mule back over atrocious roads or no roads at all, and by roundabout journeys on native riverboats... then the accommodations for all but Chinese are impossible... One usually sets up one's establishment in some temple, after turning out the beggars and lepers who infest them. At one time we had nearly forty coolies digging, breaking the rocks, wrapping (under supervision), packing and carrying. Our forty boxes of fossils were carried by coolies from our headquarters to the railroad station, a distance of perhaps half a mile, and they were big boxes too. Once you get to it railroad transportation is easy provided you stay with your boxes. We brought our forty boxes to Peking, a day's journey by train, as baggage without paying a copper except for tips.[3]

Like Grabau, all the fossil hunters dining together were experienced in the field – often working in remote places and extreme temperatures. But as they discussed matters that evening over their '*liqueurs préhistoriques*', it is likely that their talk centred as much on future projects as past success. For even after years of achievement and many tantalising clues, they had yet to uncover the biggest prize of all – a fossil of the so-called 'missing link'.

Their conviction that that Central Asia was the best place to look for traces of the beings that had theoretically filled the gap between apes and modern humans came largely from Henry Fairfield Osborn – geologist, palaeontologist, millionaire, President of the American Museum of Natural History and a figure of great influence. He was also a eugenicist and as such emphatically believed in Caucasian superiority. For men like him, and there were plenty, it was important to prove that the cradle of civilization lay not – as Darwin believed – in Africa but in more palatable Asia. The men that gathered together that April evening in Peking were not necessarily eugenicists but they did accept Osborn's scientific claim for Asia as the 'Mother of all Continents' and in an affectionate gesture sent him their 'prehistoric' menu inscribed with all their signatures.

Although Osborn's ideas had gained wide currency,[4] by 1920 they still lacked hard evidence. A lone skull that had contained a brain, midway in size between ape and man, discovered in Java in 1891,[5] pointed helpfully towards Asia but was not enough. Much more was needed if the Asian mainland was to be established as the birthplace of the human species. Finding this proof was exactly the kind of challenge that appealed to the swashbuckling explorer Roy Chapman Andrews. As the title of his autobiography, *Under a Lucky Star*, suggests, Andrews was a man in the right place at the right time. Explorer, zoologist, entrepreneur and adventurer, he had been on the staff of the American Museum since 1906, but (much to the irritation of his colleagues) had spent little of his career in New York. Ignoring the routine grind of museum administration, he had made his name (more recently linked to that of Indiana Jones) by exploring remote corners of Asia, collecting zoological specimens for the Museum and surviving numerous colourful adventures.

In 1920, fresh back to the Museum from exploring in Mongolia and confident that his extravagant plans would dovetail with Osborn's theories, Andrews promoted a project on a far grander scale than any he had previously undertaken. His prime goal was to test Osborn's ideas by looking for primitive man in the Gobi desert, but that was by no means all. He aimed to reconstruct the entire natural history of the Central Asian plateau – 'its geology, fossils past climate, and vegetation'. He also planned to collect its living mammals, birds, fish, reptiles, insects and plants and to map the unexplored parts of the Gobi. It was to be a multi-disciplinary effort lasting at least five years and, as he made clear, 'a thorough job – the biggest land expedition ever to leave the United States'.[6] Osborn's enthusiastic support coupled with Andrews' organisational talent was to result in a series of spectacular expeditions that took place in the Gobi and Mongolia between 1921 and 1930. Known collectively as the Central Asiatic Expedition (CAE), they were to be the last of their kind, for the days when the likes of Sir Aurel Stein, Baron Ferdinand von Richthoven, Francis Younghusband and Paul Pelliot could roam China at will, removing archaeological treasures to their own countries, were fast running out. Meanwhile, the CAE's intriguing mission and charismatic leader were about to catch the imagination of the whole world.

Having secured Osborn's blessing, Andrews then faced the much harder task of raising the money. But with cheques from J.P. Morgan and John D. Rockefeller Junior in his pocket, the quarter of a million dollars needed was soon within reach. 'Talk about adventures in the Gobi Desert,' Andrews wrote, 'adventures in Wall Street are just as exciting.'[7] Once a public announcement had been made, the newspapers had a field day with headlines such as 'Scientists to seek ape-man's bones' and 'Will search Asia for Missing Link'. The publicity stimulated hundreds of would-be adventurers to contact Andrews, begging him to take them with him to the Gobi. One woman wrote:

I am a lady who wants to join your expedition in any capacity. I am thirty years old. If you should answer please don't try to tell me of the dangers due to sexual feelings because they do not exist in me and cannot be aroused so that ends that argument.[8]

After months in New York picking his scientific team and marshalling supplies, Andrews together with his wife, small son and 38 tons of equipment arrived in Peking, during a particularly fierce dust storm, on 14 April 1921. Andrews already knew the city well, having been based there in the First World War while on an intelligence mission for his government. He found 'dear old hysterical Peking' much the same:

…we were greeted with a flood of rumours. Peking was certain to be attacked and looted…no one could go into the interior, smallpox was raging, it would be dangerous to do this and dangerous to do that! So with dust, war and smallpox we felt the summer was beginning rather well.[9]

The house once owned by his old friend Dr Morrison, and empty since his death, provided the perfect headquarters with its 47 rooms built around eight courtyards. Andrews described how it soon became like a small city in itself devoted to the various aspects of the expedition. 'There were living quarters for my own family, garages for eight cars, stables, a home for the storage of equipment, an office, laboratories and a complete movie-picture studio.'[10] It was to be his home for the nine years he was leader of the CAE. When not occupied with negotiating permits, buying camels, packing up supplies and equipment or studying Mandarin, Andrews and his wife, Yvette (on whom Ann Bridge based Nina Neville in *Peking Picnic*), threw themselves into the social scene – their reputation and good looks adding glamour to the endless round of parties and race-meetings.

On 16 April 1922, the eve of the expedition's departure, a gala dinner was held at the American legation.[11] 'All that day,' wrote Andrews,

> the headquarters seethed with activity. Every man was occupied with his own individual preparations for the long summer in the desert. The court-yard in front of the main laboratory was strewn with skins, boxes and equip-ment, which were being packed for shipment to New York or to go with us to Mongolia... the front court was filled with cars, and all day the whirr of motors being tested and the ring of hammers made it seem like an open-air garage.[12]

The next day, the motor-cars, piled high with baggage covered with brown tarpaulins, left Peking and within hours were winding up the steep Wanhsien Pass leading to the great plateau:

> Wonderful panoramas unfolded at every turn as we wound higher and higher... Above us loomed a rampart of basalt cliffs, crowned with the Great Wall of China, stretching with its serpentine length along the broken rim of the plateau. Roaring like the prehistoric monsters we had come to seek, our cars gained the top of the last steep slope and passed through the narrow gateway in the Wall. Before us lay Mongolia.[13]

There were many obstacles ahead – bandits, sandstorms, snakes – but the fear that most haunted Andrews was that they would not find any fossils and that his whole grandiose venture might turn into nothing more than a wild goose chase. However to everyone's relief dinosaur fossils were found only four days after leaving Peking – the gamble had paid off. But despite the vast quantities of bones the CAE collected over the subsequent years, no human remains were ever recovered. Nevertheless, returning to Peking after their first season in Mongolia, Andrews could boast that the scientific results had surpassed their greatest hopes. His team of scientists had brought back not only a wealth of rare dinosaur fossils and geological data but also many previously unknown species of living mammals. The whole operation was widely regarded as a triumph inspiring Osborn to cable: 'You have opened a new chapter in the history of life upon the earth.'[14]

But it was during the following season in the summer of 1923, when the expedition had grown to around 40 members, that they made their most thrilling discovery:

> Our arrival at the Flaming Cliffs was a great day for the Central Asiatic Expedition. We camped at three o'clock in the afternoon and almost at once the men scattered over the badlands. Before night everyone had discovered a dinosaur skull. But the real thrill came the second day when George Olsen reported that he was sure he had found some fossil eggs. We teased him a good deal but, nevertheless, were curious enough to go down with him after luncheon. Then our indifference suddenly evaporated. It was certain they really *were* eggs. Three of them were exposed and evidently had broken out of the sandstone ledge beside which they lay.[15]

The eggs caused a sensation, turning Andrews overnight into a worldwide celebrity. But there was a sting in the tail. The huge public interest surrounding them gave him the idea of auctioning one (it fetched 5,000 dollars) to raise funds for the CAE. At the time it seemed little more than a clever publicity stunt, but no one had considered what impact the sale might have in China (already seething with anti-foreign sentiment) or in Mongolia (a Communist state since 1921). In both, the auction confirmed long-held suspicions that foreign explorers were simply imperialist robbers bent on profit. The sale of the dinosaur egg marked a fundamental change in Chinese attitudes to foreign expeditions, and although Andrews was to spend a further three seasons in the field (1925, 1928 and 1930) his dealings with the authorities became increasingly confrontational.

The CAE was not the only expedition to run into political difficulties during the mid-1920s. Sven Hedin, revered for his pioneering achievements (if not his pro-German sympathies) also fell foul of the nationalism sweeping China. Hedin belonged to an older school of exploration, his chief interests remaining predominantly archaeological. His first expedition to China in

1885 had nearly been his last when he had run out of water while crossing the Taklamakan desert. Undaunted, between 1894 and 1908 he undertook three major expeditions through the mountains and deserts of Central Asia, rediscovering lost cities, drawing up the first detailed maps of Tibet and the Silk Road and lodging several months with the Panchen Lama.

In May 1927, a few days after the fossil dinner-party, Hedin left Peking for Northwest China with the Sino-Swedish expedition, sponsored by Lufthansa. It was to be his last great undertaking and one that over the next seven years would often bring him back to Peking. The aim was to lay the groundwork for a regular air service between Berlin and Peking by establishing weather stations and surveying potential landing sites. Not surprisingly, the Chinese reacted with suspicion. It was only after Hedin agreed to accept stringent conditions (much to the irritation of his Western colleagues who accused him of 'going over to the Chinese'[16]) that the expedition was finally allowed to proceed. A year later, Hedin wrote to Lufthansa:

> The educated Chinese here, and those in power, say to me 'You pretend that the Germans provide planes for you only to give you a chance to carry out aerial surveys of unexplored desert.' You want us to believe that? That poor Germany is spending these sums to allow you to look at the desert? No, the Germans have other aims, political ones. These cannot be achieved now. But in ten or twenty years when Germany is a great power once again.[17]

Although during the long months of negotiation with the Chinese authorities Hedin was a frequent visitor to the legation quarter, the British would have nothing to do with him. His active support for the Kaiser in the Great War had made him *persona non grata* with everyone – except Ann Bridge. Finding Hedin 'great fun and immensely interesting', she defied the embargo by inviting him regularly to lunch. She soon realised that her fellow countrymen were every bit as suspicious of Hedin's forthcoming expedition as the Chinese. Anxious to discover its exact purpose and route (always mindful of any threat to India), one of the diplomats appealed to Bridge for help. She was quick to see the funny side, noting:

> While the Minister was frowning on me for my unpatriotic behaviour in making friends with Hedin, British Intelligence was imploring me to use that same friendship to find out for them what they could not learn for themselves.[18]

Hedin refused to tell her exactly where he was bound but she nevertheless managed to extract the information by means of an ingenious subterfuge. One day when the explorer was at her house, she made some excuse to leave him studying a map alone with her 11-year- old daughter of whom Hedin was fond and whom Bridge had especially schooled for the purpose. After he had left, she found the little girl sitting on her bed, the atlas open on her knees and, to Bridge's delight, 'across the double spread which covered Central Asia ran a heavy black line, along which Jane, her tongue out in her concentration, was writing down names'.[19]

***

Living in a country where – even in the legation quarter – disease and death could appear suddenly without warning, Peking's foreign community knew how fortunate they were to have on the doorstep a hospital equal to the best in Europe or North America. The reason the PUMC was able to attract so much talent from the West, apart from the obvious lure of the exotic, was the exceptional research opportunities it offered its staff. Visiting medics from European capitals expressed both astonishment and envy when shown the hospital's state of the art equipment – all paid for by the Rockefeller Foundation. But in certain ways, as the professor of anatomy, Davidson Black, illustrated, the PUMC remained very different:

> During the last month I have had a large female camel living in the basement. Our physiologist chemist is doing the nitrogen metabolism on this beast and I shall take what remains. It is a treat to see this camel objecting to coming indoors. The whole neighbourhood is made aware of her objections.[20]

Camels may have been in ready supply but Chinese aversion to autopsy resulted in such a shortage of human corpses for the students to dissect that they had to be shipped up from Hong Kong.[21] 'It is much more difficult to obtain human material for study,' Black remarked, 'than it is subjects for execution!'[22]

Although Black (a Canadian) was a distinguished anatomist, his real interest lay in human evolution. Present at the dinner in April 1927, he was a popular and much respected member of the fossil hunters' group. But there was one secret he chose not to share – the fact he might at any moment drop dead from congenital heart disease. Instead of slowing him down, this made him even more determined to find the evidence that would prove man's Asian origins. His Peking neighbour, Roy Chapman Andrews, was pursuing the same goal but while his expeditions – despite all the razzamatazz – failed to find any trace of early humans, Black's team operating only a day's journey from Peking hit the jackpot in 1929, when they uncovered a human cranium, known to the world as 'Peking Man'.

Choukoutien, 40 miles south-west of Peking, lay at the foot of the Western Hills. It was reached by a twisting road that crossed the Marco Polo Bridge before arriving at the small coal-mining village, its streets crowded with camel trains, rickshaws and Ford cars.[23] Around the village were the limestone caves and opencast mines that had been investigated by Johann Andersson as promising fossil sites as early as 1918, prompting him to declare: 'Here is primitive man, all we have to do is find him.'[24] But it was not until nearly a decade later, after two teeth found there were controversially identified by Black as human, that the China Geological Survey in partnership with the PUMC launched a full-scale excavation of the site known as Dragon Bone Hill. Once again the Rockefeller Foundation provided the funding while Black became the project's executive director.

On 16 October 1927, yet another tooth emerged from the site. Reckoned to be about 500,000 years old it was better preserved than the earlier two and this time unquestionably human. Black immediately wrote to Andersson: 'We have got a beautiful *human* tooth at last! It is truly glorious news is it not?'[25] On the basis of this slim evidence, Black declared that the molar came from a previously unknown human species and genus, which (at the suggestion of his friend Amadeus Grabau) he named *Sinanthropus Pekinensis* or Peking Man. It was a bold claim and one that, coming only two years after the Scopes 'Monkey trial' in Tennessee, attracted huge publicity. Black spent most of the following year in America and Europe lecturing on the implications of the find – the tooth itself allegedly tucked into a specially designed box hanging by a gold chain from his belt.[26]

Then came the discovery for which Black and his circle had waited so long. By the end of October 1929, with the ground almost too hard to dig, the Choukoutien site was ready to close down for the winter. However, the geologist in charge of fieldwork, Pei Wen-chang (one of Professor Grabau's former students), persuaded Black and his Chinese colleagues to let him continue a few weeks longer. By 2 December even the enthusiastic Pei decided that it was time to stop and paid off the coolies. But at 4 p.m. that afternoon, despite the fading light and bitter cold, he and a few others were still working in the pit. One of those present left the following record:

> Maybe because of the cold weather, or the hour of the day, the stillness of the air was punctuated only by occasional rhythmic hammer sounds that indicated the presence of men down in the pit. 'What's that?' Pei suddenly cried out. 'A human skull!' In the silence everybody heard him. Some suggested that they take it out at once, while others objected for fear that, working rashly in the late hours, they might damage the object. 'It has been there for so many thousands of years, what harm would it do lying there for one more night?' they argued. But a long night of suspense was too much to bear. Pei thought hard and at last decided to get it out there and then.[27]

By buying up the village shop's entire stock of candles, Pei was able to produce just enough light to photograph the skull *in situ* before removing it from the cave wall, still partially embedded in rock. Taking the sodden object back to his room, he dried it out for several days before encasing it in gauze and plaster ready for its journey to Peking. Although this was only about 40 miles, Pei was aware that anything from skirmishing soldiers to bad weather might threaten his precious cargo. Prepared for the worst, on 6 December he set off for the bus stop in a rickshaw with 'Peking Man' lying hidden between his feet under his scholar's gown. Worried that the odd-shaped bundle would be searched at the city gate, he wrapped it in a couple of grubby quilts hoping that no one would suspect a student going home with his laundry. Once safely through the gate, Pei went immediately to the PUMC where, to Black's intense delight, he placed before him his great prize. 'Mr Pei is a corking field man,' Black later commented with feeling.[28]

Six months later Lampson took his small daughter to visit Black in his laboratory:

> The Skull was lying on his worktable and he was engaged in trying to piece together the tiny fragments which had become detached when the skull was taken from its original rock matrix. For this purpose he uses what looks very much like a complete dentist's outfit – all the elaborate buzzers and what not that is everybody's nightmare. So far they claim to have found bits of the skeletons of at least eleven humans in this cave, together with numberless bones of all sorts of extinct animals such as hyenas, sabre-toothed tigers, and I know not what all.[29]

Black's working pattern was unusual. A gregarious man, he enjoyed spending the evenings with his friends at the Peking Hotel before disappearing into his laboratory to work through the night only returning home to sleep in the morning. But on 15 March 1934, at the age of 49, his heart finally gave out. His friend Teilhard de Chardin reported how he was found the next morning lying at his worktable next to Peking Man.

Between Pei's discovery in 1929 and the beginning of the Sino-Japanese war in 1937, many more human fossils were recovered from Choukoutien as well as large numbers of stone tools. But while the importance of the site remains undisputed, Peking Man's unique status within the palaeontological hierarchy was lost only three years after Black's death when, joining his Java cousin, he was re-classified as *homo erectus*. Furthermore, the belief held by Black and so many of his friends that mankind originated in Asia was conclusively proved wrong when human fossils several million years older than Peking Man emerged from Africa. Nevertheless, Black's achievements together with those of his fellow dragon bone hunters were prodigious and not just related to science. For as the Chinese themselves recognised, this group of foreign scientists based in Peking had proved that Western and Chinese professionals could collaborate successfully on an equal footing. V.K. Ting, a leading intellectual, director of the China Geological survey and a close friend of Black, made the point:

> It is frankly admitted that sometimes we find cooperation between Chinese and foreigners in scientific work rather difficult…Firstly, many foreigners are suffering from a superiority complex. Subconsciously they think somewhat like this; here is a Chinese, he knows something about science, but he is Chinese nevertheless – he is different from a European, therefore we cannot treat him in the same way. At best his manners become patronizing. On the other hand, their Chinese colleagues are suffering from an inferiority complex. They become self-conscious and supersensitive, always imagining that the foreigner is laughing at them or despising them…In my dealings with Davidson Black…I never found him suffering from such a complex, and his Chinese colleagues became also free from theirs. In politics, Black was a conservative, but in his dealings with his Chinese colleagues, he forgot altogether about their nationality or race, because he realized that science was above such artificial and accidental things.[30]

Perhaps Teilhard de Chardin best summed up the camaraderie of the group when after the 'prehistoric' dinner in April 1927 (at which four of the 11 diners present were Chinese) he wrote:

Never in my life – family life included – have I spent hours so rich and cordial as that evening. As at so many other times in Peking, the occasion was pervaded by a dimly sensed triumph at the overcoming of racial, national and religious barriers.[31]

Science, it seemed, was leading where diplomacy and religion had yet to follow.

14

GATHERING MENACE

By the time of Davidson Black's death in 1934, Peking's intellectuals had a good deal more to worry about than Western notions of superiority. For, after years of tightening its grip on Manchuria, Japan finally annexed the territory in September 1931. Watching events from Peking, the diplomats remained curiously unmoved. Most took the view that it was perfectly legitimate for Japan to protect its vested interests and that having now secured such a large slice of China, it would leave the rest of the country alone. Their complacency was shattered when, on the pretext of yet another 'incident', the Japanese attacked Shanghai on 28 January 1932. The bombing and shelling continued until 3 March when a truce (largely brokered by Lampson) was at last put in place. Six days later, Tokyo converted Manchuria into 'Manchukuo' – a puppet state complete with its own puppet head in the shape of China's last emperor – Puyi.

Then, early the following year, Japanese troops marched into Jehol, the province lying immediately north-east of Peking, and were soon so close to the city that its fall seemed inevitable. Out riding on 9 March 1933, Lampson noticed 'the ominous emptiness of the countryside; all the houses closed up and their outer gates shut', adding 'there is no doubt that there is an atmosphere of anxious expectancy in the air – more so than I have known for many years'.[1] The next day, after putting up a fierce fight, hundreds of wounded Chinese soldiers poured into Peking for treatment at the PUMC. Despite all this, the commanding general found time to host Lampson and his house-party for a day's shooting at the Summer Palace:

> We paddled about the lake contentedly, every now and then blazing off at duck
> or coots as they flew overhead. Finally we landed and had refreshments at one
> of the pavilions. General Ho then bustled off to telephone to find out if there
> was any news of the war! But returned to say that nothing very striking had
> happened, and that he was therefore free to continue to shoot![2]

By 1933, his last year in China,[3] Lampson's position as the most authoritative minister in Peking was unassailable. Constantly pressed for his views by both the Chinese government and his less well-informed colleagues, he responded frankly to each: 'The last thing we wish is to be drawn into these bickerings between China and Japan,' he warned the diplomats, 'my whole instinct is that there is nothing for us to do but sit quiet and not fuss.'[4] Meanwhile he told the Chinese, who he knew were much too weak to fight Japan, that 'it was foolish for them to go on bothering their heads about Manchuria when the only thing to do was to leave that problem to solution by time and patience'. Instead he suggested that 'they concentrate on getting their internal house in order, during which period they should most carefully abstain from giving any pretext to Japan for further encroachments'.[5]

But when in May aeroplanes began dropping leaflets over Peking urging the elimination of Chiang Kai-shek, even Lampson began to question Japan's ultimate aims. He and Nelson Johnson, the only other minister to wield real influence, shared their growing disquiet at daily meetings: 'Did this really mean that the Japanese deliberately intended to dictate to China what sort of Government they were going to have? And if so, where was the end of it? The dominance of China and of Chinese policy by Japan? And if that was so, why stop at China?'[6] Johnson reported his anxieties to Washington but Lampson, not yet convinced that Japan was a threat to 'ourselves' and nervous of starting hares, refrained from telling 'his people back home'.[7] Meanwhile, as rumours of Peking's imminent occupation became ever more lurid, life in the legation quarter went happily on: 'the Oxholms, the Vellosos and Baron Sternberg came to tea and afterwards played tennis in the back garden'.[8] A few days later, on the 'great Fourth of June', Lampson sent a telegram to his old school, Eton, noting, 'Caccia[9] drafted it in Latin so I hope it will be understood.'[10]

Despite public outrage at the loss of Manchuria, Chiang Kai-shek decided not to resist. On 31 May 1933, the Nationalists signed the Tangku truce, in which they effectively recognised Manchukuo by agreeing to a vast demilitarised zone stretching far south of the Great Wall and east to Tientsin. Peking at least was spared if only for the time being. It was a humiliating deal but by accepting Japan's terms the Nationalists left themselves free to concentrate on what they saw as the more important task – the extermination of Communists or, as they termed them, 'Red bandits'. And no doubt the majority of Peking's foreign residents agreed that given a choice between Japan and Bolshevism, it was Bolshevism that posed the greater threat. Not that they knew anything about the Reds nor indeed had met any, but for years now everyone – including Lampson – had been absorbing the rumours:

> The atrocities perpetrated would be quite incredible but for the irrefutable evidence that they are true. Apparently there is a sort of communistic experiment…in a rather bleak and desolate area up country. This movement has now quite taken charge and become really insane. Whole classes are condemned to extermination: no one may live after 50, because they have passed their prime; no immoral class may be allowed to exist, e.g. marriage mediators, prostitutes and the like; capitalists and anybody having more than $5,000 are *ipso facto* criminals and executed; no children under 15 should be spared, because the world is over populated and that must be rectified. Moreover, it is essential that children should be brought up in the proper communistic spirit and for that a new generation is necessary. These doctrines are actually being put into practice, and apparently so-called lecturers tour the country, part of their procedure being to carry out executions during their lectures…the whole thing is too ghastly.[11]

There was however a small group of China specialists[12] in the American legation who were sceptical. Appalled by Japan's aggression and keen to obtain hard facts, they encouraged a young journalist from Kansas City, Edgar Snow, to find some way of contacting the Communists. Snow had already been in China five years when he arrived in Peking in March 1933 with his smart energetic wife Helen Foster Snow. Increasingly critical of Chiang Kai-shek's fascist behaviour and supine attitude to the Japanese, he needed little encouragement. But the timing could hardly have been worse. For in October 1934, the Communists slipped through the Nationalist cordon surrounding their Kiangsi Soviet (in south-east China) to embark on their epic 6,000-mile journey – the Long March. Pursued by Chiang Kai-shek's armies and hostile warlords over mountains, rivers and deserts, they suffered unimaginable hardship before establishing a new headquarters at Pao-an in northern Shansi – several hundred miles north of Sian. Although only a fraction of the 80,000 or so men women and children who began the Long March survived, once established in their new territory they were able to regroup and rebuild.

Snow signed a contract for a book on the Communists as early as 1934 but it was to be another three years before *Red Star Over China* was published. In the meantime, the Snows were far from idle. Helen, always ambitious for Edgar, pushed him hard. But she was also determined to succeed as a writer herself so that it often seemed to their friends that she was in direct competition with him. One joint venture they undertook with equal enthusiasm was the publication of an anthology of contemporary Chinese short stories aimed at the American market, entitled *Living China*. In a letter to a publisher, Snow made clear why he attached so much importance to the project:

> The important thing to me is to secure publication of some fiction about China by *Chinese*. Frankly, the thing which impelled me to embark on this work was a nausea with the impossible fiction on China by foreign and particularly by American novelists. It sickened me no little to think of thousands of my gullible countrymen reading such tripe…and innocently believing that the contents were valid of China…the difficulty now I fear may be that Americans have been reading these romantic versions of China as a kind of never-never land for so long that they won't believe real people exist here, very much like ourselves, even when the Chinese fiction, written by Chinese for Chinese, shows that. Apparently a Taoist proverb or a Confucian maxim has to be drawn across every page, men must go about talking in a remarkable sort of jargon (will the Honourable Chang permit this Less-Than-The-Dry-Grass Servant to address his August Visage, etc., etc.) which never existed outside the pages of cheap Western novels, or the work isn't considered authentic. If the Chinese write about themselves as they really think, as they really talk, and as they really are, the Western reader fed on Walns and Milns and Bredons and Bucks says knowingly that he understands this isn't the real China but only 'propaganda'.[13]

Snow's reference to Pearl Buck (whom he knew well) in this context is perhaps surprising. Buck's book *The Good Earth* (1931) had won the Pulitzer prize in 1932 precisely because it aimed to give a realistic portrayal of peasant life in China with all its hardships. The book was a huge success and the main reason Buck was awarded the Nobel Prize for Literature in 1938.

Both Snows enjoyed working on their anthology, not least because it brought them into contact with some of Peking's brightest young minds. And once Edgar began teaching journalism at Yenching University (a Christian institution founded in 1919) they met many more. Yenching's first president, Dr John Leighton Stuart, was a second-generation missionary who claimed to feel as much Chinese as American. Rejecting the crude evangelising of his parents' day, he offered his students a broad liberal arts curriculum, taught by an international faculty that included some of China's finest scholars. By early 1930s Yenching had become one of China's top universities, its success underpinned by partnerships with prominent American universities, most notably Harvard, which led to the establishment of the Harvard-Yenching Institute.

As the Long March drew to an end in October 1935, the Japanese were on the point of signing a pact with Peking's Nationalist administration in which the city and five northern provinces would be severed from the rest of China and, like Manchuria, brought under Japanese control. Because a number of Yenching students came from exiled Manchurian families, the university was particularly attuned to this latest crisis. Some of the students began to gather at the Snows' house in search of advice and sympathy. The Americans offered them their full support for, as Edgar put it, 'you can't just stand by and watch a lady you love being ravished and do nothing about it. And Peking is a very nice old lady indeed.' [14]

But it was Helen who really put her shoulder to the wheel, coming up with a string of imaginative proposals. Inspired by the 1919 Fourth of May demonstrations, she wrote to one of the student leaders:

> I hope you will make a speech to them and give them *the devil* for their inactivity and sleepiness. They are exactly like turnips. Why be a vegetable? This is a historic moment in Chinese national life, and a wonderful time for the students to declare themselves in one way or another. At least you should declare a *strike* for a week and not act as if nothing were happening. [15]

Encouraging the students to take to the streets, she suggested that they parade a coffin through Peking labelled 'the Corpse of Old China'. In fact, the protests that took place on 9 and 16 December 1935 proved so effective that they were imitated all over China, forcing the Japanese temporarily to retreat from declaring North China an autonomous region. 'I have got the impression that you do understand the Chinese youth of the present age during this crisis,' wrote one grateful young man to the Snows, 'very, very few Westerners in China so far I have met have the same "taste". Most of them misunderstand us. You know the environment is so reactionary, ordinary we dare not tell the truth [*sic*].[16]

Judged by his outward appearance, the Honourable Sir Alexander Cadogan, youngest son of the Earl of Cadogan, old Etonian, graduate of Balliol and rising star of the Foreign Office,[17] was exactly the kind of foreigner the student had in mind. The dapper Sir Alexander, with clipped moustache and neat central parting, succeeded Lampson as British Minister in 1934. He quickly accepted the general view that Japan's dominance over China, however unpalatable, was a fact of life. And as British envoy – he became Britain's first ambassador to China in 1935 – his chief role must be to encourage rapprochement between Nanking and Tokyo and protect his own country's interests. On that basis, although he was by no means unsympathetic to the students, their demonstration meant little to him beyond the irritating fact that it prevented his house-guests, Sir Frederick and Lady Leith-Ross, from spending the day at the Jade Temple as planned. As a result Sir Alexander had returned from his afternoon walk on 9 December 'to find that woman in the drawing room'.[18]

But it took more than a student demonstration or threat of Japanese invasion to keep the foreigners away from their favourite nightspot – the roof of the Peking Hotel. Helen Snow happily abandoned all political scruples when invited to waltz there by the two best dancers in town, even though one was an Italian Fascist and the other a Nazi. Adamant that only the Fascists knew how to dance, she described how 'an apolitical bridge came down when the Viennese waltz began and we maintained a silent truce till it was over'.[19] 'Silent' and 'truce' were not words uppermost in Lady Leith-Ross's mind as she watched Sir Frederick whirl the curvaceous wife of the Brazilian ambassador, Madame Barbosa, around the floor. Turning to a young British diplomat, she announced, 'I won't have Leithers dance with that Madame Baboose any longer. Go and do something about it.'[20] It was at some similar occasion on the roof of the Peking Hotel that her husband (then financial adviser to the Chinese Government) found himself sitting next to the Japanese Consul General who explained:

Japan is like a young man, very energetic and sincere, deeply in love with Miss China, a beautiful girl too. But Miss China always giving glad eye to Britain or America and rebuts Japanese approaching [*sic*]. So young Japanese gets cross with Britain and America and says, 'Hands off – I want to marry Miss China and I won't have you interfering.'

Sir Frederick replied that it seemed to him more like rape than a marriage proposal.[21]

Unlike Lampson, Cadogan did not engage emotionally with China: 'Peking is beginning to bore me again from the point of view of work,' he wrote in January 1935, 'I might as well be at home, and these little social occasions are getting on my nerves.'[22] A 'nasty Chinese lunch' was one such event and dinner with a famous Peking hostess, 'Aunt Lucy' Calhoun, another: 'Usual squash at narrow table but fortunately the Danish Minister shirked which gave me more room.'[23] The uncontrollable buzz of Aunt Lucy's hearing aid added to Sir Alexander's irritation. Mrs Calhoun whose husband had served as American minister 1909–13 was one of a number of widows and divorcees who had set up on their own in Peking. Indeed, after Lady Lampson's death in 1930 (from meningitis), it was considered so necessary to shield Sir Miles from their advances that a niece was despatched from England to act as his chaperone. At least Lampson was naturally gregarious but Cadogan's dislike of Peking's social life was so intense that he even referred to it in a letter to King George V: 'Both in Peking and in Nanking, Sir Alexander has been entertained to an extent and in a manner that is almost disconcerting. Chinese meals cause the foreigner various embarrassments, and a series involves a certain physical and spiritual strain.'[24] The King's private secretary responded sympathetically: 'First let me say that the King has no objection to your writing in the 1st person if you find this easier... Your letter was just such a one as His Majesty enjoys and next time any gossip or a spicy story would be well received.'[25]

But it was not only Chinese food and trying house-guests that caused Cadogan such annoyance: 'Stopped at the Metropolitan Hotel to see exhibition of most contemptible modern Chinese pictures. Never saw such daubs.' Nor does he seem to have formed close relationships with his diplomatic colleagues: 'B. came for a longish chat but said nothing of interest – nor for that matter did I.' And to make matters worse, the Japanese with their shrill bugles, military exercises and speeding cars were getting on everyone's nerves. 'Aeroplanes flying all morning low over the embassy,' noted Cadogan in his diary, 'I instructed the Military Attaché to see his Jap colleague and ask what they thought they were doing and to hint that the thing was becoming a bore.'[26] By the time Sir Alexander, an early opponent of appeasement, left China a few months later, he had concluded that negotiations with Japan were a waste of time since they would do nothing to halt the country's aggression.

Cadogan's grumpiness was caused in part by constant travel to Nanking and elsewhere, and by frequent ill health. At one point he wrote to a friend: 'All my family [his wife, Lady Theodosia, and three daughters] are down with scarlet fever...I therefore, continue to be in quarantine, and to lead the life of a leper, which is beastly and depressing.'[27] Given Peking's small social circle, it is likely that the Cadogans and Snows met (possibly at Mrs Calhoun's where Edgar and Helen were also regulars), but they could not have had much to say to one another. Sir Alexander despised all journalists commenting after a brush with the *Manchester Guardian*, 'really these newspapermen – even the best – are *so* tiresome. I shall never tell any of them anything again.'[28] To left-leaning Americans like the Snows, meanwhile, Sir Alexander and Lady Theodosia must have seemed the very embodiment of redundant empire.

Six months after the December demonstrations, Snow received a letter written in invisible ink inviting him to visit the Communists at their north-west headquarters in Yenan. A few days later, as Helen recorded in her memoir, 'Ed packed up his sleeping bag, his Camel cigarettes, his Gillette razor blades, and a can of Maxwell House coffee, feverish with excitement, and with inoculations.' With various cameras hanging round his neck, he petted the puppies, said goodbye to the servants who had all lined up at the gate and took off into the night. 'It was dark midnight with no light on the streets but the bobbing ricksha lanterns...overhead were the immense desert stars and a crescent moon...We were silent except, except for the slow pad-pad of the jogging rickshawmen.' Catching the train by the skin of his teeth, Ed, 'stood on the steps, grinning as if he were Caesar at one of his triumphs, and saluted "Heil Hitler" as the noisy, coal-burning locomotive wheezed on its way.'[29]

When Snow returned to Peking nearly six months later he brought with him not only a stack of notebooks filled with the personal interviews he had conducted with the Communist leaders but a mass of information on every aspect of their lives – what they ate, where they slept, how they amused and educated themselves, their aspirations, philosophy and long-term strategies. No wonder, as Helen recorded, when he reached home 'he capered around the room...exploding with pride and achievement'.[30] A few days later, in more sober mood, he wrote an account of his adventures to Randall Gould, editor of the *Shanghai Evening Post and Mercury*:

The journey to the Red districts did involve a certain amount of weighing of destinies, and we-live-but-onces of course because I had nothing to weigh against all the lurid tales on which we have been fed for years except my confidence in one or two youths in whom I believed. But it turned out to be quite tame, and except for a couple of days when I was running nip and tuck with some bandits (not Reds) I never felt in any danger. In fact the trick was easier done than said. The difficulty now is to get something on paper as my still small voice tells me it should be written, and get it published.[31]

The extraordinary response to *Red Star Over China*[32] took Snow by surprise. In the first weeks after its publication in Britain in 1937, it sold over 100,000 copies. The reason for its success was simply that Snow had for the first time, and in a highly readable style, portrayed the Communist leaders as human-beings, presenting them as a sympathetic, well-disciplined group that some day might quite credibly govern China. This was startling news not just to the foreigners but also to the Chinese. The book did not of course convince everyone. Many critics accused Snow of succumbing to Communist propaganda, an accusation supported by the fact he submitted his transcripts to be edited and approved by Party officials.

The letters Edgar exchanged with his wife when he was living with the Communists reveal the frayed state of their marriage – it ended in divorce in 1949. Alone in Peking, Helen relied heavily on the companionship of her beloved Gobi – a greyhound given to them by Sven Hedin. 'Regards to Gobi,' Edgar wrote to her when he had been gone a few weeks, 'but for God's sake keep him out of the bed. It's not only fleas, you will get a louse carrying typhus or cholera or anything. Remember what he eats. Don't be a sentimental old maid.'[33] Given their vastly different political orientation any personal contact between Nazi sympathiser Hedin and Edgar Snow seems improbable. But although Peking's foreign community remained small during the 1930s, its increasingly varied mix gave rise to a number of surprising friendships including that between the Snows and Teilhard de Chardin. In her memoir, Helen describes how the three of them liked to walk on the Tartar wall (Gobi in tow) discussing among other things the Jesuit's efforts to unite science and God.

By the time Teilhard met the Snows in 1933 he had been based in China for a decade. His reputation as a distinguished geologist and palaeontologist (much enhanced by his role in the discovery of Peking Man) was widely recognised, but his efforts to persuade the Catholic Church to integrate science and evolution into its world-view had met with utter failure. Although his religious theories (published after his death) attracted a global following, his superiors regarded them as little short of blasphemy. Spirit and matter may have been two sides of the same coin for Teilhard but they were emphatically not for the Vatican, which not only insisted on his exile to China but also refused him permission to publish any of his religious writings. Many of his friends, including Helen Snow, encouraged him to leave the Jesuits but this was never a serious option. Convinced that ultimately the Church must recognise the validity of his arguments, he chose to remain on the inside. 'I know that my book has arrived safely in Rome and has been under consideration for three months,' he wrote in 1941, 'I don't dare to hope for favourable news: and yet isn't this just the time for a Catholic to speak openly and as a Christian on lines determined by the best scientific thought of today?'[34] Apparently not, for the book in question, *The Phenomenon of Man*, was turned down by the Vatican and not published until after Teilhard's death in 1955.

For such a sensitive man and one so concerned with the human condition, Teilhard was surprisingly detached from China: 'Inside the villages, swarming like ants are the Chinese,' he wrote not long after his arrival there, 'not evil, but primitive, inert, earthy, leading their humdrum lives in a mental twilight, and instinctively hostile to Occidentals, whose benefits they avail themselves of, but whom they regard basically as undesirables and trouble-makers.'[35] Despite the 23 years he was to spend based in the country, Teilhard remained deeply rooted in his own European values, unconvinced that China, would ever be capable of holding its own in the modern world.

As far as the foreign community was concerned, the rough treatment meted out to Teilhard by the Catholic Church only added to his mystique. One diplomat thought him 'by far the most impressive and interesting personality living in Peking', describing how he would 'stride into receptions, resplendent in his robes on return from some long expedition into the Gobi Desert or elsewhere'.[36] 'That great devil of a priest,' wrote another friend, 'clear as crystal, about whom there was nothing clerical, unctuous, turgid or shady. Silhouetted in a moon door in impeccably tailored clerical black, walking, both hands extended in greeting, through the ambiguous shadows of a wintry Chinese garden, his face like old wood on which the lines were prematurely etched... a man of extraordinary charm... carrying with him a mysterious aura of secret sorrow and a legend of persecution by his Church that made him irresistible.'[37] Women certainly found him so and Helen Snow was not alone in noticing the 'fine lines at the corners of his blue-grey eyes reflecting humour and alertness' or the way he sat 'tensely on the edge of a chair, lifting his face toward the speaker, eyes crinkling with anticipation and attention.'[38]

One woman in particular fell deeply in love with him. Lucile Swan was an American sculptor who, like many other artists and writers in the 1930s, had come to Peking for a short visit and decided to stay. A divorcee, she first met Teilhard in the autumn of 1929 at a party given by Amadeus Grabau for his scientific friends. She was immediately drawn to the priest: 'For the first time in years I felt young and full of hope again.'[39] That evening marked the beginning of an intense relationship revealed in the hundreds of letters they exchanged between 1932 and Teilhard's death in 1955. To the 'fine-featured, amply bosomed and hipped' Swan,[40] the platonic nature of their love affair was to bring as much anguish as joy, 'it seems to me I love more completely every day,' she wrote in 1934, 'he is the man I've been dreaming to find all my life – except why did God put in that little joke of making him a priest?'[41] Lucile also urged Teilhard to leave the Jesuits not just because she longed to consummate their relationship but also because she wanted him free to spread his religious beliefs: 'They are so sane and intelligent and so appealing to the world of today which needs and *longs* for the very thing that he has to give whereas his church neither wants nor condones it…if they would only kick him out.'[42] But as they never did, Lucile was forced to sublimate her desires in her sculpture which included two busts of Teilhard and a reconstruction of Peking Man.

In 1934, Teilhard noted that the China Geological Survey had started 'migrating to Nanking'[43] by moving there its library and unique collection of specimens. It was not the only institution in Peking to do so. Many universities also began dismantling their faculties and libraries. And a year earlier, on a visit to the Forbidden City, Lampson was horrified to see dozens of showcases stripped bare. The explanation given to him by the Director of the Palace Museum was that many of the Museum's contents had been sent away as a safety precaution. He asked Lampson whether, in the event of a Japanese invasion, the remaining treasures could be lodged in the legation quarter – a request Lampson regretfully felt forced to turn down.

Although by the beginning of 1936 Peking was still technically unoccupied, the Japanese were everywhere. Khaki-coloured motor trucks drove at reckless speeds along the main thoroughfares knocking down any coolie or cart too slow to move out of the way. Japanese drugstores, beer parlours and brothels multiplied, fundamentally changing the appearance of some of Peking's best-known streets, while Japanese goods smuggled into the country – including vast quantities of heroin and morphine – were intended to wreck the economy.

In his classic memoir, *Through China's Wall*, Graham Peck, a young American artist who arrived in Peking in January 1936, set the scene: 'In groups of ten or twenty the duck-bottomed little empire-builders promenaded every day through the shopping districts, grinning like canary-fed cats. In increasing numbers they drilled in the open spaces around the Legations, marching and counter-marching with their officers posting before them like monkeys on the backs of the huge Russian horses they affected.'[44] Many moderate Japanese diplomats serving in China at the time were appalled by their country's aggression, but by the mid-1930s they had long since ceased to have any influence over their military masters.

It was against this background that Helen Snow (not to be outdone by her husband) left Peking for Sian on 21 April 1937, determined to make her own pilgrimage to the Communists. But the Nationalist authorities, equally determined to stop her, kept her under such close surveillance that she was unable to leave Sian. In Helen however, they had met their match:

> At 12.30 I put on as many layers of clothing as I could under my tan camel's hair slacks and matching camel's hair coat...I pulled on my ancient and honorable blue suede beret and tucked all my curls under it...Like a truant schoolgirl seeking to escape detection at a bed check, I arranged pillows and blankets into a person-shaped mound in the bed...I loaded my handbag with the bare essentials for my expedition: a Waterman fountain pen with a very fine point, lipstick, powder, cold cream, a couple of handkerchiefs and all my money in a thin roll of paper bills. I put on my Crookes' lens sunglasses and sat tensely at the window looking at the moonlight outside.[45]

Displaying considerable courage, she escaped that night from the Sian Guest House and with the help of an American businessman reached a Communist-held town. To Edgar, waiting nervously in Peking for news, Helen's gallant cavalier sent the following letter:

> It would no doubt amuse you if I could give you even a slight idea of how burned up the local so-called secret service are here, but not so amusing was the difficulty I had of keeping my own good name. I have heard that there are women who are good travellers and make the grade in a bit of adventure – but I hope you will pardon me for observing that your wife is not one of these, if such exist, and should not be allowed to run around without the gentle hand of restraint ever at her elbow.[46]

For a young woman who liked smart clothes and dancing Vienna waltzes, life in the Communist caves of Yenan came as a shock. Expecting something more in the nature of a boy-scout camp, Helen instead found herself confronting tuberculosis, dysentery, rats, hunger filth – and human nature. Despite this, her interviews with Mao, Chou En-lai, Chu Teh and others (including many women), although never receiving the acclaim accorded to Edgar's, were a substantial achievement. 'I was not the best kind of visitor for Yenan,' she admitted, 'though I was willing to adapt to my environment *almost* the whole way,' [47] – the '*almost*' being her lipstick. She was thankful when she was at last able to arrange her return journey, although that also proved far from uneventful. But the Peking to which Helen eventually returned in October had in her absence suffered a profound trauma. On 8 August 1937, Japanese troops marched into the city unopposed. Peking had finally fallen.

15
LAST DAYS OF PARADISE

Although the 1930s was such a bleak decade for Peking, it was during these years that foreign scholars, writers and artists flocked to the city as never before. Disillusioned with post-war Europe (described by one of them as a 'sucked orange'[1]) they found in Peking an entrancing survival from a vanished world – an exquisite way of life still virtually untouched by modernity. As the American scholar Laurence Sickman put it: 'Peking was the only city in the world where physical and social traditions a millennium old had survived into the twentieth century.'[2] Utterly seduced, many foreign intellectuals planned to spend the rest of their days there, living surrounded by beautiful objects in the tranquillity of a courtyard house, their every need catered for by delightfully eccentric servants – and all on next to nothing. That they should have discovered this paradise just as it was about to be swept away was a tragedy that many chose to ignore. Instead, they immersed themselves in Peking's cultural riches, hoping that somehow despite the odds their charmed existence would last forever.

A favourite meeting place was the *Librairie Française*, Henri Vetch's bookshop in the Peking Hotel. There 'you met everyone who was really interested in China,' noted Helen Snow, 'and could spend whole afternoons talking.'[3] Certainly Vetch, described by Sir Edmund Backhouse as 'a charming cosmopolitan', loved nothing more than to spend hours discussing linguistics and literature with his customers, often leaving them, as one observer recorded, dazed by the 'excited and eccentric explanations of his ideas pursued with all the ingenuity that enthusiasts commonly devote to impossible propositions.'[4] Vetch was also a successful publisher, counting among his authors, Backhouse and Teilhard de Chardin – whose scientific papers at least, the Vatican made no attempt to censure.

Close to Vetch's bookstore, at the top of the stairs facing the hotel's entrance, was another famous foreign enterprise – The Camel Bell. Owned by the resourceful Helen Burton, the shop overflowed with every conceivable oriental object likely to tempt the large parties of tourists that periodically descended on Peking from cruise ships anchored at Tientsin. Seeing no conflict between left-wing politics and expensive clothes, Helen Snow enjoyed modelling Burton's ball gowns and opera cloaks for the tourists: 'I would dance the Vienna waltz – the orchestra always played waltzes when I arrived – and next morning the visitors would appear at the shop to order similar gowns.'[5] Originally from North Dakota, the statuesque Burton, her platinum blonde hair piled high on her head in a plait, had arrived in Peking via Honolulu in 1920. By the time her first venture (a sweet factory) failed, she had already spotted the potential in the tourist market and for the next 22 years – until the war burst everyone's bubble – never looked back. 'I have just gone ga-ga with purchases,' wrote a typical tourist:

> Embroideries, coats (a fur-lined one for little Mary) porcelain plates, a stone
> Buddha life size, sardes jars and a complete room of old Chineeze wall paper,
> four lovely trunks of lacquer and leather, six camphor wood chests and two *huge*
> camphor armoires.[6]

The Camel Bell's location in the Peking Hotel meant that Burton always knew exactly who was in town. George Bernard Shaw, Pearl Buck and Anna May Wong were among the long list of celebrities invited to her legendary parties held either in her courtyard house or at her temple in the Western Hills. In both places Burton adorned every available surface with exotic objects – jewellery, jade, silks and ceramics, thus providing yet further temptation for her guests whose purse strings loosened with each glass of champagne. 'I have a lighthouse mind,' Helen Burton once said, 'it revolves.'[7] And to help her keep everything revolving profitably, she adopted four Chinese girls whom she took everywhere – even aboard *The Empress of Britain*, the only ship to boast its own branch of the Camel Bell. Her Christmas egg-nog party was a social must: 'Helen's house looked beautiful as usual,' wrote one American guest:

> Out in the courtyard was a tree covered with paper poinsettia and flashing lights. It was rather bewildering but lovely. She looked tremendously gay in red with huge gold leaves and red glass berries at her throat. Her girls were also in red – little Mei Li's hair topped with a poinsettia – simply darling.[8]

In Helen Burton's seamlessly entrepreneurial world, there was little distinction between home and business, friend and client, family and employee.

Burton was clearly one of the women on whom the writer and connoisseur Harold Acton based 'Mrs Mascot' in his wonderfully funny satire of 1930s Peking – *Peonies and Ponies*. But as Acton, who lived in the city, 1932–9, pointed out, when it came to Peking's foreign community, fact was far stranger than fiction:

> There was a German scientist, for instance, whose sexual foibles would have interested Havelock Ellis. During the rainy season he was wont to repair to one of the parks and strip naked, but the sensation of cold water on his flesh did not suffice, and he remunerated the gardeners handsomely for emulating an extra rainfall. And a devoted married couple in the Legation Quarter used to flog each other punctually on Sunday mornings, so that their screams accompanied the church bells…[9]

In his writings on Peking, Acton makes no mention of an event that shook the foreign community to its core – the murder of a 17-year-old schoolgirl, Pamela Werner, in December 1936. She was found dumped by the Tartar City wall close to where the Snows lived – her skull crushed and her internal organs cut out. One of the Scotland Yard detectives sent from Shanghai to deal with the case told Helen Snow, his face pale green, that it was the most gruesome crime he had ever encountered. Rumours and theories were rife. Was it a maniac, a warning to foreigners, terrorism or a case of mistaken identity? The crime was never solved but the investigation uncovered a murky world of sex and drugs in which a number of Peking's leading foreign residents were apparently implicated. Paradise, it seemed, had a dark underbelly.

Although Acton's characters in *Peonies and Ponies* are only amalgams of real people, there is a striking resemblance between the scholarly 'Philip Flower' and the American sinologist George N. Kates. Kates' book – *The Years that Were Fat* – is an account of the seven years he spent in Peking,

1933–41. Inspired by an encounter with Chinese poetry, Kates abandoned Harvard, Oxford and a consultancy in Hollywood to seek his intellectual fortune in Peking as a 'Chinese' scholar. Determined from the start to shun Western ways, he even arrived in a third-class railway carriage – an act of inexcusable eccentricity in the eyes of the foreign community. Much to his satisfaction, Kates was able to rent a courtyard house uncontaminated by Westerners:

> No electric light, no wooden floors (brick covered with matting sufficed), no heating apparatus except several cast-iron stoves, and no plumbing did I ever install…I did not rip out the pretty geometric window tracery, there were no unsightly wires, no clumsy digging for ill-concealed pipes or ducts. Nothing marred the excellent lines of the large well-proportioned inner court…and so my house, while extremely comfortable, remained more authentically Chinese than any that I can recall belonging to Western friends. [10]

Unlike other foreign occupants of old Chinese houses, he does not mention the 'stink-bugs' that would drop unexpectedly from the ceiling on to dinner plates, the centipedes and scorpions lurking in slippers or the 'feather' bugs secreted behind papered walls that scratched relentlessly through the night.

Convinced, like the fictitious Philip Flower, that within his Western body lurked a Chinese soul, Kates wanted to meet the Chinese on their own ground and be accepted as one of them: 'It so often seems, when I look back,' he confided to a friend, 'that everything that happened before I came to China happened to *another* me. What that me desired it found here, and having found, desires only not to be separated from.'[11] He deplored the expatriates' lifestyle – summed up in his view by their taste in 'dull, expensive porcelains and garish Mandarin robes'. In any case, Kates (nicknamed 'the oyster') soon established that the rigorous life of a Chinese scholar did not mix well with the legation quarter. 'The Diplomatic Corps one has to keep rather completely clear of, or else one receives "commands" to vapid and entirely foreign parties of all sorts.'[12] Each morning, Kates rose early to attend classes at Peking University where, sitting on a hard wooden bench in a Chinese gown, he absorbed esoteric lectures on such subjects as the structure of early Buddhist society.

But even the ascetic Kates was not immune to gossip – especially when it involved his smart Bostonian friends, many of who visited Peking in the 1930s. After accompanying a large group of them (including the writer

John Marquand and landscape architect Fletcher Steele) to a monastery not far from Peking, he wrote to a friend:

> Such regal goings-on you never did see! Mrs Edward Robinson[13] went in state. Chairs, bearers, lanterns, runners, even a spring bed carried up the mountain for the lady to sleep on when she got to the top. It was a pageant; especially when the 'Duchess of Manchester' (for so she was called here) was given Prince Kung's imperial (and rather precariously *old*) chair – to be carried *down* the mountain again.[14]

A few classrooms away from Kates in the Peking National University (founded in 1897 it was the oldest institution of its kind in the city), Harold Acton taught English literature. Throughout the 1930s, Peking's universities employed increasing numbers of foreign teachers many of whom, such as Ivor Richards, William Empson, John King Fairbank and Baron de Staël-Holstein, to name but a few, were outstanding scholars. Acton took his responsibilities very seriously, forming a close bond with the students ('long soliloquies seemed perfectly natural to them'[15]) and admiring their cheerfulness in the face of their poverty, poor prospects and the escalating Japanese threat. 'This zest for life,' he wrote, 'was sharpened by a keen consciousness of the rhythm of nature, a deep sentiment of man's harmony with the universe, which we in Europe have lost – if we ever possessed it.'[16] Acton therefore held Richards and his 'Cambridge henchmen' in deep contempt for their efforts to introduce Basic English[17] to China: 'With their brilliant mnemonic gifts and their hereditary love of fine language,' Acton wrote, 'the Chinese are the last people to be seduced by this emasculate jargon.'[18]

In 1936, Acton moved into Dr Morrison's house – unoccupied since Roy Chapman Andrews' departure four years earlier. He embellished the court-yards with ornamental rocks, white lilacs and crab-apple trees, deriving, like Kates, deep pleasure from his domestic arrangements. But he also built a swimming pool and created an English lawn – desecrations that would have appalled the American. In this elegant courtyard house, one of the finest in Peking, Acton had ample space to hang his pictures and arrange his collection of Chinese art. He

> wandered through these halls of mellow carving, where every object had some happy associations, and watched flocks of doves circling above the courtyards with whistles under their tails, and swallows darting from roof to roof or twittering under the eaves.[19]

Not everyone was impressed. After dining one evening in the celebrated house, 23-year-old Winifred, daughter of the American military attaché, Colonel Joseph Stilwell, recorded her disappointment:

> The rooms are bare and the curios he chooses I don't care for. But he has some treasures and the food was good. He had invited the prettiest Englishman with curly hair and long curly eyelashes who surprisingly enough was easy to talk to.[20]

'Vinegar Joe' Stilwell, who in 1942 would become commander of the US forces in the China-Burma-India theatre and Allied Chief of Staff to Chiang Kai-shek, had more in common with the aesthetic Harold Acton than his prickly, limey-hater reputation might suggest – not least a deep love of Chinese art. Stilwell had an excellent eye and it is tempting to imagine this 'tough, gruff, battle-scarred' soldier[21] in the thick of the Burmese jungle occasionally allowing his thoughts to turn to his collection of exquisitely carved ivory fan handles. Fluent in Mandarin and having in the course of his military duties travelled all over China (often incognito in the roughest of conditions), Stilwell knew the country and its people better than almost any foreigner in Peking. Certainly, he was the only one to have spent four months directing 800 Chinese coolies in the building of an 80-mile-long road in Shansi province – a feat he accomplished when a language student in the early 1920s.

In common with Harold Acton, the Stilwell family had an unusually wide circle of Chinese friends. Prominent among them was the last emperor's cousin Prince Puju, one of only two contemporary artists Acton considered equal to the ancient masters and with whom he himself studied for a while. His own efforts, though, were soon out-shone by the Prince's star pupil, Alison Stilwell. Apart from the distinction of being the first human baby born in the PUMC (a camel beat her by a few hours), she was the first foreigner to take up Chinese painting seriously. Her work won high praise even from discerning Chinese – a remarkable achievement for an American teenager. The Prince lived in a magnificent palace where each spring, 'at the first explosion into blossom of his cherry trees and lilacs', he would invite his friends to a garden party. In a town given to endless entertainment, this, Acton noted, was still an exceptional event especially for the handful of foreigners present:

> Extremely old and fragile Manchu dignitaries and loyalists who had lived in retirement since the revolution and were invisible on other occasions, retaining their queues and long fingernails and the courtesies of a serener day, assembled

here to pay homage to the Prince who had as good a claim to the Dragon Throne as the late emperor, and to feast their tired eyes on flowers in hallowed ground.[22]

Acton's enthusiastic accounts of Peking encouraged other English literati to visit the city. Delighting in all it had to offer, some of them wrote books about their experiences, much to the irritation of Lewis Arlington, one of Peking's more colourful foreign residents. Acton, who collaborated with Arlington on a book about the Chinese theatre, described him as 'bald as a coot yet something of a beau' whose 'blue eyes sparkled with the flame of youthful endeavour'.[23] By the mid-1930s he had lived in China for more than half a century and was therefore well qualified to co-author the highly regarded guide book – *In Search of Old Peking* (1935). But as a self-educated American who had been a cowboy and seaman before finding employment with the Chinese Maritime Customs, he had little time for the 'literary tourists' now descending on Peking, complaining that 'there ain't one that don't try to pick my brains then they go back home and write books on old Cathay'.[24]

Quite possibly, Osbert Sitwell was one of the literary tourists Arlington had in mind. Sitwell's book *Escape with Me* (dedicated to Harold Acton and Laurence Sickman) records his travels through Cambodia and China in 1934, and his four-month sojourn in Peking. One of the book's more memorable passages describes a visit he made with friends to the Eunuchs' Temple, a few miles west of Peking, on an icy winter's day:

> We turned into a court, and immediately from behind the paper windows could distinguish the chinking of tea-bowls and a sound of high-pitched gossip and chatter. Knocking at the door, a momentary silence ensued, and then a hubbub of eager voices bade us enter. When we opened the door, we found a cluster of excited, inquisitive old faces round us.

Sitwell was struck by the contrast between the eunuchs' current poverty and their former lives in the Forbidden City – so full of extravagance, ritual and gossip. After their wholesale expulsion in 1924, many had ended up living in this temple – a cheerless building next to the foreigners' golf club. No longer did they wear 'splendid or impressive robes, but dark-coloured and stained gowns. No one ever visited them and so there was nothing about which to talk.'[25]

In January 1936, Julian Bell ('a half fledgling sort of a person', according to the writer Robert Byron, with 'a most ridiculous Bloomsbury voice'[26]) wrote

187

to his mother, Vanessa, from Peking: 'this is the nicest town in the world: the only great capital besides Paris – full of queers.'[27] He had a point for it was true that a good many of the foreigners who migrated to Peking in the 1930s were homosexual, drawn there, like others before them, by China's relaxed attitude to male love. Having long been accepted as an integral part of society, and practised quite openly by mandarin and coolie alike, homosexuality in Peking attracted none of the moral outrage so familiar in the West – except from foreign diehards. Acton, tongue in cheek, recorded their disapproval in *Peonies and Ponies* when Mrs Mascot, blaming the failure of some enterprise on the fact that she did not get on with the 'degenerates', complains that they are getting the run of the place. 'Take Elivira; she keeps open house for them; they fairly swarm around her. I dare say she's tarred with the same brush.'[28]

But the Mrs Mascots were easily ignored and in Peking the 'degenerates' had discovered an idyllic existence where they could relish every exotic new experience free from legal constraint. Heterosexuals were equally seduced by Peking's night-life, as John Blofeld (aged 22 when he arrived in Peking in 1934) makes charmingly plain in his book *City of Lingering Splendour*. What is more, all these pleasures were possible on very little money. Robert Byron, who spent the winter of 1935–6 in the city writing his masterpiece *The Road to Oxiana*, noted in a letter to his mother that when Acton's private income temporarily dried up, he was able to live in a lovely house with a large establishment of servants on the 200 pounds a year he received as a university lecturer – and still have something left over for collecting. 'You and Father could live like princes,' he added, 'plus about 60 pounds each for the journey one-way. So if you ever feel you can't bear England any more, there is always Peiping!'[29] A couple of years earlier, the Marquis of Ormonde had seriously considered recouping his finances by letting his ancestral home, Kilkenny Castle, and renting a courtyard house.[30] If war had not intervened, Peking might well have developed into a sanctuary for impoverished members of the British upper class.

Because the foreigners' living expenses in Peking were so small, even the less well off among them were able to indulge in the local passion for 'curios'. Laurence Sickman's brilliant eye and deep knowledge of Chinese art was so much admired within Acton's circle that soon no excursion was complete without him. Boys carried chits from house to house arranging shopping trips, dinners and expeditions to temples: 'Are you by any chance free tonight?' wrote David Horner (Osbert Sitwell's companion) to Larry Sickman. 'Osbert says he can't live without you as you are the only person who appreciates his buckles and general good taste!' adding in a postscript, 'I can't live without you either.'[31]

Sickman first went to Peking in 1930 on a Harvard-Yenching fellowship to further his studies in Chinese art and language. The following year, the brand new Nelson Gallery in Kansas City commissioned him to buy objects for its embryonic oriental collection. 'Tell KC to get ready to sell their pants,' Sickman wrote to his former Harvard tutor in 1933, 'About the best piece of sculpture – not Buddhist – ever to come out of China will be on the way soon.'[32] The Museum's timing was perfect since the early 1930s proved the heyday for foreign collectors of Chinese art. One reason was the building of a railway along the Yellow River valley right through the heartland of China's ancient culture. The new railroad cut across thousands of tombs, releasing their precious contents into the hands of the local gentry who rapidly sold them on to dealers – mainly in Peking and Shanghai. It was, in Sickman's words, 'a regular-cloak-and-dagger business'. Once in Peking, the really important pieces were never displayed openly. Instead runners were despatched to inform potential buyers who were then led into the dealer's inner sanctum to view the latest arrival. For Sickman, the complex bargaining procedure, as well as the manoeuvring between competing international buyers, turned the whole process into 'a wonderful game' – one moreover that he was only too happy to share with his friends.[33]

***

The literati were not the only foreigners in Peking to hope that the disagreeable political situation might simply fade away. By the mid-1930s the majority of ministers had been promoted to ambassadors and were now spending most of their time in Nanking. But when Sir Hughe Knatchbull-Hugessen arrived in China on 15 September 1936, it was in Peking that he and his family first settled. A few weeks later he wrote to his predecessor, Cadogan, in London:

> Writing now it seems clear the Japanese do not intend to go to extremes – at least that is my strong feeling. I am inclined to write off the possibility of the present Sino-Japanese difficulties leading to serious trouble, certainly to war.

Keen, like his predecessors, to promote Britain's trade interests, he added, 'I think we are on a very good wicket watered and rolled for us by our Japanese friend. I hope that on it we shall make substantial commercial scores.'[34]

At first his 21-year-old daughter, Elisabeth, found embassy life in Peking 'tepid' – but not for long:

> We repaired to the Club for what I imagined would be a quiet evening of Animal Grab and Snap. Instead there were crowds of people and after Gerry and Clifford had poured a few sherries down and over us we joined in the free fight for food. Then the riot started: Alethea dropped an entire plate of spaghetti on the floor...Beer was upset in every direction and Franz revealed a strange tendency to throw tomatoes at everyone...We tore home heaved up the carpets, threw a record on the gramophone, yelled for some whisky and waltzed madly for a bit...Suddenly we were all in the APC Mess playing golf with glasses and playing ball with bottles and breaking records on each other's heads and sliding on the floor...On the pavement outside we sang the Marseillaise and Auld Lang Syne – just for fun.[35]

Nor did her life become any less exciting when several months later a stray bullet struck her while she was out riding with friends. Luckily the enterprising Third Secretary was with the party:

> Gerry discovered the bullet neatly lodged in my forehead. With astounding quickness he decided it must be removed at once. 'God dammit,' he yelled, 'Has no-one got a knife?' Nobody had. So he rummaged in his pocket and produced the Chancery key and some iodine. After a good deal of poking and prodding the bullet was levered out of my head.[36]

Two years later she married him.

Her father was not so fortunate when, six months after Elisabeth's accident, a Japanese aeroplane strafed the car in which he and members of his staff were travelling not far from Shanghai. A bullet grazed his spine causing serious injury. Although the Japanese official, rapidly despatched to Peitaiho to apologise to Lady Knatchbull-Hugessen, 'shook' all over with embarrassment, his apology, Elisabeth recorded in her diary,

> ...was a rather awkward affair. It was hard to know what answer to give – I couldn't say 'Oh don't mention it' and anyhow he spoilt the effect rather by saying he had to hurry away now as the aeroplane was wanted back to go and bomb Nankow.[37]

The press had a field day, for no story could have underlined more sensationally just how fast the old order was unravelling. Over the years, the Sino-Japanese conflict had become a familiar backdrop to the foreigners' existence in China but had mostly left them personally unscathed. The attack on the British Ambassador's car, despite its prominent Union Jack, marked a sinister new turn of events. Four months later it was the Americans' turn when the Japanese made an even bolder 'mistake' by sinking the USS Panay, on the Yangtze.

**

On the evening of 7 July 1937 the American ambassador, Nelson Johnson, hosted an informal boat party on the Pei Hai in the Imperial City. Among the guests were Colonel and Mrs Stilwell. Their eldest daughter, Nancy, described the occasion:

> We anchored in the middle of the lake from where you could see a lovely marble bridge, lights from numerous teahouses reflected in the water and the Dagoba – creamy white in the moonlight. After supper we drifted slowly down to the far end and back poled by two men on either side of the barge. We sang all kinds of songs accompanied by Mr Johnson who plays the guitar splendidly.[38]

The next morning her father learned that while they were floating on the lake, fighting had broken out between Chinese and Japanese troops at the Marco Polo Bridge, eight miles from Peking. Although at the time its significance was far from obvious, it was the incident that finally ignited the eight-year long Sino-Japanese war.

Graham Peck first heard the news later that day at a cocktail party – woven into snatches of Peking gossip:

> He performs in the costume of a Louis XIV blackamoor and boasts he's the only man alive who can dance on a kettledrum without breaking it... With that complexion she certainly does herself no favour by getting tattooed...

> The Japanese claim they advanced to rescue a lost soldier, but now they've found that the man in question had just retired into a bush for reasons which were nobody's business but his own...

Initially, the fighting around Peking was only sporadic but it soon intensified. Martial law was imposed, street barricades erected and the gates kept shut although no fighting took place in the city itself. Old China hands confidently predicted the crisis would soon pass, but over-excited tourists could be heard exclaiming: 'It's like having been at Sarajevo.' It was, as Peck observed, a curious situation for the foreigners:

> ...with all the unpleasantness kept outside the walls and only the excitement filtering in it was hard to make a tragic thing of it. The war seemed no more than one of those pleasantly novel and exciting group inconveniences, like a small blizzard or a cloudburst, which throw every one together in more or less comic misfortune and so increase conviviality.[39]

But by the end of the month the fighting was serious enough for the diplomats to summon their nationals into the legation quarter. 'Awakened on Wednesday by *tremendous* bombardment', wrote Dorothea, (wife of Ivor Richards) in her journal on 28 July, 'About 11am we packed rucksacks and walked to the Legation Quarter climbing over various barricades.' For those who remembered the Boxer uprising or Peking's many subsequent crises, it was a familiar scene. Tents sprouted over the well-watered lawns along with signs to lavatories and dining rooms as people poured into the quarter. 'A polyglot assortment I can tell you,' wrote Captain John Letcher, an American marine officer, to his mother: 'Missionaries, Eurasians, Chinese and Russian wives of Americans and all their progeny. One couple brought in nine children and a goat to give milk for the baby.'[40] As usual, dozens of stateless Russian prostitutes turned up. Equally predictable was the rivalry between the British and Americans. The latter, so it was claimed, only charged 50 cents a day for lodging and three meals (including canned beans and pineapple), while the British served bad food at high prices and made sure that class distinctions were 'delicately but firmly drawn'.[41] Rumours, gossip and fear over a possible outbreak of cholera kept everyone occupied although it was impossible to get any real news. Even broadcasts from London, Dorothea Richards complained, covered little beyond the Wimbledon tennis tournament.[42]

Yet by the time the Japanese army marched triumphantly into Peking on 8 August everyone had been allowed to return home. 'Strange to see so little change after such cataclysmic happenings,' wrote Dorothea in her journal.[43] And it was true that within days – for the foreigners at least – life had more or less returned to normal. As Peck sat in his courtyard shortly after the occupation, he heard the faint sound of music. Looking towards the Peking Hotel he could see 'along one shoulder of it tiny figures moving about in a flat area of radiance' and realised that the roof had reopened for dancing.[44] It was, in fact, on the dance-floor that the foreigners heard their first real news of the war.

In between dances, 'men in white mess-jackets and ladies in chiffon gowns' clustered around the few journalists who had ventured beyond the walls, eager to hear their reports of ditches clogged with rotting corpses swelling and bursting in the heat, bloated horses and scattered body parts, and – worst of all – the moans and screams of the wounded as they lay hidden among the crops. Yet Captain Letcher, one of the few foreigners actually to have seen the carnage, wrote home a few days later,

> ...it is a very good time to buy things out here because with all the uncertainty the shop keepers are willing to sell their goods cheap. I just hope that we don't have to go in such a hurry that we will have to leave all our things behind.[45]

A group of foreigners now returned daily to the roof of the Peking Hotel – not to dance but to view the fighting. Sitting comfortably in white metal chairs among tubs of flowering oleanders, Peck recalled how they could see in the distance 'the delicate blue wall of the Western Hills and before it the flat green plain billowing with unbroken foliage'. Only the aeroplanes disturbed the tranquillity, 'dipping and weaving like persistent bumblebees'. The foreigners were too far away to observe the bombs actually drop, but at intervals 'a puff of white smoke would mushroom up from the floor of the plain and after a moment would come the shimmering detonation, only a faint boom on the warm breeze'.[46] Later in August, Stilwell wrote to his wife (away at the beach with the children):

> This is a hell of a life. And the worst of it is that I can't tell you whether it is clearing a bit or about to get worse. The atmosphere is sad and gloomy, and there is a pall over everything. Jesus, to think the blow has fallen, actually fallen already is enough to make you sick physically. Maybe I'll feel better when you all get back, but I'm lower than a snake's belly right now.[47]

For the Chinese, existence under the Japanese occupation grew daily grimmer but, as the war receded from Peking, life for the foreigners settled back into its familiar rhythms. By October the racecourse, having been a battlefield all summer, was in full operation, and Captain Letcher could report that 'today in the warm fall sunshine a crowd of Chinese and foreigners watched the races and bet on the ponies as if nothing had ever happened'.[48]

But it had happened. And as the years of occupation slipped by it was increasingly obvious even to the most sanguine foreigner that life had radically changed. As Kates observed, the Westerner lived 'more and more like a man who although physically comfortable knows that he has a fatal disease, clawing even at that moment in the dark at his vitals'.[49] Japanese attitudes to foreigners became increasingly arrogant – particularly towards the Americans and British. There were daily anti-Western demonstrations in which large numbers of Chinese were forced to take part while slogans proclaiming 'Down with Britain' or 'Asia for the Asiatics' were plastered everywhere. Businesses packed up due to an embargo on raw materials and the disruption of international finance.

Governments now actively encouraged their nationals to leave, and on 10 September 1937 Mrs Stilwell went to the station to say goodbye to the dozens of American families departing that day for home:

> 'It was a sad scene,' she wrote, 'for amahs were weeping, husbands wiping tears from their eyes, and wives crying openly. The Marine band played its usual helpful tunes ending with Auld Lang Syne. Then one of the longest trains I've ever seen pulled out of Chien Men station. On board were some of our favourite Chinese friends who were hoping to reach Hong Kong, although no place seemed to be safe for them. Everyone was restless and anxious. It was so easy for us to say not to worry, for we are Americans.'[50]

A year later, in October 1938, Mrs Stilwell noted that 'the darling of Peking', Aunt Lucy Calhoun, had sent out invitations to her first 'At Home' of the season. It was a brave effort but everyone knew that it was a far cry from former parties like the one she had given a several years earlier when her guests, in full evening dress, had boarded a barge and been towed under a full moon along the canal through hundreds of floating paper lanterns, each lit by its own candle.[51] In any case, as most of the diplomats were now in Nanking, much of the social glamour had vanished. Occasionally, there was an attempt to recapture the old atmosphere, but Captain Letcher was not fooled:

> The French gave a ball at their Embassy with a great deal of champagne and a cold buffet groaning with food. All of Peking's social world was there but most of them are rather ludicrous. Very small frogs in a very small pond acting like they were big frogs in an ocean.[52]

Teilhard de Chardin was pleased to see the French now making the running in Peking and asserting their 'ancient spirit of dignity and independence which automatically reappears in moments of crisis',[53] but he had little else to celebrate. After 15-odd years of roaming across China, he had since the occupation not even been able to visit the Peking Man site only 40 miles away: 'It's impossible to do any digging at Chou-Kou-Tien', he wrote to his brother, 'as it is caught between Japanese troops in the plain and the Reds based in the mountains.'[54]

Shortages and soaring prices hit everyone, causing Harold Acton to be thankful for his chickens and vegetable garden. 'We ran out of kitchen coal yesterday,' wrote Doot Stilwell to her sister in January 1939, 'and find there is no more in town. They are sending it all to Japan. The joys of winter in China!'[55] In desperation, their coal supplier wrote to Colonel Stilwell:

Dear Sir,

From yesterday morning, I have two carriages (Horse-Car) walk on the street. Was rob away to the Japanese Army. I think you have the Japanese friend and please you heart and soul to want the carriage for me that I am very thinks.

Yours faithfully,

(I think the office helped me.)   Shuang Chu Shing *[sic]*[56]

A few months later the Stilwell family also left but not before – in a last gesture of farewell to old Peking – Vinegar Joe had invited 12 rickshaw boys to a banquet in his house.

On 3 September 1939 Britain declared war on Germany. Shortly afterwards Teilhard de Chardin wrote to his brother:

Here apart from the official news, we are still quite in the dark about things in Europe, and its very difficult to get the feel of what is happening. At such a distance all these events seem to have something unreal about them, a sort of dream one can't understand.[57]

One reality however was all too evident – the souring of relationships within the foreign community. 'The Peking Club seethes with hatred,' wrote a Canadian interior decorator, 'also the hotel lobbies where people in small groups sit and glare at people in other groups.' On the other hand she admired the way the Chinese went on with their lives as if nothing were happening, only wishing that the foreigners possessed more of their stoicism.[58]

In fact, by mid-1940 most of the foreigners had left. Those that stayed did so because Peking was their home and they had nowhere else to go, or because they had a business to protect. Missionaries remained out of a sense of duty and stateless Russian refugees from necessity. A few optimists hung on to the hope that they might yet retrieve their former lives. But Teilhard de Chardin knew better when he wrote 'we are living through an end – the end in particular of the old European influence'.[59] On 7 December 1941 the Japanese attacked Pearl Harbour. The next day, Peking's foreigners awoke to the unpleasant discovery that the party was well and truly over.

16
AFTER THE PARTY

This morning there is only one announcement. No other news will be read. The Japanese Air Force has attacked Pearl Harbour. The United States Pacific Fleet has been destroyed. A state of war now exists between Japan on the one side and the United States of America and Great Britain on the other.[1]

Although war had long been expected, the news still came as a shock to Peking's remaining foreigners as they listened to the wireless on the morning of 8 December 1941. Yet for those committed to the Allied cause it was also a relief. The fact that America was at last in the war gave fresh hope to Europeans and Chinese alike. But if victory for both now seemed more possible in the long term, the immediate future held only uncertainty. 'My life seemed to have stopped,' wrote one English resident, Hope Danby, 'I was as helpless as a wooden puppet dangling on a wire in mid-air. The past was gone, the present unreal and the future a blank.'[2]

The Japanese wasted no time in taking over the legation quarter. Marching in before dawn they sealed the gates, leaving those returning home from a gala ball at the Peking Hotel marooned outside in the snow. "Machine guns" aimed at the 140 men of the US Marine guard were mounted on the section of the Tartar wall that their former comrades had defended so tenaciously during the Boxer siege. Although the Japanese gave Colonel William Ashurst until noon to decide, in reality he had little choice but surrender. Other foreign institutions, among them Yenching University and the PUMC, were also rapidly occupied. Intent on finding the Peking Man fossils, the Japanese made a thorough search of the PUMC but, even after subjecting the staff to intense questioning, came up with nothing. A Swiss professor of parasitology at the college, Dr Reinhold Hoeppli, was appointed honorary consul responsible for American and British interests – a post he was to fill with distinction. Throughout the day Japanese officials appeared at foreign residences to make inventories of possessions and warn of the terrible consequences awaiting any individual discovered listening to the BBC or concealing a firearm. Everyone had to be registered, each foreigner receiving an identity card and correspond-ing armband – green for friends, white for neutrals and red for enemies. Since the Japanese regarded Vichy as an ally, the French were allowed to carry on as normal – a position Teilhard de Chardin found humiliating, writing home to France: 'We don't feel very proud in the presence of the Anglo-Saxons.'[3] Meanwhile the movements of all Americans, British, Australians, Dutch, Russians, Canadians, Greeks and Indians were strictly monitored (although the Japanese were curiously sympathetic to anyone requesting a visit to the dentist), their bank accounts were frozen, their businesses closed down and their assets seized. For Japan's enemies it was a new and frightening world.

Some responded better than others. Bertram Hale, head of the Thomas Cook office, and his wife Hilda were nothing if not resourceful. When in 1939 the Japanese had opened a brothel next door to their courtyard house, they had taken their young daughters and servants to join a small foreign com-munity living by the racecourse at Paomachang, just outside the city. With a large household to support but no money or car, they had little to live on but their wits.

> We lucky ones living in the countryside carried on quite a tidy little barter busi-ness. The Hales would swap eggs for tomatoes, Elsie Henning would exchange potatoes for apricots, Gladys Finalyson would offer her homespun wool for veg-etables and Charles Peacock, who had a contract with the wine-making monks at the Shala Monastery, would swap a bottle of wine for a boiling fowl or some of our homemade sausage. We all lived within visiting range of each other, and this bartering game added some interest to our lives.[4]

A network of sunken roads running between the fields outside Peking gave excellent cover for clandestine operations. Few were more successful than Hilda's sausage-making business, which she initially funded by selling a ring to the wife of a Swiss diplomat. In the dead of night, when no Japanese were around, three of her Chinese boys bicycled to a neighbouring farm to collect a slaughtered pig. 'Then all the servants went to work on our large kitchen table. After cook Wang had prepared the sausage meat, they used funnels and wooden plungers to hand-stuff the casings before twisting the sausages into the required lengths.'[5] The following day one of the boys would take the sausages to the Peking Club – now run by the Japanese, Germans and Italians – where they proved so popular that orders were soon coming in from as far away as Tientsin.

It was with schemes such as this and support from the Chinese, who in consequence often put their own lives at risk, that families like the Hales managed to cope. Others evicted from their homes, or for whom the situation just became too difficult, took refuge in their respective embassies where, like 20-year-old Katy Talati, they soon learned to make the best of things. 'Life in the British Embassy during that brief period from January 1942 to March 1943 was a pleasant time,' she wrote, 'I was really happy there.' Originally from Bombay, the Talatis were a prominent Parsee family who had settled in Peking in the early part of the century and had over the years built up a number of successful businesses. The three Talati daughters had been strictly brought up so for Katy this sudden change of lifestyle, with friends calling in every evening, was a welcome novelty. Meals were a communal affair eaten in the ambassador's residence, giving Katy plenty of opportunity to study her fellow inmates. They were an odd mix ranging from a bohemian modern dancer to Mr Scratch, a narrow-minded, fundamentalist Christian. Among Katy's new friends was none other than Peking's most enigmatic foreign resident – Sir Edmund Backhouse.

> A tall, distinguished, elderly gentleman with a long white beard and flowing white hair, dressed in long Chinese robes and a formal Chinese waistcoat. On his head he always wore a black silk skullcap with a red plaited button on top. We loved him and were carried away by his fabulous stories of his life and intimate friendship with the Empress Dowager and other members of the Chinese Imperial family. They kept us riveted and he, I am sure, was in his element with such an adoring audience.[6]

Since his return to Peking after the First World War, Backhouse had led an increasingly reclusive life, going to great lengths to avoid his fellow Westerners. If he passed one while out in his rickshaw, he would cover his face with a handkerchief. He did however stay in touch with a few loyal friends – the Anglican Bishop, Dr Norris, his publisher Henri Vetch and Mrs Danby – who always referred to him as 'the Professor'. In 1935, Sir Alexander Cadogan recorded a rare visit Backhouse made to the British Embassy:

> Backhouse came to lunch! He hasn't been out for years. Woodruff dug him out for us. He was very nervous but very agreeable and would be very interesting if one had time to draw him out. He told us he had seen Ch'ien Lung! Explanation was that he had visited the tomb just after they had been sacked and the coffins broken open and there they all were, Ch'ien Lung, the Empress Dowager and all![7]

Given Backhouse's reputation, his fellow evacuees were astonished to find him so gregarious. The Backhouse they came to know was a charming old man whose rich fund of stories was a welcome distraction from their current plight. His only ambition, so he told them, was to end his days at a secluded temple in the Western Hills. Little did they know that, with Dr Hoeppli's encouragement, this gentle scholar was on the point of writing a memoir so scurrilous and outrageous that it was to remain unpublished until 2011.[8]

In the meantime, while most enemy aliens tried to adjust to life under their new masters, others determined on escape. Having long been convinced that war between America and Japan was inevitable, Carel Brondgeest, a Dutch engineer in charge of the legation quarter's electrical plant, had been planning his getaway for months.

> I considered all possibilities and routes of escape very carefully. It was soon apparent that my only chance lay in a long trek overland to Free China. Once I had made up my mind, I lost no time in making all possible preparations while I was still free.[9]

He was not alone. Michael Lindsay, a British teacher at Yenching University, and his young Chinese bride, Hsiao Li, had for many weeks been smuggling radio parts out to Chinese guerrillas operating in the hills near Peking. At a meeting held three days before Pearl Harbour, Yenching's president, Dr Leighton Stuart, urged his younger foreign staff to escape. But it was not a decision to be taken lightly, for however unpalatable the prospect of internment under the Japanese, life as a fugitive in the Western Hills in the depths of a North China winter was not an easy option. A couple of young women, accustomed only to wearing high heels, worried that they might not be able

to walk far in flat shoes. Hsaio Li told them to start practising. The Lindsays decided to leave on 10 December, allowing time for Michael to keep an
appointment with his dentist. But when they heard the news on the morning
of 8 December, toothache was forgotten as they seized their rucksacks and
revolvers and fled. It was not until after the war that they learned the Japanese
had arrived ten minutes later to arrest them.

Unlike the Lindsays (who at Yenching University were already outside
the city walls) Brondgeest's first challenge was to get through one of Peking's
heavily guarded gates. Anticipating the problem, he had left a rucksack with
a farmer 20 miles south of Peking, packed with the bare essentials. A friend
from a neutral country had agreed to drive him out of the city when the
time came.

> The 31 January arrived with a brilliant sky, a cold clear Peking day. The ground
> was hard and dry with frost. In the course of the morning, I asked Mr Yamamoto
> casually for a few hours' leave in the evening, and this to my relief and joy he
> unhesitatingly granted. I changed my suit for more practical clothes for the jour-
> ney ahead – heavy flannel shirt, woollen sweater, fur-lined jacket and cap, leather
> gauntlets, and a pair of American army boots. Fortunately the Chinese guards
> rarely took their duties very seriously when their Japanese masters were out of
> sight and so my friend had little trouble in persuading them to let us through
> the gates. We raced at top speed to the place where I had arranged to meet René
> d'Anjou, some eight miles distant. He was waiting there all right and…so we
> started on our long trek to Chunking – about 1,000 miles as the crow flies. But
> we were not birds and it took us eight months to cover over two thousand miles.[10]

After extraordinary adventures (including their daughter's birth in a remote
mountain village in the middle of a Japanese offensive and their son's in a cave),
the Lindsays also made it to safety. In May 1944 they arrived in Yenan, the
Communist headquarters, where they were to remain until the end of the war.[11]

But escape was only for the hardy few. And, as had happened so often before
in Peking, once the immediate crisis receded, life went on much as usual. Lack
of ready cash was the biggest problem forcing many foreigners to sell their valu-
ables and curios. But despite having to replace their gin with vodka and reduce
five course meals to three, most of them survived 1942 reasonably well while
those in real need received American and British government loans through a
welfare committee. While it was true that life for enemy aliens had lost much
of its lustre, it would still have been perfectly tolerable had it not been for

the nagging worry of internment. As rumours of its imminent approach grew stronger, some pinned their hopes on repatriation. Miss Bowden-Smith, the admiral's daughter, who had arrived in Peking 30 years earlier on the eve of revolution, was among the lucky few to be evacuated with Allied diplomats in the summer of 1942. She nevertheless departed with great sadness, having fully expected to spend the rest of her life in Peking. Her friend Dr Margaret Phillips, who had over the years so often been part of the crowd on the streets of Peking, watching history unfold, was also offered repatriation but turned it down. She had lived in the city 25 years and had nowhere else to go. She decided to stay and take her chances.

***

The long expected blow fell in a letter sent out by the Japanese to all enemy aliens. Bertram and Hilda Hale received theirs on 13 March 1943:

Notice

You are herby notified that for reasons of military necessity the Japanese authorities have decided to transfer all enemy nationals residing in Peking to the Civilian Assembly Centre at Weihsien, Shantung. Accordingly you (and members of your family) are requested to make all necessary preparations in conformance with the following:

A. Assembly
    1. Place of assembly – Former American Embassy Compound.
    2. Date and time – March 25th 1943 at 1.00 o'clock pm.
    3. Each individual is requested to bring his own supper.

B. Articles which may be taken to the Civilian Assembly Centre
    1. Beds and bedding.
    2. Clothing.
    3. Articles of daily necessity and personal effects, excluding cameras, field glasses, microscopes, radios, maps or charts.
    4. Articles for sport and amusement, several books, garden implements and stocked provisions if desired.
    5. Tableware (knives, forks, spoons, dishes, table-linen and the like).
    6. For every hundred persons, one typewriter, sewing machine, phonograph and card-table will be allowed.[12]

The reference to 'table-linen' was comforting since it seemed hardly likely that they would need napkins in a concentration camp. Another document reassuringly described Weihsien (a small town 300 miles south of Peking in the middle of Shantung) as a place where 'every comfort of Western culture will be yours'.[13] Not all enemy aliens were on the list. Because of his age and poor health, Backhouse (having refused repatriation) was allowed to remain in the legation quarter under the care of Dr Hoeppli. Nor was the Talati family included – an omission that paradoxically caused them great distress. 'We felt that we were being singled out as not being true Brits and it made us feel very vulnerable,' Katy explained: 'Our friends congratulated us on our good luck, but we protested at being left behind. Everyone was astonished that we chose to go.'[14] It was a decision they soon came to regret.

On the appointed day, an assorted crowd of 300 or so foreigners gathered in the American compound. Among them were missionaries, nuns, doctors from the PUMC and Yenching teachers – as well as a large group of bearded and hooded monks. Bertram Hale also spotted a couple of Thomas Cook tourists, utterly bewildered by this unexpected extension to their holiday. The foreigners, ranging in age from six months to 85 years, came in all shapes and sizes and from every sort of background. The only thing they had in common (besides too many possessions), wrote Langdon Gilkey, a young American teacher from Yenching, was '...a queer combination of excitement and apprehension. Were we bound for a camping vacation [one man had brought along his golf clubs] or the torturer's rack?'[15] Their first challenge, recorded Katy Talati, was the mile-long walk to the station.

> The Chinese were made to line the streets on the way to witness our humiliation. The Japanese barked their orders and we had to pick up our belongings and start walking. Many of the people in this procession had never carried baggage before, let alone walked any distance with it. We had travelled by rickshaw or cars and there were always more porters than one needed, eager to earn a few coppers by handling anything that need to be carried. Now we had this new and horrible experience of carrying, dragging, pulling our possessions along while being marched under guard.[16]

The foreigners – as the Japanese intended – made an absurd spectacle, leading Gilkey to believe that it was on 'that burdened crawl to the station that the era of Western dominance in Asia ended'.[17] The long, overcrowded train journey to Weihsien with no food, locked lavatories and two changes did little to revive the foreigners' spirits. For those with small children it was a particular nightmare causing Hilda Hale a rush of gratitude to her servants for having thought to pack both picnic and potty.

The camp where they were to spend the next two and a half years was a former Protestant mission compound named 'Courtyard of the Happy Way'. Drab beyond words, it was damp, cold, unfurnished and ankle-deep in rubbish. If this was not bad enough, the British businessman who greeted them had even more shocking news. No Chinese were allowed in the camp. 'No *Chinese*?' wrote Gilkey in *Shantung Compound*, his gripping account of Weihsien. 'Who would cook the food and feed the fires necessary for life and warmth? I could *feel* the familiar comforts of being provided with heat, food, warm water, and clean clothes peeling off – and a quite new life beginning.'[18] Yet although conditions were unquestionably tough at Weihsien, it was relatively humane compared with other camps. Certainly the guards could be cruel but they never tortured or killed any of the several thousand internees brought there from all over North China, while some went out of their way to be friendly. From the start the Japanese authorities handed over the running of the camp to the internees, instructing them to form nine committees: General Affairs, Discipline, Labour, Education, Supplies, Quarters, Medicine, Engineering and Finance. No women, it seems, were appointed to any of the committees although roughly half the camp's population was female. A top priority was to clean up the latrines: 'When I pushed the rickety door open just a fraction of an inch,' wrote Katy Talati, 'the stench hit me. There were several holes in the ground, heaped high with ordure, and no means of flushing anything away. It was a moment of heart stopping despair and degradation.' With nearly a century of foreign privilege now buried under a sea of excrement, it was also one of high symbolism.

But within a few weeks the camp had been cleaned up, kitchens organised, the wrecked hospital made operational and quarters given some semblance of home. Schools were set up for the 300-odd children and regular entertainments put on in the church, while additional provisions (such as eggs and jam) were supplied by a flourishing black market. 'This poorly prepared and, indeed, almost desperate group,' wrote Gilkey, 'had transformed itself into a coherent civilization, able to cope with its basic material problems and day by day to raise the level of its life on all fronts.'[19] For Gilkey, who was later to become a distinguished liberal theologian, Weihsien proved a decisive experience, providing him with an ideal laboratory in which to study human nature.

And, as a member of the housing committee, he soon came up against one of its most basic drivers – territory. It rapidly became clear that neither rational argument nor moral persuasion would have the slightest effect on Weihsien's inmates when self-interest was at stake – least of all the missionaries. 'Nothing indicates so clearly the fixed belief in the innate goodness of humans,' Gilkey later wrote, 'as does the confidence that when the chips are down, and we are revealed for what we "really are," we will all be good to each other. Nothing could be so totally in error.'[20] Yet, as he was the first to acknowledge, there was also much to praise. 'We were determined to remain cheerful and show that we could take it,' Katy Talati recalled. 'There was a general atmosphere of camaraderie and people put their hearts and energy into making the best of a bad situation.'

One inmate who did more than most to raise morale was Helen Burton. To everyone's delight, she appeared at roll call on 4 July 1943 draped from head to foot in the Stars and Stripes. On the same day she opened an exchange shop in a disused hut – the 'White Elephant Bell',

> Oh the Elephant Bell, the Elephant Bell
> Just think of the tales its chimes could tell
> Of hearts made lighter and hearts made gay
> By living and giving the getting way.
> On the Rivers of Trade you cast your bread
> Only to find you get cake instead
> Those narrow shoes that gave you pain
> Are just the thing for Mary Jane
>
> You scorn the brush, the comb, the file
> That would make some other trader smile
> The cot you can't find a place to keep
> Would give another his first good sleep.
> Oh the Elephant Bell, the Elephant Bell
> With its gay little song of buy and sell.[21]

The shop was a triumph, its knitted woollen caps, overalls and lavatory paper providing every bit as much pleasure for its customers as had the Camel Bell's jades and silks in former days. Shortly after it opened a fur coat was exchanged for a pot of jam, illustrating just how radically and rapidly values had altered. But Helen Burton's internment soon ended when, along with several hundred

other Americans, she was repatriated in September 1943. She settled in Honolulu, never to return to China and never again to see her adopted Chinese
daughters.

Another group also left Weihsien after only six months, but for a very
different reason. A number of the Peking monks had teamed up with the
daughters of fundamentalist missionaries. Innocent though these friendships
were, they caused both the Catholic hierarchy and the girls' anti-papist fathers
far greater anguish than any heathen aggressor. The papal legate in Tokyo
was instructed to request the Japanese government to re-classify the monks
as neutral citizens of the Vatican rather than enemy aliens. As a result, and to
everyone's deep regret (not least the young men themselves), they were sent
back to Peking to resume their monastic life.

On their return there, the monks no doubt received a warm welcome from
Teilhard de Chardin, now living at the French legation where he had set up
an Institute of Geobiology. There he managed to work and publish (thanks
to Vetch) much of the material he had accumulated during his long years in
China.[22] But even this absorbing occupation did little to raise Teilhard's spirits.
Writing to Lucile Swan (who had left Peking just before Pearl Harbour) he
hints at the drabness of his life:

> Socially speaking, Peking is almost completely deflated. As you probably know
> the national enemies have been concentrated in Weihsien and as a result of this
> emigration, the circle of friends has become so narrow! Houghton, Leighton
> Stuart and Bowen are still kept 'au secret' in a house, in town. They are well
> but nobody can see them – even Hoeppli – who has become one of the most
> popular figures in Peking since becoming Swiss consul for Anglo-American
> interests.[23]

Kept under strict house arrest for the duration of the war, Dr Houghton,
president of the PUMC, Trevor Bowen, its chief administrator, and Dr
Leighton Stuart spent much of their time playing badminton and anagrams,
their hardships, as Leighton Stuart later recorded, being 'limited to loneliness,
monotony and haunting suspense',[24] Bowen suffered more than the others as
he was for a time imprisoned in a cage by the Japanese while they attempted to
extract from him the whereabouts of Peking Man. Bowen had no idea where
the Choukoutien fossils were but nor did anyone else. The intention had been
to send them to America with the legation marine guard then awaiting repatriation.[25] But although it seems likely that the fossils reached the coast, they

subsequently vanished without trace. Exhaustive efforts to find them after the war came to nothing and, despite many imaginative theories, the mystery has never been solved. However not all was lost. Perfect casts of the fossils survived intact, together with Lucile Swan's reconstruction bust of Peking Man. At the time though, news of their disappearance can only have added to Teilhard de Chardin's gloom.

While Teilhard was editing such worthy publications as *The Chinese Neolithic, Geology of the Western Hills* and *The Granitization of China*, Edmund Backhouse (living nearby at a German boarding house in the former Austrian legation) was absorbed in a literary project of a very different nature. By May 1943 he had completed the first volume of his memoirs – *Décadence Mandchoue* – commissioned by his regular companion and protector, Dr Hoeppli. The Swiss consul greatly treasured his friendship with Backhouse, because, as he explained in a postscript to the memoirs:

> Sir Edmund, having moved for many years in a vanished world, brilliant in art and literature, and at an extraordinary oriental court, could in his conversation bring it all back so vividly that the historical persons whom he had once met seemed alive and spoke through him.[26]

Hoeppli, seduced like so many others before him by Backhouse's charm and plausibility, was so convinced that his remarkable story should be preserved for posterity that he offered to pay Backhouse to write his autobiography.

From the obsessively pornographic account that emerged (a second volume, entitled *The Dead Past*, chronicled Backhouse's pre-China years) few would guess that Backhouse had only a couple of months earlier converted to Roman Catholicism. For, in Hoeppli's words, the memoir exposes him as 'a person who, notwithstanding age and ailments, still harboured a strong sexuality and who, after some external inhibitions had been overcome, revealed with lascivious pleasure the erotic part of his personality'.[27] And this was to put it mildly. Expanding on his no-doubt authentic experiences in Peking's homosexual bordellos such as 'The Hall of Chaste Joys', Backhouse allowed a lifetime of sexual fantasies to run wild. The long list of celebrated contemporaries he claimed to have bedded included Lord Rosebery, Paul Verlaine and, most conspicuously, the Empress Dowager – the last no less than a couple of hundred times. As with his former fabrications, Backhouse supplied such a wealth of circumstantial detail that even the solidly reliable Dr Hoeppli was convinced that this pornographic extravaganza was essentially true. Backhouse, who spent his last months being cared for by nuns at St Michael's hospital in the legation quarter, died on 8 January 1944. After Hoeppli's own death 30 years later, Backhouse's manuscript was handed to Professor Trevor-Roper and is now in Oxford University's Bodleian Library.

***

In Weihsien, meanwhile, conditions were deteriorating. By the summer of 1944 not only were far fewer rations entering the camp but by the time food reached the kitchens much of it had already rotted in the heat. Constantly hungry, in poor health and with no immediate hope of release, the internees began to lose heart. Nor was their mood improved by the discovery that children as young as 12 and 13 had been conducting regular sex orgies in a basement of one of the buildings. It was Eric Liddell, the 1924 Olympic gold medallist, who in the wake of this scandal did more than anyone to retrieve the situation. He threw himself into organising track events for the teenagers, Scottish dancing, one-act plays and puppet shows, as well as teaching them chess and science. 'It is rare indeed when a person has the good fortune to meet a saint,' wrote Langdon Gilkey, 'but he came as close to it as anyone I have ever known.'[28] When Liddell died from a brain tumour on 21 February 1945, the entire camp – especially its teenagers – was bereft.

Three months later, on 8 May 1945, the European war ended. Although a great boost to morale, the Allied victory brought no immediate relief to Weihsien. On the contrary, it so incensed the Japanese commandant that he made them stand outside all night, 'both for the victory and for knowing about it', recorded Katy Talati. With no end to their ordeal in sight, the 1,500 internees (of whom around 1,000 were British) had little choice but to struggle on with the daily grind of keeping themselves alive. To make matters worse it was an even hotter summer than usual. Then, on 17 August, the miracle happened. The drone of an aeroplane became plainly audible – 'quite different from the chug-chug-chug of a Japanese plane', noted Katy Talati. As they all rushed out on to the baseball field a huge plane roared overhead just above the treetops, its US markings plainly visible. Gilkey described the scene:

> At this point the excitement was too great for any of us to contain. It surged up within us, a flood of joyful feeling, sweeping aside all our restraints and making us its captives... proper middle-aged Englishmen and women were cheering

or swearing. Others were laughing hysterically, or crying like babies. All were moved to an ecstasy of feeling that carried them quite out of their normal selves as the great plane banked and circled over the camp three times... Then a sharp gasp went up as fifteen hundred people stared in stark wonder... the plane's underside suddenly opened. Out of it, wonder of wonders, floated seven men in parachutes! This was the height of the incredible! Not only were they coming here some day, they were here *today*.

The 'Duck Mission', as the rescue team was officially named, consisted of only seven men who parachuted from the plane at the dangerously low height of 435 feet, landing in a field of maize about a mile from the camp. 'Then the explosion occurred,' wrote Gilkey.

> Every last one of us started as with one mind toward the gate. Without pausing even a second to consider the danger involved, we poured like some gushing human torrent down the short road. This avalanche hit the great front gate, burst it open, and streamed past the guards.[29]

The internees carried their rescuers shoulder high back to the camp where in a moment of high tension the Japanese guards briefly raised their rifles before lowering them again as common sense prevailed. Shortly afterwards the camp commandant surrendered to American authority as a band struck up with 'Happy Days Are Here Again'. There followed an orgy of food and freedom as over the next few days people enjoyed picnics by the river, countryside walks and excursions to the nearby town. But it was not long before the first exhilaration of freedom began to evaporate. 'After all our hardships,' wrote Katy Talati, 'it hardly seemed possible that we could grow used to our newfound comforts but the novelty soon wore off and the only thing we now longed for was to return to our former lives.'[30]

17
END GAME

Now that the war was over, most foreigners took it for granted that things would soon return to normal. Those who had lived in Peking were particularly optimistic since, despite eight years of Japanese occupation, the city had escaped the destruction inflicted on so many others. Yet again Peking had weathered the storm and few doubted that once the post-war confusion had cleared, it would swiftly regain its former charm. Old China hands looked forward to resuming life at the club – tennis, tiffin and cocktails on the veranda.

For those left at Weihsien it was therefore particularly frustrating to find themselves still there weeks after liberation, and with no immediate hope of evacuation. The main problem was transport. Soon after Japan's defeat, skirmishes between the Nationalists and Communists added to the disruption of the railways which were in any case quite unable to cope with the post-war demand. 'Our disappointment at not being able to pick up our former lives in a civilized world cast a terrible gloom over the camp,' wrote Hilda Hale. 'Food we had. Freedom we had not.' But morale sank even lower when in mid-September a British colonel flew into Weihsien from Chungking, China's wartime capital. Addressing 1,000 fellow countrymen, he told them that their colonial life in China was over. Their houses, shops and warehouses had all been wrecked and looted and there would be no compensation. The Treaty Port system was finished. Foreigners were no longer welcome and protection of their former residential areas was no longer possible. Extraterritoriality had ended.[1] Any foreigner choosing to live in China must now do so under Chinese law. The colonel wound up with a word of advice: 'Go home or find jobs in other parts of the British Empire such as Australia, Canada or New Zealand.' 'Listening to him,' wrote Hilda Hale, 'we found it hard to believe the war was over and we were the victors.'[2]

Despite the colonel's bleak message many internees still chose to return to Peking. Although they no longer expected to regain their old life, they did hope to salvage some property. However, it was not until mid-October that the Americans were finally able to airlift the last of them to Peking and Tientsin. For Katy Talati, seated in the cockpit with the young pilots, it was a thrilling ride. Flying low over Peking, she had a perfect view of its great landmarks – the Temple of Heaven, the Forbidden City, the Bell and Drum Towers, the Tartar city wall and Coal Hill. From the sky all looked reassuringly normal, although once on the ground she noticed a number of changes. Cars with charcoal burners strapped to the back (a Japanese invention to counter petrol shortages) were among the odder sights. A more attractive legacy was the quantities of silk kimonos to be seen on sale everywhere, a reminder that it was now the Japanese who were desperate for money although financial chaos and rampant inflation meant that ready cash was a problem for everyone. But the most noticeable change to strike the returning internees was the huge influx of American personnel, both civilian and military.

One American army officer knew Peking better than most. A couple of days after the formal Japanese surrender in Nanking on 9 September 1945, Major Laurence Sickman flew into Peking on a B25. His official mission was to take possession of Japanese intelligence documents, but when an unexpected opportunity arose to buy some important Ming paintings, it proved irresistible. Borrowing from the 250,000 dollars stashed away in a suitcase belonging to the Quartermaster Corps, he secured yet more masterpieces for the Nelson-Atkins Museum. On the return flight to Chungking these were stowed in the plane's bomb bay along with dozens of samurai swords.[3] After a spell at General Macarthur's headquarters in Tokyo, advising in the arts and monuments section, Sickman returned to Kansas where, appropriately enough, he was appointed in 1953, director of the Nelson-Atkins Museum.

When Lieutenant Walter J.P. Curley Junior (later US ambassador to France and Ireland) arrived in China in September 1945, he was astonished to find the Marine Corps relying heavily on Japanese soldiers. 'We still have a couple of battalions of Japs who are, in truth, part and parcel of our III Amphibious

Corps,' he wrote to his parents, 'they are guarding rail-lines, warehouses and outposts for us. They are excellent soldiers – at least they are 1000% better than the Chinese.' As ADC to General Worton of the US Marines, he soon came to realise that such anomalies were commonplace in post-Hiroshima China: 'North China is a firecracker,' he wrote home, 'there are a lot of sparks flying around from the Communists, the bandits, the Marines, the Japanese, the puppet troops etc. It just depends on what sparks will strike the fuse.'[4]

Three months later, General George C. Marshall arrived in China hoping to sort out the mess. Although he spent most of his time in Chungking and Nanking, the executive headquarters of the tripartite peace commission (Americans, Nationalists and Communists) was established in Peking at the PUMC. But with neither of the warring factions prepared to compromise on any of the fundamental issues, let alone give up any territory seized after the Japanese surrender, it was a hopeless task. Marshall relieved his frustration by watching a movie every night and eating ice cream: 'How he does like his ice cream,' wrote one of his aides, 'my admiration for him is tempered only by a wish that he would stop trying to make me smoke less. Just because he stopped….'[5]

For young Curley, meanwhile, it was not all work. 'China is absolutely fabulous!' he wrote home, 'it is not at all surprising to have a running gun fight in the afternoon and attend a formal official dinner at night – dining from gold plates, drinking champagne and vodka, and eating Peking duck – served by liveried Chinese servants.'[6] After months of fighting in the Pacific, girls were a high priority:

> Tonight General Rockey's aide and I are going out with Gisela and the ex-German Ambassador to Japan's daughter, Ullie Ott. We're going into the Mongol City for some Mongolian chow. (We can't be seen in the more public but less interesting places with Germans, so we go to these far more intriguing places.) Germans or not, fraternization or not, these two girls are as attractive, refined, and good-humoured as any I have ever met.[7]

He was also very taken with Madame Chiang Kai-shek – admiring her perfect English almost as much as her perfect figure. He met her in December 1945 at the time when the Generalissimo was making his first visit to Peking in 11 years. 'I must hand it to him,' Curley noted, 'because this place up here is really bristling with Communists who are out for his (and our) neck.' Accompanying General Worton to a 'picnic' arranged by Madame Chiang, the 23-year-old Marine officer had one of the 'grandest experiences' of his life:

"We went to the Forbidden City which had been emptied of visitors so we had the whole place to ourselves...After three hours of visiting the various parts, we retired to one of the heretofore unopened Emperor's chambers where the Madame had arranged a fabulous luncheon for us. We were waited on by all the retainers that she had brought from Chungking. She insisted that she take the 'young fellows' in tow and that Al Gorman and I be her luncheon partners. She said she was sick of talking business, so we would just be crazy together down at the other end of the table."[8]

But despite such memorable occasions, by the beginning of 1946, Walter Curley, in common with everyone else in uniform, just longed to go home:

At first it was downright interesting – but now it is thoroughly peeving, maddening and dangerous. *Every* Marine in China is fed up. The important and most farcical circumstance of all is our actual presence here in China, and the way our mission is being accomplished. In a strict military sense we are doing a good, thorough job of disarming the Japs and repatriating them. But our government officials out here and the policies they are carrying out are stupid and incomprehensible...All the foreigners here (French, British etc.) are amazed and disappointed at the way our government is facing some of the problems. There is terrific feeling growing against the Russians; everybody is afraid of them. Russian soldiers in civilian clothes are filtering into Peking and Tientsin by the hundreds.[9]

Lieutenant Curley left China in March 1946, the same month as did Hilda Hale and her family. The Hales had soon realised that the colonel was right – their life in China was over. So after retrieving a few possessions (hidden by their Chinese neighbours behind a false wall) and selling their house (from where at night the civil war was only too audible) they made plans to move to Hong Kong. Bertram went on ahead leaving Hilda to pack up and, as it turned out, to become involved in the strangest party ever to take place at the Peking Club. In mid-December 1945 Mao Tse-tung allegedly made a brief clandestine visit to Peking. Two British secret service agents, on a mission to establish contact with the Communists, came up with the idea of introducing him to the Weihsien internees. According to Hilda, one of the agents, Rex Hardinge (author of several 'Sexton Blake' stories), asked her to help host the party:

It was a very cold, wet night when we assembled at the club. Mao was accompanied by five other officials and his first wife. I was amazed how much alike he and his wife looked – the same heavy build, round face, and wide smile.

I was also impressed by their plump hands and gentle handshakes. The whole party was dressed alike in blue cotton uniforms and the famous Mao caps that became a Communist trademark. Mao met each of the internees and asked about their treatment in camp. I told him that no one had been physically abused, but we had all been humiliated under conditions we were not used to and that food had been scarce. So that was our meeting with Mao. It was very brief – hardly worth the effort – but it did happen.[10]

By the time Teilhard de Chardin sailed for France in April 1946,[11] the steady stream of departing foreigners had turned into a flood. Nevertheless, at the beginning of the following year, a hard core of Westerners remained. With no end to the civil war in sight, they could not have been much cheered to learn that General Marshall was also packing up. He left China on 8 January 1947, the same day Melby wrote in his diary:

Marshall's farewell 'a plague on all your houses' statement has the Chinese vacillating between stunned silence and anguished screams. The dismay is compounded by the announcement he is to be Secretary of State, which leaves them with no illusions as to what they can expect from the United States at this time. It was typical of him that he took off almost unnoticed and that his new job was kept completely secret until he was in the air and beyond reach of supplication.[12]

With the exit of the Peace Commission in the spring of 1947, the PUMC was at last free to revert to its proper function although there too life was to be very different. A week after General Marshall's departure, the Rockefeller Foundation severed its support of the PUMC with a final cheque of ten million dollars. Since 1915 the Foundation had poured 45 million dollars into the medical college – the largest grant it had ever given a single project: 'Insofar as the Foundation is concerned, it completes the task undertaken in 1915, when the creation of a modern medical school in China was agreed upon…The Rockefeller Foundation can do no more.'[13] Significantly, when the PUMC reopened its doors to 22 medical students in October 1947, apart from three foreigners (Reinhold Hoeppli among them) the faculty was now entirely Chinese.

By the summer of 1948, the foreign community had dwindled dramatically. Even diehards like Dr Margaret Phillips and the Talati family realised that it was time to go: 'There were all kinds of farewell parties for us.' Katy recorded, 'and it was said that if the Talatis were leaving Peking it must surely be the end'.

Having lived so long in China it was hard to choose where to settle but they eventually decided on Britain despite having never even visited it. 'What a shock to see the docks piled high with huge quantities of rubbish,' wrote Katy when they arrived at Tilbury in September, 'and what a come down from our imagined views of England.'[14]

***

Apart from the diplomats and missionaries who had little option but to stay at their posts, those foreigners still in Peking now consisted mainly of Russian émigrés and individuals either too old or too poor to contemplate moving. Their plight was pathetic, noted the American sinologist Derk Bodde in his book *Peking Diary: A Year of Revolution*, 'now they have almost nothing and before them lies the prospect of even less'.[15] Bucking the trend, Bodde had arrived in Peking with his Russian wife and small son on 22 August 1948. Among the first Fulbright scholars, he joined a small group of Western teachers and academics who had made a firm decision to stay – come what may.

Prominent among them was the British poet William Empson, regarded as one of the most brilliant literary critics of the twentieth century. Having lived briefly in Peking at the time of the Japanese invasion in 1937, he had returned a decade later with his wife Hetta and two young sons to take up a teaching post at Peking University. In common with other foreign teachers scattered throughout Peking's various colleges, he had great sympathy for his students whose lives were made a misery by the Nationalist authorities. Their dreadful living conditions and anxiety over the civil war were hardly conducive to study, but despite this Empson cut them no slack. I.A. Richards's *Philosophy of Rhetoric* and A.C. Bradley's *Hegel's Theory of Tragedy* were among the texts he expected them to read. However, by the end of the 1948 summer term, even he decided that since his students had shown so little interest in metaphysical or modern poetry, he would drop John Donne and T.S. Eliot from the syllabus. In addition to his normal classes, Empson bicycled out each week to Tsinghua University (about seven miles west of Peking), sometimes braving freezing weather, gunfire or the secret police, to deliver a lecture on Shakespeare, noting that even the appallingly difficult language of the major Shakespeare plays did little to deter his students.[16]

Although the Bohemian Empsons (theirs was a very open marriage) and their circle made a striking contrast to Peking's former diplomatic set, they did share one tradition – a love of fancy-dress parties. And despite all the practical difficulties now confronting the foreigners, 1948 was 'a semi-gilded time with gaiety running high before the gathering storm', according to the wife of one academic.[17] Hetta Empson, admired for her 'statuesque looks and flamboyant gregariousness', was the inspiration behind many of the exotic parties indulged in by the small band of Westerners in those last months of the old China. Moreover, that summer (just four months before the Communist troops entered the city) the British Council heralded its new cultural centre and library with a series of events culminating in Hetta's production of *An Inspector Calls*.[18] By then the daily struggle with hyperinflation was a major part of everyone's existence, its absurd consequences becoming all too plain to Empson when he tried to buy an airline ticket to America:

> One could not give a cheque for the ticket, because that would take a day to pass
> through the bank, and then be worth much less. We carried to the airline office
> a military duffle-bag full of the highest denomination of paper money, and four
> men counted it all day; towards the fall of eve, with patient triumph, they said:
> 'You're two million short', but I was just in time to get this extra sop out of the
> bank, and the ticket was won.[19]

While the foreigners distracted themselves with plays and parties, increasing numbers of students, harried and beaten up by the Nationalists, abandoned their studies to join the Reds. Furthermore, by the time the Communist forces, re-named the People's Liberation Army (PLA), had taken Manchuria in November 1948, disenchantment with Chiang Kai-shek was so widespread that most of Peking now regarded Mao as the lesser of two evils. 'Peiping was not a city of heroes', reported *Life* magazine,

> ... the people expected the Communists would take the city and they preferred
> that to seeing it damaged by battle. They were not especially craven, everywhere
> the desire for peace was doing as much as the Communists to destroy Chiang
> Kai-shek's China.[20]

Meanwhile, something approaching hysteria was gripping the Americans, noted Derk Bodde in his diary on 4 November. The US Consulate had the previous day issued a circular urging its nationals, in view of the worsening military situation, to consider evacuation while transport was still available. And at a party held three days later at the Soviet Consulate, at which most of 'Peking' was present, there was only one topic of conversation – whether or not to leave. The purpose of the reception was to celebrate the 31st anniversary of the Bolshevik revolution, but with the Consul General, Sergei Tikhvinskii, resplendent in his blue diplomatic uniform, the flowing cocktails and string orchestra struggling to be heard above the hubbub, it was for some guests a poignant reminder of former legation parties, and of a world now on the brink of extinction.

Acutely aware that the old order was about to perish, *Life* flew in Henri Cartier Bresson to photograph its last moments. He arrived on 4 December 1948, when, so the magazine reported, 'ice was decking the lakes which mirror the gold roofs of the old Ming palaces and Communist armies were driving Peiping's defenders behind the city's high gray walls'. Many of his photographs capture the serenity that Peking so often displayed at times of crisis. Even as the Communists encircled their city, Peking's citizens were photographed practising tai chi, skating, browsing through bookstalls or airing their pet birds.[21]

On the day Cartier Bresson arrived in Peking, Mary Ferguson (registrar at the PUMC since 1928) cabled New York, 'All quiet here.'[22] But the illusion was shattered when on 13 December heavy firing was heard west of the city and the gates were closed. The siege of Peking had begun and was to last six weeks. The following day Cartier Bresson just managed to board one of the last scheduled flights while the Lutherans began operating 'St Paul', an aeroplane intended only for the evacuation of their own missionaries but which was soon overflowing with Chinese and Westerners alike – all frantic to escape. With the telephones still working, 'wild rumours raced each other across the city', recalled Ralph Lapwood, a missionary at Yenching university, ' "Chiang Kai-shek is going to resign," "Madame Sun Yat-sen is in Peking," "American soldiers are landing to protect Tientsin," "Fu Tso-yi [the Mayor of Peking] has surrendered." '[23] His boss, the acting president of Yenching, warned his staff to expect conflicts between 'Marxist ways and the dictates of Christian conscience', but optimistically believed that if they all cooperated with the new regime these could be peacefully resolved.[24]

Meanwhile at the airfield to the south of Peking, people were fighting their way on to aeroplanes even as the Communists began shelling the runway. Bodde noted how

Many important personages were on the field at the time, ready to be evacuated. Some jumped into the planes which immediately roared off, but others ran for cover. The baggage, which they left strewn over the ground, was promptly looted by the soldiers on guard. Family members became separated during the excitement, some succeeding in boarding the planes but others (including one small baby) being left behind on the ground.[25]

Inside the city, efforts were already underway to complete two new airstrips – one on the former polo field on the glacis outside the legation quarter and another in the park surrounding the Temple of Heaven where, Bodde recorded, no fewer than 400 trees – most of them ancient cypresses – were destroyed in the process.[26] The pilots likened the crude runways to ripe Camembert because the bumpy take-offs caused so many passengers to be sick. 'First one would puke, and then they'd all puke in a chorus of vomiting,' recollected Captain Felix Smith. 'The smell of vomit in the cabin was so bad that after landing in Shanghai, we'd climb out of the cockpit window, walk back along the top of the airplane, and jump off the tail.'[27] Among those desperate to fly out was Michael Horvath whose father, the Russian émigré leader General Horvath, had died in Peking in 1937. But, as he recalled, the queues were so long it would take him a month to work his way to the front. Unable to get away, Horvath was subsequently imprisoned for more than six years before being allowed to join his family in Canada.[28] Others, like the Soviet Consul General who had been in Manchuria assisting Russian refugees, were equally desperate to fly back *into* Peking. Finally, after accepting help from the Americans, Tikhvinskii managed 'to squeeze into a two-engine transport plane, packed to overflowing with refugees, sitting or lying in a heap on the metal floor of the plane covered in flour dust'.[29]

By 22 December 1948, Yenching had already been 'liberated' but this did not prevent the college's 100-strong choir from giving a vigorous rendering of *Messiah*. Lapwood noted the striking contrast between the newly arrived People's Army, 'absolutely indigenous and drawing its strength directly from the peasants' and 'our sophisticated and westernised students singing a European oratorio in English'.[30] At the PUMC in the meantime, work carried on as normal. On Christmas Eve, as it began snowing, ten members of the 1943 class celebrated their graduation with carols round a Christmas tree.

Aside from such nostalgic moments, the foreigners' mood that Christmas was, in the words of Bodde,

> …one of dullness and boredom…The curfew, the billeting of soldiers, in almost all of Peking's parks and beauty spots, the exodus of so many friends for the South, the cessation of letters from the outside world, the scantiness of news

in our single-sheet newspapers, the lack of water and electricity, the desperate struggle for existence of so many poor people, the hectic military movement on the streets which makes one want to stay at home as much as possible and the almost complete curtailment of social activities – all these make of this once lovely city a place unrecognizably drab and dreary.[31]

Then, on 23 January 1949, he wrote:

The momentous news of the week is that the siege of Peking is now officially over. Fu Tso-yi has surrendered…in the twinkling of an eye the aspect of the city has been changed from that of impending attack to a semblance of peace.[32]

Eight days later, Tikhvinskii stood with his family and colleagues at the open gates of the Soviet Consulate:

At about noon, the People's Liberation Army triumphantly entered Peking…moved northwards along the wide main road, passed the city gates…and turned eastwards along the main street of the legation quarter. Unlike the other streets full of joyful crowds, Legation Street was deserted. Intimidated by anti-communist propaganda, the diplomats had locked their gates facing the street and blocked them from inside with trucks and cars. The soldiers moved continuously along Legation Street in orderly fashion, dressed in their brand new warm winter uniforms. Their faces weathered by the northern winds, these heroes of the victorious battles in north-east China rode on captured American jeeps armed with American carbines seized from the KMT. Artillery units manned cars pulling captured American field-guns and anti-aircraft guns on chains. Enclosed by cavalry, the procession continued for more than an hour. Our street fell quiet again but on all sides of the huge city we could hear the sounds of festive music and the joyous cries of the masses who had come out to greet their army.[33]

The formal victory parade took place in the middle of a dust storm on 3 February when again the PLA showed off the mass of American military equipment captured from the KMT. The foreigners were more impressed by the soldiers' impeccable conduct for, as Mary Ferguson noted, they commandeered nothing, paid for what they bought and were generally extraordinarily well behaved.[34] This time thousands of students and workers also took part in the parade though their paper banners and portraits of Mao were soon torn to shreds by the wind and dust. Summing up the mood, Hetta Empson cabled home: 'now great feeling general relief'.[35]

After such a dramatic build up, the Communist takeover of Peking proved something of an anti-climax. Once the gates had re-opened and services had been restored, it seemed to the foreigners that, on the surface at least, the city functioned much as before. But inevitably their own lives became more restricted as they were dogged by complicated registration procedures, threatening interviews and travel embargos. With the banning of all foreign newspapers and journalists it was difficult to find any reliable news except what could be gleaned from the radio. Another problem was the fact that although there was little sign of anti-foreign feeling among ordinary people, the authorities refused to establish any kind of dialogue with the Westerners or their consulates, thus leaving them without diplomatic representation. Not surprisingly, the Soviet Consul General received rather different treatment. On 17 July 1949 Tikhvinskii was invited to dine with Mao at his country residence:

> It was already getting dark when the car which had been sent for us arrived at the estate 20 kilometres from the city, hidden by centuries-old Cyprus and pine trees. The car made its way up a long road winding through trees, until it stopped at the gates of an old Buddhist monastery surrounded by a high, white stone wall.

Once inside the gates, he watched as Mao emerged from one of the buildings, 'tall, thick-set, slightly stooped' and slowly walked towards him across a carved stone bridge. Like Hilda Hale, Tikhvinskii particularly noted the softness of his handshake.[36]

On that hot July night, while Tikhvinskii and Mao sat discussing Sun Yat-sen, HMS *Amethyst*[37] and the fate of the Chinese bourgeoisie, less favoured foreigners were planning one last glorious party before the Communist shutters finally came down on privilege and profligacy. Organised by Hetta Empson, it took place under a full moon in a particularly fine courtyard house belonging to one of Peking's oldest families. By then the Yu clan were all too aware that it could only be a matter of time before they were forced to give up their house with its exquisite garden and see their large extended family dispersed. David Kidd, a young American who 'pre liberation' had taught at Tsinghua University, was married to a daughter of the house. In his book, *Peking Story*, he describes the occasion:

> From all parts of the city, the guests began to arrive, emerging from one pedicab after another, their costumes greatly amusing the gateman. After some thirty

or forty had come, I began to detect trends in the choice of costume. Most Europeans came as traditional Chinese – mandarin officials, empresses, or singsong girls. The younger Chinese came as Indians, in saris and turbans and the Indians (largely exchange students) came as Communists in Party 'cadre uniforms'… Aimee, in a red skirt, wearing paper roses in her hair and carrying a tambourine, was a Spanish gypsy, and there was the inevitable sprinkling of sheeted Arabs. Hetta Empson came as Schererazade, in a sort of breastplate of colored beads that caused a certain amount of controlled giggling among the younger Chinese women. Eugene Chiang wore an unbelievable pink tweed business suit and a turban made of nine yards of pink chiffon…Walter Brown, an American teacher costumed as a harem keeper, arrived with the elegant Charlotte Horstmann, born of a Chinese mandarin father and a German mother…who came as a Manchu princess in an embroidered gown and kingfisher feather crown. We expected no less.

The guests wandered through the garden sipping cocktails or danced in the Hall of Ancient Pines, 'tripping over their hems and trailing their veils in polkas, Lambeth walks, and congas'. Since the revolution the Lambeth Walk and Conga had become the most popular Western dances in Peking, as it was hoped that they looked like the kind of healthy mass-participation dances which the Communists were likely to approve. But even as one British diplomat danced with a Mongolian princess (unaware that she was actually a Mongolian prince), Communist soldiers armed with grenades and bayonets were gathering at the gate.[38]

With such outbursts of imperialist behaviour, it was perhaps not surprising that, as the year wore on, suspicion of Westerners grew. Bodde noted how the foreigners, restricted in their movements and harried by bureaucracy, became increasingly embittered. He left Peking in August 1949, but Mary Ferguson was still there the following month by which time the whole city was caught up in preparation for the formal establishment of the People's Republic of China. She noted the mounting excitement among the students at the PUMC as they received instructions through their respective unions to acquire the grey cotton uniforms they were expected to wear on the day and to be ready to take part in the parade.[39]

When the great day arrived on 1 October 1949, Tikhvinskii went to the station to meet the Soviet delegation. He recorded how he and his colleagues were surprised when,

... several soldiers appeared on the platform gently supporting the new Foreign Minister, Chou En-lai on each side, his eyes closed, white as a sheet, mechanically placing one foot in front of another as they moved towards us. His aide quietly asked us not to wake him and explained that his chief had not slept for four days and nights while he directed the founding session of the People's Political Consultation Conference almost single handed.[40]

Tikhvinskii remembered the morning as bright and sunny but Empson recalled it as being damp and grey when he and Hetta set off in pedicabs to witness the formal birth of the new China. At precisely 3 pm the official ceremony was declared open. Mao slowly raised a red standard with five stars on a tall flagpole in the centre of Tiananmen Square. Then, while massed bands played the new national anthem, the artillery fired 28 salutes symbolising, as Tikhvinskii put it, 'the 28 years of struggle for victory over reactionary forces by the Communist Party of China'.[41] Empson had expected to be bored by the ceremony, but in the event was deeply moved. 'You may believe that what is being celebrated will turn out a delusion,' he later wrote, 'but history is full of gloomy afterthoughts. Here you have celebrated a victory of revolt against tyrants, supported by the countryside alone, practically with their bare hands... if anything in history is impressive you are bound to feel that is.'[42]

David Kidd and his wife were also among the crowds hoping to see something of the historic occasion. They eventually found a perch on the roof of a former American army truck parked to the west of Tiananmen Square. In the distance they could just make out familiar landmarks of the legation quarter, the Wagons-Lits Hotel, and the American Consulate's radio tower. But on that day all eyes were turned towards the Gate of Heavenly Peace in front of the Forbidden City, where, Kidd recorded, could be seen China's new leaders, looking 'oddly stiff and mechanical, like opera singers seen from the third balcony'.[43] From there, in his curiously high-pitched tones, Chairman Mao proclaimed the establishment of the People's Republic of China. While he spoke, behind him huge scarlet flags fluttered against the rust-red of the palace walls. The Peking that the foreigners had for nearly a century both loved and looted was gone forever.

***

Old Peking has vanished, swept away by China's resurgence. And if much of the architecture of the city has changed beyond recognition, so too has that image of China once perpetuated by the expatriates who are the subject of this book and whose insensitivity and ignorance were to leave such a scar. China played its own part of course in mutual misunderstanding, and the foreigners had no crystal ball. Nevertheless (with honourable exceptions) they stand guilty of a massive failure of imagination. Had they been more astute and less incurious, keener to nurture China's self-confidence rather than undermine it, had they not lived so insistently in their own bubble and had they been, above all, less convinced of their own superiority, their legacy in China might not now be regarded with quite such contempt and China's recovery of its former prestige would surely have proved less traumatic.

ARCHIVAL SOURCES

Archives of American Art, Washington, DC

British Library, Oriental and India Office Collections

College of the Holy Cross, archives and special collections, Worcester, MA

Columbia University (Oral History Research Office, COHO), New York

Georgetown University, Washington, DC

Gloucestershire Archives, Gloucester

Harry Ransom Humanities Research Center, University of Texas at Austin

HSBC Archives, London

Hoover Institution Library and Archives, Stanford University, California

Hull University Archives, Hull History Centre

Imperial War Museum, Department of Documents, London

Indiana University Library

John Rylands University Library, University of Manchester

Joyner Library, East Carolina University, Greeneville NC

Lancashire Record Office, Preston

National Archives, Kew

National Army Museum, London

Nelson-Atkins Museum of Art Archives, Kansas City

Newcastle University Library, Northumberland

New York Public Library

Reuters Archives, London

Royal Society of Asian Affairs

Royal Asiatic Society

School of Oriental and African Studies (SOAS), University of London

Suffolk Record Office, Ipswich

Surrey Historical Society, Woking

Thomas Cook Archives, Peterborough

Thomson Reuters Archives, London

University of Chicago, Harriet Monroe Collection

University of Cambridge
    Churchill Archives Centre at Churchill College
    Newnham College archives
    The Old Library, Magdalene College
    University Library
University of Oxford
    Bodleian Library
    St Antony's College archives

NOTES

Prologue

1. Alfred Viscount Northcliffe, *My Journey Round the World*, Lord Robert Cecil and St John Harmsworth (eds.), London: John Lane, 1923, p. 145.
2. Elizabeth Kendall, *A Wayfarer in China*, Boston: Houghton Mifflin, 1913, p. 229.
3. It was common knowledge, according to a senior American doctor working in *Peking*, that for some reason, German night soil fetched the highest prices – British the lowest. Dr John Grant, *Reminiscences*, oral history, Columbia University, p. 524.
4. Berkeley Gage, *It's Been a Marvellous Party*, London: Privately printed, 1989, p. 62.
5. Gertrude Bell to her father, 27 April 1903, Gertrude Bell Archive, University of Newcastle.
6. Harold Acton, *Peonies and Ponies*, Oxford: Oxford University Press, 1983, p. 45.
7. Teilhard de Chardin to his brother, 14 January 1924, quoted in Claude Cuénot, *Teilhard de Chardin*, translated by Vincent Colimore, Baltimore: Helicon, 1965, p. 52.
8. George B. Barbour Collection, letters dated 26 March and 4 April 1926, Hoover Institution Archives, Box 1.
9. Dorothea Richards, Journal, 20 March 1930, The Old Library, Magdalene College, University of Cambridge.
10. John King Fairbank, *Chinabound*, New York: Harper & Row, 1983, p. 66.
11. Memorandum from A.W.G. Randall to Austen Chamberlain, 8 November 1926, British Library, India Office records, L/PS/11/272.
12. Quoted in Harry L. Shapiro, 'Davidson Black: An Appreciation'; B.A. Sigmon and J.S. Cybulski (eds.), *Papers in Honor of Davidson Black*, Toronto: University of Toronto Press, p. 26.
13. Quoted in Vincent Sheean, *Personal History*, London: Hamish Hamilton, 1969, p. 281. Originally published as: *In Search of History*, London: Hamish Hamilton, 1935.
14. Owen O'Malley, *The Phantom Caravan*, London: John Murray, 1954, pp. 99–100.
15. Lampson diary, 1 September 1939, St Antony's College Archives, University of Oxford.
16. John Dewey and Harriet Dewey, *Letters from China and Japan (1920)*, New York: E.P. Dutton, 1920, letter of 24 July 1919, p. 302.
17. Lampson diary, 14 February 1932.
18. Rhodes James (ed.), *Winston Churchill: His Complete Speeches 1897–1963*, vol. III (1914–22), 8 July 1920, New York: Chelsea House Publishers, 1974, p. 3011.

Chapter 1

1. Lancelot Giles, *The Siege of the Peking Legations*, Nedlands: University of Western Australia Press, 1970, p. 177.
2. Mary Hooker, *Behind the Scenes in Peking*, Oxford: Oxford University Press, 1987, p. 175.
3. Ibid., p. 176.
4. Quoted in Sir Roger Keyes, *Adventures Ashore & Afloat*, London: G.G. Harrap, 1939, p. 290; Keyes to his mother, n.d.
5. Austria-Hungary, Belgium, France, Germany, Great Britain, Italy, Japan, the Netherlands, Russia, Spain and the USA.
6. J.K. Fairbank, K.F. Bruner and E.M. Matheson (eds.), *The I.G. in Peking: Letters of Robert Hart, Chinese Maritime Customs, 1868–1907*, Letter 1171, 27 May 1900. Cambridge, MA: Harvard University Press, 1975, vol. 2.
7. Sir Robert Hart, *These from the Land of Sinim*, London: Chapman & Hall, 1901, p. 11.
8. Putnam Weale, *Indiscreet Letters from Peking*, Engelska: Dodo Press, 2005, p. 11.
9. Giles, *The Siege of the Peking Legations*, p. 72.
10. Ibid, p. 34.
11. Hooker, *Behind the Scenes in Peking*, p. 43.
12. Francis G. Poole, Diary, 20 June 1900, National Army Museum, London.
13. Quoted from Sir Claude MacDonald's account of the Boxer uprising, in Henry Keown-Boyd, *The Fists of Righteous Harmony*, London: Leo Cooper, 1991, p. 92.
14. Allen, *The Siege of the Peking Legations*, p. 108.
15. Poole, Diary, 22 June 1900.
16. Lo Hui-min (ed.), *The Correspondence of G.E. Morrison*, Cambridge, NY: CUP, 1976–78, Morrison to V. Chirol, vol. 1, p. 118, 2 March 1899.
17. Ibid., Morrison to Moberly Bell, pp. 148–50, 20 October 1900.
18. Hooker, *Behind the Scenes in Peking*, pp. 66–8.
19. Poole, Diary, 26 June 1900.
20. Weale, *Indiscreet Letters from Peking*, p. 95.
21. Allen, *The Siege of the Peking Legations*, p. 104.
22. Hooker, *Behind the Scenes in Peking*, pp. 144–5.
23. William Meyrick Hewlett, *Diary of the Siege of the Peking Legations*, published as a supplement to *The Harrovian*, November 1900, p. 65.
24. Hooker, *Behind the Scenes in Peking*, pp. 129–30.
25. G.E. Morrison, *The Times*, 13 October 1900.
26. Hooker, *Behind the Scenes in Peking*, pp. 127–8.
27. Chamot received many honours after the siege. He and his wife moved to San Francisco where he built two large houses, established a menagerie and kept a yacht. His property was destroyed in the 1906 earthquake and he died a pauper at 43, having divorced his wife.
28. W. Lord, *The Good Years*, New York: Harper, 1960, p. 27.
29. Poole, Diary, 15 July 1900.
30. Shiba was later appointed military attaché to London and was decorated by King Edward VII. He died after a suicide attempt on hearing of Emperor Hirohito's surrender in 1945.

31. Hooker, *Behind the Scenes in Peking*, pp. 134–5.
32. G. Casserly, *The Land of the Boxers*, London: Longman, 1903, p. 53.
33. Jessie Ransome, *Story of the Siege Hospital in Peking*, London: SPCK, 1901.

Chapter 2

1. Quoted in Peter Fleming, *The Siege at Peking*, London: Readers Union, 1960, p. 137.
2. Ibid.
3. Allen, *The Siege of the Peking Legations*, p. 213.
4. Ibid., p. 229.
5. Press cutting inserted into William Thomas Swift's diary, 16 July 1900, Gloucestershire Public Record Office, D3981.
6. Juliet Bredon, *Sir Robert Hart*, London: Hutchinson, 1909, p. 214.
7. Allen, *The Siege of the Peking Legations*, p. 260.
8. Quoted in Diana Preston, *The Boxer Rebellion*, London: Robinson, 2002, p. 221; S.D. Butler, *Old Gimlet Eye*, New York: Farrar and Rinehart, 1933.
9. Gwalior, Bikanir and Alsur Jung.
10. Casserly, *The Land of the Boxers*, p. 54.
11. Roger Keyes to Beatrice Jackson, 6 September 1900, quoted in Frederic A. Sharf and Peter Harrington, *The Boxer Rebellion*, London: Greenhill Books, 2000, p. 202.
12. Ibid., p. 199.
13. Lieutenant William Harllee, quoted in Lennox-Boyd, *Boxer Rebellion*, p. 167.
14. Casserly, *The Land of the Boxers*, p. 99.
15. Arnold Henry Savage Landor, *China and the Allies*, London: Heinemann, 1901, vol. 2, p. 227.
16. Sarah Pike Conger, *Letters from China*, London: Hodder & Stoughton, 1909, p. 163.
17. Arthur H. Smith, *China in Convulsion*, New York: Fleming H. Revell, 1901, vol. 2, pp. 519–20.
18. John Ker, 18 August 1900, private collection.
19. Nigel Oliphant, *A Diary of the Siege of the Legations in Peking*, London: Longmans, 1901, pp. 173–85.
20. Landor, *China and the Allies*, p. 359.
21. Ibid., pp. 359–80.
22. Quoted in Sharf and Harrington, *The Boxer Rebellion*, pp. 222–3.
23. Hooker, *Behind the Scenes in Peking*, p. 190.
24. Quoted in Cyril Pearl, *Morrison of Peking*, Sydney: Angus & Robertson, 1967, p. 131.
25. Quoted in Sharf and Harrington, *The Boxer Rebellion*, p. 225.
26. Casserly, *The Land of the Boxers*, p. 89.
27. Hooker, *Behind the Scenes in Peking*, p. 201.
28. Conger, *Letters from China*, p. 239.
29. Landor, *China and the Allies*, p. 334.
30. Pierre Loti, *Les Derniers Jours de Pékin*, Paris: Calmann Levy, 1902, reprinted in facsimile by Elibron Classics, 2006, pp. 122–3.

31. Ibid., pp. 92–3.
32. Conger, *Letters from China*, p. 194.
33. Casserley, *The Land of the Boxers*, p. 102.
34. Conger, *Letters from China*, p. 188.
35. Loti, *Les Derniers Jours de Pékin*, pp. 448–51.

Chapter 3

1. A.B Freeman-Mitford (later Lord Redesdale), *The Attaché at Peking*, London: Macmillan, 1900, p. xliv.
2. First Opium War 1839–42; Second Opium War 1856–60.
3. Nanking 1842; Tientsin 1858; Peking 1860.
4. Lord Elgin to Lord Carnarvon, 31 October 1860, private collection, London
5. Quoted in S.C.M. Paine, *Imperial Rivals*, Armonk, NY: M.E. Sharpe, *c.*1996, p. 79; *Complete Account of Barbarian Management*, vol. 19, Hsien Feng 69 ts'e 42a *yeh*.
6. Treaty of Wanghsia, 1844.
7. David Field Rennie, *Peking and the Pekingese*, London: John Murray, 1865, vol. 1, p. 32. Reprinted in facsimile by Elibron Classics 2005.
8. Ibid.
9. Ibid., p. ix.
10. Ibid., pp. 99, 174.
11. *Peking*ese dogs can be traced back as far as 2000 BC. Much favoured by Chinese emperors, they were sometimes given the title of Viceroy or styled as Imperial Guardsmen. They are often depicted on vases, screens, pottery and sculpture. Their breeding reached its height in the Tao Kuang period (1821–51).
12. See Madame de Bourboulon, *Shang-Hai à Moscou*, Paris: Hachette, 1866. Reprinted by the Long Riders' Guild Press, n.d. See: thelongridersguild.com
13. Ibid., p. 95.
14. Hart, *The I.G. in Peking*, vol. 2, Letter 874, 15 January 1893.
15. de Bourboulon, *Shang-Hai à Moscou*, p. 43.
16. See P.A. Cohen, *History in Three Keys*, New York: Columbia University Press, *c.*1997, pp. 93, 322.
17. Rennie, *Peking and the Pekingese*, vol. 1, p. 276.
18. A.E. Moule, *New China and Old*, London: Seeley, 1891, p. 309.
19. Rennie, *Peking and the Pekingese*, vol. 1, p. 216.
20. Quoted in Hart, *The I.G. in Peking*, p. 8; *The Times*, 10 January 1909.
21. Ibid.; *North China Daily News*, 21 February 1928.
22. Hart, *The I.G. in Peking*, vol. 1, Letter 705, 23 June 1889.
23. Ibid., vol. 2, Letter 981, 4 August 1895.
24. Rennie, *Peking and the Pekingese*, vol. 1, p. 264.
25. Charles Stewart Addis, memoir, n.d., HSBC archives, S016/002c.
26. Ibid.
27. Eleanor Hillier, memoir, Hillier papers, HSBC archives, London.

Chapter 4

1. Hart, *The I.G. in Peking*, vol. 2, Letter 1174, 8 September 1900.
2. Ibid., Letter 1182, 1 November 1900.
3. Ibid., Letter 1185, 26 November 1900.
4. W.J. Garnett, 19 February 1906, Lancashire Record Office, 775 DDQ 9/10/17.
5. Ibid., 20 November 1905, LRO, DDQ 9/12/12.
6. Quoted in, Peter Thompson and Robert Macklin, *The Man Who Died Twice*, Crows Nest, NSW: Allen & Unwin, 2004, p. 203.
7. Gertrude Bell, 5 May 1903, Gertrude Bell papers, Newcastle University.
8. Hart. *The I.G. in Peking*, vol. 2, Letter 1231, 12 January 1902.
9. Sarah Pike Conger, *Letters from China*, Chicago: McClurg, 1910, pp. 215–6.
10. Gertrude Bell, 27 April 1903.
11. Ibid., 21 April 1903.
12. Hart, *The I.G. in Peking*, vol. 2, Letter 1298, 27 October 1903.
13. Conger, *Letters from China,* p. 224.
14. Ibid., p. 217.
15. Ibid., p. 220.
16. Satow diaries, 20 January 1902, published by lulu.com.
17. Lady Susan Townley, *My Chinese Note-Book*, London: Methuen, 1904, pp. 271–2.
18. Ibid., p. 278.
19. Hart, *The I.G. in Peking*, vol. 2, Letter 1292, 6 September 1903.
20. Ibid., Letter 1320, 6 March, 1904.
21. Katherine Carl, *With the Empress Dowager in Peking*, London: KPI, 1986, pp. 217–8.
22. Ibid., pp. 10–1.
23. Garnett, 12 September 1906, LRO, DDQ 9/12/37.
24. Townley, *My Chinese Note-Book*, pp. 279–80.
25. Garnett, 27 May 1906, LRO, DDQ 9/12/27.
26. Quoted in Marina Warner, *The Dragon Empress*, London: Hamish Hamilton, 1972, title page.
27. Garnett, 26 February 1906, LRO, DDQ 9/12/20.
28. Ibid.
29. Ibid., 1 February 1907, LRO, DDQ 9/13/4.
30. Malcolm A. Robertson, 4 March 1907, Churchill Archives Centre, Churchill College, RBTN box 2.
31. Garnett, 26 November 1906, LRO, DDQ 9/12/44.
32. Colonel Clarence Dalrymple Bruce, Edinburgh: William Blackwood, 1907.
33. Garnett, 17 February 1908, LRO, DDQ 9/13/33.
34. Ibid., 25 December 1907, LRO, DDQ 9/13/29.
35. Ibid., 1 January 1907, LRO, DDQ 9/14/6.
36. Interview with Paula von Rosthorn's great-nephew, Thomas Pinschoff.
37. Garnett, 27 March 1907, LRO, DDQ 9/13/8.
38. Luigi Barzini, *Peking to Paris*, London: E. Grant Richards, 1907, p. 44.
39. Ibid., pp. 67–8.

40. Ibid., p. 65.
41. Hart, *The I.G. in Peking*, vol. 2, Letter 1298, 27 October 1903.
42. Robert Hart to the Duke of Manchester, 1 November 1882, Bodleian Library, Hart papers, D.320 (113).
43. Quoted in Thompson and Macklin, *The Man Who Died Twice*, p. 131.
44. W.A.P. Martin, *A Cycle of Cathay*, London: Oliphant, Anderson and Ferrier, 1896, p. 411.
45. Hart, *The I.G. in Peking*, vol. 2, Letter 1437.
46. Ibid., vol. 1, Letter 550, 21 December 1885.
47. Ibid., vol. 2, Letter 1434, 18 May 1907.
48. M.A. Robertson to Lord Cranley, 4 March 1907, Surrey History Society, G173/24/44.

Chapter 5

1. Lady Jordan to Garnett, 10 December 1908, LRO, DDQ 9/9/13.
2. Quoted in Cyril Pearl, *Morrison of Peking*, 1967, p. 189.
3. G.E. Morrison, *An Australian in China, Being the Narrative of a Quiet Journey Across China to Burma*, London: Horace Cox, 1895.
4. Lo Hui-min (ed.), *The Correspondence of G.E. Morrison*, Cambridge, NY: CUP, 1976–8, vol. 1, p. 52; 26 May 1987.
5. Bell, 5 May 1903.
6. Morrison to J.O.P. Bland, 24 April 1903, Bland Papers, University of Toronto Library.
7. Hugh Trevor-Roper, *A Hidden Life*, London: Macmillan, 1976; later re-published as *The Hermit of Peking*, Penguin, 1978.
8. Gertrude Bell to her father, 21 April 1903.
9. Hart to Smith, 18 June 1901; quoted in Smith, *China in Convulsion*, p. 596.
10. Trevor-Roper, *A Hidden Life*, p. 212.
11. Henri Borel, *The New China*, London: T.F. Unwin, 1912, pp. 150–2.
12. H. McAleavy, *A Dream of Tartary*, London: Allen & Unwin, 1963, p. 186.
13. Marshall Broomhall (ed.), *Martyred Missionaries*, London: Morgan & Scott, 1901, p. viii.
14. F.L. Norris, *China*, London: Mowbray, 1908, pp. 200–1.
15. Ibid, p. 5.
16. Lord William Gascoyne-Cecil, *Changing China*, London: James Nisbet, 1910, p. 222.
17. Broomhall, *Martyred Missionaries*, p. xii.
18. Norris, *China*, p. 202.
19. See J.G. Lutz, *China and the Christian Colleges*, Ithaca: Cornell University Press, 1971, pp. 98–9.
20. Affiliated with Yenching University in 1919.
21. Gertrude Bell to her father, 5 May 1903.
22. M.A. Robertson, 12 September 1906, Churchill Archives Centre, Churchill College, GBR/0014/RBTN, Box 2.
23. Garnett, 30 May 1907, LRO, DDQ 9/13/13.
24. Ibid., 23, 30 April 1907, LRO, DDQ 9/13/10 and DDQ 9/10/39.

25. Ibid., 30 April 1907, LRO, DDQ 9/10/39.
26. Gascoyne-Cecil, *Changing China*, p. 4.
27. For example H. Borel, *The New China*, London: T.F. Unwin, 1912; W.Y. Fullerton and C.E. Wilson, *New China*, London: Morgan Scott, 1910; E.A. Ross, *The Changing Chinese*, New York: The Century Co., 1911.
28. Count Preben F. Ahlefeldt-Laurvig, 6 October 1908, Baker-Lloyd papers, Gloucestershire Record Office, D3549.
29. D.I. Abrikosov, *Revelations of a Russian Diplomat*, Seattle: University of Washington Press, 1964, p. 163.

Chapter 6

1. Wuhan is the name given to the area covering three cities: Hankow, Wuchang and Hanyang.
2. Percy Loraine to his father, 23 November 1911; Suffolk Record Office, HA61.
3. Ahlefeldt Laurvig to G.E. Lloyd-Baker, 22 March 1911, GRO, D3549/27.
4. Paul S. Reinsch, *An American Diplomat in China*, New York: Doubleday, 1922, p. 1.
5. W.W. Yen was foreign minister (1920–22) and between 1920 and 1926 served as prime minister five times. He was appointed minister to Berlin in 1912 and was the first Chinese ambassador to the Soviet Union.
6. W.W. Yen, *East-West Kaleidoscope*, typescript copy, pp. 122–3, Hoover Institution Archives.
7. Alice Bowden-Smith, Newnham College Roll Letter, 1912, p. 39; Newnham College Archives, Cambridge.
8. Loraine, 23 November 1911, SRO, HA61.
9. Quoted in Cyril Pearl, *Morrison of Peking*, p. 242.
10. Reinsch, *An American Diplomat in China*, p. 2
11. Quoted in Cyril Pearl, *Morrison of Peking*, p. 243; Liang Chi-chao, scholar and reformer.
12. D.I. Abrikosov, *Revelations of a Russian Diplomat*, p. 167.
13. Lady Hosie, *Two Gentlemen of China*, London: Seeley Service, 1924, p. 37.
14. Daniele Varè diary, 10 February 1913, private collection.
15. Quoted in Cyril Pearl, *Morrison of Peking*, p. 245.
16. Abrikosov, *Revelations of a Russian Diplomat*, p. 169.
17. Ibid., p. 246.
18. Quoted in Cyril Pearl, *Morrison of Peking*, p. 249.
19. J.O.P. Bland, *Recent Events and Present Policies in China*, London: Heinemann, 1912, p. 469.
20. Quoted in Cyril Pearl, *Morrison of Peking*, p. 273.
21. Quoted in Hugh Trevor-Roper, *A Hidden Life*, p. 88.
22. Morrison to Lady Blake, 9 August 1911, in Lo Hui-min (ed.), *The Correspondence of G.E. Morrison*, vol. 1, p. 614.
23. Garnett, LRO, DDQ 9/13/10.
24. Hart, *The I.G. in Peking*, vol. 1, Letter 393; 26 December 1882.
25. Borel, *The New China*, pp. 33–5.
26. Reinsch, *An American Diplomat in China*, p. 30.

27. Varè diary, 21 January 1913.
28. Garnett, 10 January 1906, LRO, DDQ 9/14/2.
29. Ibid., 11 February, 1913.
30. Ahlefeldt-Laurvig to G.E. Baker-Lloyd, 22 March 1911, GRO, D3549/27.
31. Abrikosov, *Revelations of a Russian Diplomat*, p. 154.
32. Daniele Varè, *Laughing Diplomat*, London: John Murray, 1938, p. 119.
33. Mythical mischievous creatures who lurk in trees throwing rotten fruit at passers-by. They align themselves to no one.
34. Varè, *Laughing Diplomat*, p. 119.
35. Hosie, *Two Gentlemen of China*, p. 32.
36. Bowden-Smith, Newnham College Roll Letter, 1912, pp. 39, 46, Newnham College Archives.
37. M.A. Robertson to his mother, 16 April 1907, Churchill Archives Centre, RBTN, Box 2.
38. Reinsch, *An American Diplomat in China*, pp. 60–1.
39. Quoted in Jonathan Spence, *The Search for Modern China*, New York: W.W. Norton, 1999, pp. 278–9; J. Reed, *The Missionary Mind and American East Asia Policy, 1911–1914*, Harvard University Press 1983, pp. 36–7.
40. Abrikosov, *Revelations of a Russian Diplomat*, p. 170.
41. Lo Hui-min (ed.), *Correspondence of G.E. Morrison*, vol. 1, p. 611; 9 June 1911.
42. Ibid., vol. 2, p. 286; 30 January 1914.
43. W.W. Yen, *East West Kaleidoscope,* p. 132.
44. Ibid., p. 289.
45. Ibid., p. 290.
46. T. Hillier, *Leda and the Goose*, London: Longmans, 1954, p. 8.
47. Varè diary, 18 March 1913.
48. Lo Hui-min (ed.), *Correspondence of G.E. Morrison*, vol. 1, p. 657; 12 November 1911.
49. Ibid., vol. 2, pp. 257–8; 27 November 1913.

Chapter 7

1. Marion Carnegie to Garnett, 26 November 1906, LRO, DDQ 9/12/44.
2. Garnett, LRO, DDQ 9/13/22.
3. Varè diary, 21 July 1913.
4. Garnett, 21 August 1907, LRO, DDQ 9/10/47.
5. Varè diary, 7 February 1913.
6. T. Hodgson Liddell, RBA, *China, Its Marvel and Mystery,* London: George Allen, 1909.
7. Varè diary, 6 June 1913.
8. Varè, *Laughing Diplomat*, pp. 120–1.
9. Varè diary, 6 August 1914.
10. Ibid., 7 August 1914.
11. Jordan to Sir Walter Langley, 26 August 1914, NA, FO 350/11.
12. Jordan to Langley, 25 October 1914, NA, FO 350/11.
13. Ahlefeldt-Laurvig to G.E. Baker-Lloyd, 4 December 1914; GRO, Baker-Lloyd papers, D3549/27.

14. They form the core of the Pelliot Collection in the Bibliothèque Nationale and the Musée Guimet in Paris.
15. *North China Herald*, 26 June, 1915, vol. CXV.
16. Jordan to Sir Beilby Alston, September 1914, NA, FO 350/11.
17. Jordan to Langley, 23 February 1914, NA, FO 350/11.
18. Reinsch, *An American Diplomat in China*, p. 161.
19. *The New York Times*, 11 July 1918.
20. Jordan to Langley, 26 August 1914, NA, FO 350/11.
21. Quoted in Cyril Pearl, *Morrison of Peking*, p. 310.
22. Ibid., p. 308.
23. Jordan to Alston, 2 December 1914, NA, 350/11.
24. *The New York Times*, 2 May 1915.
25. Morrison to Prothero, 5 April 1916, in Lo Hui-min (ed.), *Correspondence of G.E. Morrison*, vol. 2, p. 507.
26. Langley to Jordan, 30 April 1915, NA, FO 350/14.
27. Hugh Trevor-Roper, *Hermit of Peking*, Harmondsworth: Penguin, 1978, p. 172.
28. Jordan to Alston, 1 February 1916, NA FO 350/15.
29. Quoted in Cyril Pearl, *Morrison of Peking*, p. 315.
30. Alston to Teichman, 10 June 1916, NA, FO 800/31.
31. Quoted in Cyril Pearl, *Morrison of Peking*, p. 320.
32. Ibid., p. 327; Morrison to Tsai Ting-kan.
33. Jordan to Langley, 16 April 1916, NA FO 350/15.
34. Daughter of Chicago millionaire, Charles R. Crane, American Minister to China 1920–1.
35. Ellen N. LaMotte, *Peking Dust*, New York: Century, 1919, pp. 74–5.
36. Ibid., pp. 14–5.
37. Ibid., pp. 26–7.
38. Jordan to Langley, 1 February 1916, NA, FO 350/15.
39. LaMotte, *Peking Dust*, pp. 161–2.

Chapter 8

1. Alston to Lord Balfour, NA, FO 371/2912.
2. Clifford H. Phillips, *The Lady Named Thunder*, Edmonton: University of Alberta Press, 2003, p. 237.
3. Reinsch, *An American Diplomat in China*, p. 272.
4. Charles Drage, *Servants of the Dragon Throne*, London: Peter Dawnay, 1966, p. 264.
5. Henry McAleavy, *A Dream of Tartary*, 1963, p. 110. The author's sources were almost exclusively Chinese or Japanese.
6. Lo Hui-min (ed.), *The Correspondence of G.E. Morrison*, p. 605; 4 July 1917.
7. McAleavy, *A Dream of Tartary*, p. 114.
8. Saint-John Perse, *Letters of Saint-John Perse*, translated and edited by A.J. Knodel, Princeton: Princeton University Press, 1979, pp. 268–73.
9. McAleavy, *A Dream of Tartary*, p. 116.

10. NA, FO 371/2912.
11. Grandfather of WW2 hero, Raoul Wallenberg, credited with saving 15,000 Jews.
12. Varè, *Laughing Diplomat*, p. 137.
13. Varè diary, 30 September 1914.
14. Jordan to Langley, 26 January 1914, NA, 350/12.
15. Ibid., 17 September 1914.
16. Lo Hui-min (ed.), *Correspondence of G.E. Morrison*, vol. 2, p. 757; Ting Wen-chiang to Morrison, 14 May 1919.
17. Alston to Balfour, despatch No. 305, 11 December 1917, NA, FO 371/2913.
18. Jordan to Langley, 28 July 1915, NA, FO 350/14.
19. Intercepted German letter, October 1916, NA, FO 371/2658.
20. Quoted in Xu, Guoqi, *China and the Great War*, Cambridge: CUP, 2005; Harry B. Wilmer, 'Chinese Coolies in France', *North China Herald*, 21 September 1918, p. 131.
21. NA, FO 228/1967.
22. Jordan to Langley, NA, FO 371/3290.
23. Reinsch, *An American Diplomat in China*, p. 156.
24. Ibid., p. 157.
25. Alston to Teichman, 16 August 1916, NA, FO 800/31.
26. Sir Miles Lampson to Sir John Tilley, 3 March 1918, NA, FO 371/3290.
27. Jordan despatch, 3 March 1918, NA, FO 371/3290.
28. See Cyril Pearl, *Morrison of Peking*, p. 334.
29. *The North China Morning Herald*, 22 December, 1917.
30. NA, FO 350/16.
31. Abrikosov, *Revelations of a Russian Diplomat,* 1964, pp. 146–7.
32. Varè, diary, 1–7 April 1914.
33. Jordan to Langley, 13 June 1916, NA, FO 350/15.
34. Ibid., 28 August 1916, NA, FO 350/16.
35. Jordan to Macleay, 15 January 1918, NA, FO 350/16.
36. Varè, *Laughing Diplomat*, p. 148.
37. Ibid.

Chapter 9

1. Quoted in Xu, Guoqi, *China and the Great War*, p. 245.
2. Lo Hui-min (ed.), *The Correspondence of G.E. Morrison*, vol. 2, p. 727; C.D. Bruce to Morrison, 3 March 1919.
3. Sir Alexander Hosie had served as commercial attaché and commissioner for opium at the British Legation. He was later appointed Consul General in Szechuan, Chihli and Shansi.
4. Hosie, 'Travels Abroad', No. 12, Royal Society for Asian Affairs /M/214.
5. A. Leger *The Letters of Saint-John Perse*, to Philippe Berthelot, 3 January 1917, p. 261.
6. Jordan despatch, British Library, L/PS/11/147.
7. Quoted in Cyril Pearl, *Morrison of Peking*, p. 375. Morrison diary, 31 December 1918
8. A. Leger, *The Letters of Saint-John Perse*, to Berthelot, 21 April 1920, p. 353.

9. Reinsh, *An American Diplomat in China*, p. 361.

10. Jordan to Langley, 16 April, 1916, NA, FO 350/16.

11. Jordan to Lord Bryce, 25 February 1919, NA, FO 350/16.

12. Lo Hui-min (ed.), *Correspondence of G.E. Morrison*, vol. 2, p. 806; 20 March 1920.

13. Aglen to Bowra, 28 April 1924, SOAS, GB 0103 MS 211355.

14. Hosie, 'Commandeered for Service in the British Legation', RSAA/M/214.

15. Aglen to Acheson, 26 November 1922, SOAS, GB 0130 MS 211355.

16. John Dewey and Alice Chipman Dewey, *Letters from China and Japan*, New York: E.P. Dutton, 1920, p. 247.

17. Bertrand Russell, *Autobiography of Bertrand Russell*, London: Allen & Unwin, 1968, vol. 2, p. 137; Letter to *The Nation*, 28 October 1920.

18. Dora Russell, *The Tamarisk Tree*, London: Elek/Pemberton, 1975, vol. 1, p. 115.

19. Bertrand Russell, *Autobiography of Bertrand Russell*, p. 141.

20. Yuen Chao-ren. Mathematician and translator.

21. Dora Russell, *The Tamarisk Tree*, p. 116.

22. Bertrand Russell, *Autobiography of Bertrand Russell*, vol. 2, p. 132.

23. Margaret Aitchison, *Doctor and the Dragon*, Basingstoke: Pickering Paperbacks, 1983.

24. Dr John B. Grant, *Reminiscences*, oral history, Columbia University 1961.

25. Quoted in John Z. Bowers, *Western Medicine in a Chinese Palace*, New York: Josiah Macy Jr. Foundation, 1972, p. 72; F.G. Peabody, *Francis Weld Peabody, 1881–1927*, p. 53.

26. Benson diary, 24 May 1920.

27. A policy introduced by US Secretary of State, John Hay in 1898 promoting free trade between the powers and China.

28. Bertrand Russell, *Autobiography of Bertrand Russell*, vol. 2, p. 129.

29. *A Chinese Appeal to Christendom Concerning Christian Missions*, 1911, published under the pseudonym, Lin Shao Yang; *Letters to a Missionary*, 1918.

30. *Puyi, From Emperor to Citizen*, translated by W.J.F. Jenner, Beijing: Foreign Languages Press, 1989, p. 112.

31. *Twilight in the Forbidden City*, Oxford: Oxford University Press, 1987, p. 167.

32. Benson diary, 30 June 1920.

33. Power to Coulton, 23 December 1931, Power papers, Girton College, Cambridge.

34. Quoted in Maxine Berg, *A Woman in History: Eileen Power, 1989–1940*. Cambridge: CUP, 1996, p. 174; Johnston to Sir James Stewart Lockhart, 14 October 1929, 2 February 1930.

35. Probhat Kumar Mukherji, *Life of Tagore*, New Delhi: Indian Book Co., 1975, p. 45.

36. Johnston, *Twilight in the Forbidden City*, p. 347.

37. Mukherji, *Life of Tagore*, pp. 54–5.

Chapter 10

1. Alice Green Hoffman, 21 November 1924; J.Y. Joyner Library, East Carolina University, MS/127.

2. Molly Orpen-Palmer, January 1921, private collection.

3. Hosie, Royal Society for Asian Affairs, RSAA/M/214.

4. Ann Bridge, *The Ginger Griffin*, London: Chatto & Windus, 1934, pp. 83, 86.
5. Orpen-Palmer, 4 January 1921.
6. Ibid., August 1922.
7. Stella Benson diary, 30 May 1920, Cambridge University Library, MS ADD 6762-6803.
8 A. Leger, *Letters of Saint-John Perse*, p. 262, note 1.
9. Bridge, *The Ginger Griffin*, p. 64.
10. Drage, *Servants of the Dragon Throne*, p. 273.
11. Bridge, *The Ginger Griffin*, pp. 71–2.
12. Benson diary, 12 August 1920.
13. Alice Green Hoffman papers, East Carolina University, Joyner Library.
14. Frances Butcher, 10 August 1923, SOAS, PP MS/30/2.
15. Brigadier L.F. Field, unpublished memoir, Imperial War Museum, Dept of Documents: cat. ref. LFF.
16. Eric Teichman to Mary Anne O'Malley, 28 January 1928, Harry Ransom Humanities Research Centre, University of Texas, at Austin, Bridge papers, Box 20.6.
17. Benson diary, 28 July, 1920.
18. Ibid., 29 July.
19. Orpen-Palmer, July 1922.
20. Ann Bridge, *Peking Picnic*, London: Chatto & Windus, 1932, p. 51.
21. Bridge, *Peking Picnic*; Bridge, *The Ginger Griffin*; Bridge, *Four-Part Setting*, London: Chatto & Windus, 1942.
22. Mary Anne O'Malley, circular letter, 18 and 22 February 1926, HRHRC, Bridge papers, Box 19.9.
23. Ibid., 30 March 1927, Box 20.2.
24. Bridge, *Peking Picnic*, p. 16.
25. Mary Anne O'Malley, circular letter, 12 January 1926, HRHRC, Bridge papers, Box 19.9.
26. Ibid., 28 May 1926, Box 19.9.
27. Ibid., 2 February 1926, Box 20.2.
28. Ibid., 28 May 1926, Box 19.9.

Chapter 11

1. *Time*, 11 August 1924.
2. Benson diary, 30 June 1920.
3. Ibid., 12 July 1920.
4. Vera Vishnyakova-Akimova, *Two Years in Revolutionary China, 1925–27*, translated by Steven I. Levine, Cambridge, MA: East Asian Research Center, Harvard University, 1971, p. 36.
5. Quoted in Jonathan Spence, *To Change China*, 1969, pp. 190–1; M.I. Kazanin, *In the Headquarters of Blyukher*, Memoir, Moscow, p. 70.
6. Vishnyakova-Akimova, *Two Years in Revolutionary China*, p. 29.
7. Valerii Pereleshin (main author), *Russian Literary and Ecclesiastical Life in Manchuria and China from 1920 to 1952*, Thomas Hauth (ed.), The Hague: Leuxenhoff, 1996, p. xiv.

8. Harry A. Franck, *Wandering in Northern China*, London: London University Press, 1924, p. 222.

9. Kitai i russkaia emigratsiia v dnevnikakh I.I. i A.N. Serebrennikovykh, eds. A.A. Khisamutdinov and S.M. Liandres, 5 vols, Moscow and Stanford: ROSSPEN and Hoover Institution Press, 2006–, p. 92, 29 December 1920. Translated for the author by Patrick Miles.

10. Ibid., 6 January, 23 February 1921, pp. 93, 100.

11. Ibid., 4 January 1921, p. 93.

12. Varè, *Laughing Diplomat*, p. 144.

13. Franck, *Wandering in Northern China*, pp. 222–3.

14. Cecil Lewis, *So Long Ago So Far Away*, London: Luzac Oriental, 1997, pp. 112–3.

15. Doushka Williams obituary, *Independent*, 4 August 2005.

16. Lewis, *So Long Ago So Far Away*, p. 36.

17. Ibid., pp. 86–7.

18. Harold Fleming, 25 August 1923, New York Library, Fleming papers.

19. Han Suyin, *A Mortal Flower*, London: Jonathan Cape, 1966, p. 198.

20. Orpen-Palmer, August 1923.

21. George B. Barbour papers, letter from Dorothy Barbour, 5 October 1926, Hoover Institution Archives.

22. Vishnyakova-Akimova, *Two Years in Revolutionary China*, p. 38.

23. O'Malley to Sydney Waterlow, 28 January 1927, private correspondence.

24. Quoted in Spence, *To Change China*, p. 192.

25. Phillips, *The Lady Named Thunder*, pp. 288–9.

26. George B. Barbour papers, letter from George B. Barbour, March 1925, Hoover Institution Archives.

27. Phillips, *The Lady Named Thunder*, pp. 288–9.

28. *North China Herald*, 17 September 1927.

29. Lampson to Ramsey MacDonald, 26 July 1927, John Rylands Library, RMD/10/4.

30. NA, FO 371/12430 (F820).

31. W. Strang, memorandum, 9 April 1927, NA, CAB/24/186.

32. Quoted in Jonathan Spence, *The Gate of Heavenly Peace*, New York: Viking Press, 1981, p. 207; Liang Qichao, letter to his sons, 30 March 1927, Nianpu, p. 727.

33. Anonymous letter, 23 April 1927, forwarded to Stanley Baldwin by Edward S.M. Perowne, NA, FO228/3618.

34. George B. Barbour papers, letter from George B. Barbour, 6 April 1927, Hoover Institution Archives.

35. British legation circular, 17 May 1927, NA, FO233/166.

36. Moore Bennett, 21 May 1927, NA, FO/233/166.

37. Mary Anne O'Malley, 2 February 1927, HRHRC, Bridge papers, Box 20.2.

38. Quoted in Jonathan Spence, *The Search for Modern China*, p. 332.

39. Ann Bridge, *The Ginger Griffin*, pp. 309–10.

40. Mary Anne O'Malley, 30 March and 5 April 1927, HRHRC, Bridge papers, Box 20.2.

41. Quoted in Spence, *To Change China*, p. 198; Victor Serge, *Memoirs of a Revolutionary, 1901–41*, Oxford: Oxford University Press, 1963, p. 217.

42. Minute by Ashley-Gwatkin, 11 December 1927, NA, FCO 371/12407; quoted in David C. Wilson, 'Britain and the Kuomintang 1924–28', unpublished PhD thesis, University of London 1973, SOAS, p. 631.

Chapter 12

1. Lampson diary, 1 June 1928.
2. William J. Oudendyck, *Ways and By-Ways in Diplomacy*, London: Peter Davis, 1939, p. 359.
3. Quoted in Wilson, 'Britain and the Kuomintang 1924–28', p. 696; 22 January 1927, FO 371/12399.
4. Lampson diary, 25 February 1927.
5. *Time*, 22 October 1928.
6. John Blofeld, *City of Lingering Splendour*, Boston & Shaftesbury: Shambhala, 1989, p. 17.
7. Lampson diary, 21 July 1928.
8. Varè, *Laughing Diplomat*, p. 355.
9. Ibid., p. 356.
10. Ibid., p. 393.
11. Lampson diary, 15 November 1930.
12. Ibid., 26 November 1930.
13. Quoted in Wilson, 'Britain and the Kuomintang 1924–28', p. 627; Lampson to Foreign office 1928.
14. Lampson diary, 3 June 1929.
15. Varè, *Laughing Diplomat*, p. 369.
16. Lampson diary, 1 June 1929.
17. Oudendyck, *Ways and By-Ways in Diplomacy*, p. 367.

Chapter 13

1. Allan Mazur, 'Amadeus Grabau in China: 1920–46', *Carbonates and Evaporites*, vol. 21, no. 1, March 2006, p. 60. The signed menu is in the archives of the American Museum of Natural History.
2. The group consisted of Sven Hedin, J. Gunnar Andersson, V.K. Ting, J.S. Lee, W.H. Wong, S.G. King, Walter Granger, Amadeus Grabau, P. Teilhard de Chardin, George B. Barbour, Davidson Black.
3. Quoted in Mazur, 'Grabau in China', p. 57.
4. Osborn, *Science*, 13 April, 1900. Another influential palaeontologist, William Diller Matthew endorsed and elaborated on Osborn's views in: *Climate and Evolution*, 1915.
5. Discovered by Eugene Dubois in 1891.
6. Roy Chapman Andrews, *Under a Lucky Star*, New York: Blue Ribbon Books, 1945, p. 163.
7. Ibid., p. 169.
8. Ibid., p. 176.
9. Ibid., p. 179.
10. Roy Chapman Andrews et al., *New Conquest of Central Asia*, New York: American Museum of Natural History, 1932, p. 18.

11. At this stage it was still called the *Third Asiatic Expedition* but was later re-named, with its successors, *Central Asiatic Expedition*.
12. Andrews et al., *New Conquest of Central Asia*, p. 21.
13. Andrews, *Under a Lucky Star*, p. 185.
14. Ibid., p. 200.
15. Ibid., p. 213.
16. Teilhard de Chardin, *Letters from a Traveller*, 1962; 13 April 1929, p. 154.
17. Quoted in George Kish, *To the Heart of Asia,* Ann Arbor: University of Michigan Press, 1984, p. 115; Hedin to Lufthansa, 4 April 1928.
18. Ann Bridge, *Facts and Fictions*, New York: McGraw-Hill, 1968, p. 26.
19. Ibid., p. 27.
20. Quoted in Harry L. Shapiro, 'Davidson Black: An Appreciation', in B.A. Sigmon and J.S. Cybulski (eds.), *Papers in Honor of Davidson Black*, Toronto: University of Toronto press, *c.* 1981, p. 24; Davidson Black, to B.E. Read, 5 December 1919.
21. Grant, *Reminiscences*, p. 209.
22. Dora Hood, *Davidson Black*, Toronto: University of Toronto Press, 1964, p. 50.
23. Barbour, newspaper article, *Brooklyn Daily Eagle*, 16 February, 1930.
24. George Barbour, *In the Field with Teilhard de Chardin*, New York: Herder & Herder, 1965, p. 43.
25. Jia Lanpo and Huang Weiwen, *The Story of Peking Man*, translated by Yin Zhiqi, Beijng: Foreign Language Press, 1990, p. 49.
26. Quoted in Mazur, 'Amadeus Grabau in China', p. 70.
27. Quoted in Jia Lanpo, *The Story of Peking Man*, pp. 64–5; Jia Lanpo diary.
28. Quoted in Lanpo, *The Story of Peking Man*, p. 68; Black to Elliot Smith, n.d. [December 1929].
29. Lampson diary, 27 June 1930.
30. Sigmon and Cybulski, 'Papers in Honor of Davidson Black', p. 26.
31. Quoted in Mazur, 'Amadeus Grabau in China', p. 70; Pierre Teilhard de Chardin, *Letters to Two Friends*, New York: New American Library, 1968, p. 71.

Chapter 14

1. Lampson diary, 9 March 1933.
2. Ibid., 12 April 1933.
3. Lampson was posted to Cairo 1936–46.
4. Lampson diary, 17 April 1933.
5. Ibid., 13 April 1933.
6. Ibid., 17 May 1933.
7. Ibid., 8 June 1933.
8. Ibid., 23 May 1933.
9. Harold Caccia was later ambassador to Washington and head of the Foreign Office.
10. Lampson diary, 4 June 1933.
11. Ibid., 18 February 1928.
12. John Stewart Service, John Paton-Davies, O. Edmund Clubb and Raymond Ludden who were all later to be victims of McCarthyism in the 1950s.

13. 10 May 1935, Nym Wales Collection, Edgar Snow to Henle, 10 May 1935, Box 24, Folder 649, Hoover Institution Archives.

14. Edgar Snow, *Journey to the Beginning*, New York: Random House, 1972, p. 139.

15. H.F. Snow to Chang Chao-lin, undated 1935, Nym Wales papers, Box 11, Folder 369.

16. Yeh Te-kuang to E. and H.F. Snow, 10 February 1936, Nym Wales papers, Box 11, Folder 379.

17. Cadogan was appointed head of the Foreign Office 1938–46 and Britain's first ambassador to the UN 1946–50.

18. Cadogan diary, 9 December 1935, Archives Centre, Churchill College, Cadogan papers, ACAD1/3.

19. Helen Foster Snow, *My China Years*, London: George Harrap, 1984, p. 152.

20. Sir Berkeley Gage, *A Marvellous Party*, London: Limited edition, 300 copies, 1989, p. 54.

21. Sir Frederick Leith-Ross, *Money Talks*, London: Hutchinson, 1968, p. 215.

22. Cadogan diary, 28 January 1935, ACAD 1/3.

23. Ibid., 25 January 1935.

24. Cadogan, to King George V, 29 January 1935, ACAD 4/1.

25. Clive Wigram to Cadogan, 1 April 1935, ACAD 4/1.

26. Cadogan diary, 6 December 1935, ACAD 1/3.

27. Cadogan to Archibald Rose, 6 May 1935, ACAD 4/1.

28. Cadogan diary, 11 October 1935, ACAD 1/3.

29. Snow, *My China Years*, p. 181.

30. Ibid., p. 198.

31. Snow to Gould, 24 November 1936, Nym Wales papers, Box 18, Folder 489.

32. Edgar Snow, *Red Star Over China*, London: Gollancz, 1937.

33. Snow to H.F. Snow, 12 July 1935, Nym Wales papers, Box 28, Folder 766.

34. Teilhard de Chardin, *Letters from a Traveller*, 1962, p. 284; Teilhard de Chardin to Claude Aragonnès (Marguerite Teilhard-Chambon), 12 July 1941.

35. Claude Cuènot, *Teilhard de Chardin*, translated by V. Colimore, Baltimore: Helicon, 1965, p. 53; March 1924.

36. Gage, *It's Been A Marvellous Party*, p. 53.

37. Henry de Monfried; Quoted in Mary and Ellen Lukas, *Teilhard: A Biography*, London: Collins, 1977, p. 110.

38. H.F. Snow, *My China Years*, 1984, p. 100.

39. Quoted in Thomas M., King, S.J. and Mary Wood Gilbert (eds.), *The Letters of Teilhard de Chardin and Lucile Swan*, Scranton: University of Scranton Press, 2001, p. xx.

40. Ibid., p. xviii.

41. Ibid., 14 October 1934, p. 23.

42. Ibid., pp. 20–1.

43. Teilhard to Walter Granger, Georgetown University, Teilhard/Granger correspondence, Folder 12; 4 October 1934.

44. Graham Peck, *Through China's Wall*, London: Readers Union, 1945, p. 33.

45. H.F. Snow, *My China Years*, pp. 249–50.

46. Kempton Fitch to Edgar Snow, Nym Wales papers, Box 20 (550); 1 May 1937.

47. H.F. Snow, *My China Years*, p. 275.

Chapter 15

1. Peter Quennell; Quoted in Harold Acton, *Memoirs of an Aesthete*, London: Methuen, 1948, p. 353.
2. Michael Churchman (ed.), *Laurence Sickman: A Tribute*, Kansas City: Nelson-Atkins Museum of Art, 1988, p. 40.
3. H.F. Snow, *My China Years*, p. 86.
4. Keith Stevens, 'Henri Vetch (1898–1978): Soldier, Bookseller and Publisher', in *Royal Asiatic Society Journal* (Hong Kong branch) 2008, p. 128.
5. H.F. Snow, *My China Years*, p. 86.
6. Nan Smith, 25 February 1937, private collection.
7. *The Sunday Star-Bulletin*, Honolulu, 11 July 1971.
8. Mrs Winifred Stilwell, unpublished memoir, private collection.
9. Acton, *Memoirs of an Aesthete*, p. 379.
10 George N. Kates, *The Years that Were Fat*, Oxford, New York: Oxford University Press, 1989, pp. 21–2.
11. Kates to Henry Francis, Archives of American Art, Henry Sayles Francis papers; 30 November 1935.
12. Ibid., 10 February 1935.
13. Widow of Edward Robinson, director of the Metropolitan Museum, New York, 1910–31.
14. Kates to Mrs Francis, Archives of American Art, Henry Sayles Francis papers; 23 September 1934.
15. Acton, *Memoirs of an Aesthete*, p. 333.
16. Ibid., p. 344.
17. An English-based controlled language created by Charles K. Ogden as an international auxiliary language. I.A. Richards promoted its use in schools in China.
18. Acton, *Memoirs of an Aesthete*, pp. 340–1.
19. Ibid., p. 363.
20. Winifred (Doot) Stilwell to her sister, 15 March 1939, private collection.
21. Agnes Smedley, *Battle Hymn of China*, New York: Knopf, 1943, p. 107.
22. Acton, *Memoirs of an Aesthete*, p. 374.
23. Ibid., p. 358.
24. Quoted in Hope Danby, *My Boy Chang*, London: Gollancz, 1955, p. 63.
25. Osbert Sitwell, *Escape with Me*, London: Macmillan, 1939, pp. 314, 316.
26. Lucy Butler (ed.), *Robert Byron, Letters Home*, London: Murray, 1991, p. 267.
27. Julian Bell, *Essays, Poems and Letters*, London: Hogarth Press, 1938, p. 75; Julian Bell to Vanessa Bell, 18 January 1936.
28. Acton, *Peonies and Ponies*, p. 93.
29. Butler (ed.), *Robert Byron*, p. 258; 30 November 1935.
30. Lampson diary, 14 April 1933.
31. David Horner to Sickman, Nelson-Atkins Museum of Art Archives, Sickman papers; n.d., [1934].
32. Ibid., Sickman to Langdon Warner, 30 April 1933.
33. Churchman (ed.), *Laurence Sickman*, p. 26.

34. Sir Hughe Knatchbull-Hugessen to Cadogan, 4 November 1936, Archives Centre Churchill College, KNAT 2/39.
35. Elisabeth Knatchbull-Hugessen, diary, 7 December 1936, private collection.
36. Ibid., 2 February 1937.
37. Ibid., 27 August 1937.
38. Nancy Easterbrook (née Stilwell) memoir, n.d., private collection.
39. Peck, *Through China's Wall*, pp. 252, 257, 258.
40. Roger B. Jeans and Katie Letcher Lyle (eds.), *Good-bye to Old Peking*, Athens, OH: Ohio University Press, 1998, p. 61.
41. Peck, *Through China's Wall*, p. 276.
42. Dorothea Richards diary, 28 July 1937, Richards papers, the Old Library, Magdalene College, Cambridge University.
43. Ibid., 1 August 1937.
44. Peck, *Through China's Wall*, p. 279.
45. Jeans and Letcher Lyle (eds.), *Good-bye to Old Peking*, 31 August 1937, p. 68.
46. Peck, *Through China's Wall*, p. 278.
47. Mrs Stilwell, memoir.
48. Jeans and Letcher Lyle (eds.), *Good-bye to Old Peking*, 10 October 1937, p. 75.
49. Kates, *The Years that Were Fat*, p. 258.
50. Mrs Stilwell, memoir.
51. Kates, letter to Mrs Francis, Archives of American Art, Henry Sayles Francis papers; 5 September 1933.
52. Jeans and Letcher Lyle (eds.), *Good-bye to Old Peking*, 10 February 1939, p. 149.
53. Teilhard de Chardin, *Letters from a Traveller*, p. 243; 25 June 1938.
54. Ibid., p. 241, 6 June 1938.
55. Doot Stilwell, 8 January 1939.
56. Mrs Stilwell, memoir.
57. Teilhard de Chardin, *Letters from a Traveller*, p. 246; 24 September 1939.
58. Nellie Hussey, archives and special collections, College of the Holy Cross, Worcester, MA; 15 July 1940.
59. Teilhard de Chardin, *Letters from a Traveller*, p. 257; 8 February 1940.

Chapter 16

1. Quoted in Hope Danby, *My Boy Chang*, p. 161.
2. Ibid., p. 163.
3. Teilhard de Chardin, *Letters from a Traveller*, p. 280; 20 March 1940.
4. Hilda L. Hale, *Indomitably Yours*, privately published, Victoria, BC: n.d., p. 162.
5. Ibid., p. 163.
6. Katy Talati, unpublished memoir.
7. Cadogan diary, 12 January 1935, Archives Centre Churchill College ACAD1/3.
8. Backhouse, Sir Edmund, *Décadence Mandchoue: The China Memoirs of Sir Edmund Trelawny Backhouse*, Derek Sandhaus (ed.), Hong Kong: Earnshaw Books, 2011.

9. Collection no. 81120, Carel A.M. Brondgeest MS., Hoover Institution Archives.
10. Ibid.
11. See Hsiao Li Lindsay, *Bold Plum: With the Guerrillas in China's War against Japan*, Morrisville, NC: Lulu Press, 2007.
12. Hale, *Indomitably Yours*, pp. 168–9.
13. Langdon Gilkey, *Shantung Compound*, London: Blond, 1967, p. 1.
14. Talati memoir.
15. Gilkey, *Shantung Compound*, p. 2.
16. Talati memoir.
17. Gilkey, *Shantung Compound*, p. 4.
18. Ibid., p. 5.
19. Gilkey, *Shantung Compound*, p. 35.
20. Ibid., p. 92.
21. Hale, *Indomitably Yours*, p. 211.
22. Quoted in Barbour, *In the Field with Teilhard de Chardin*, p. 113.
23. Thomas, King and Wood Gilbert (eds.), *The Letters of Teilhard de Chardin and Lucile Swan*, p. 159; 13 April 1943.
24. Quoted in Allan Mazur, *A Romance in Natural History*, p. 418.
25. The marines were not in the end repatriated but spent the war in an internment camp near Shanghai.
26. Quoted in Hugh Trevor-Roper, *Hermit of Peking*, Harmondsworth: Penguin, 1978, p. 282.
27. Ibid., pp. 280–1.
28. Gilkey, *Shantung Compound*, p. 192.
29. Ibid., p. 208.
30. Talati memoir.

Chapter 17

1. The treaty abolishing extraterritoriality was signed by Great Britain and the USA in Chungking on 11 January 1943.
2. Hale, *Indomitably Yours*, pp. 231–2 and Talati memoir.
3. Churchman (ed.), *Laurence Sickman: A Tribute*, p. 21.
4. Walter J.P. Curley Jr., 10 November 1945, private collection.
5. John F. Melby, *The Mandate of Heaven*, London: Chatto & Windus, 1969, p. 151.
6. Curley, 29 September 1949.
7. Ibid., 5 November 1945.
8. Ibid., 18 December 1945.
9. Curley, 1 January 1946.
10. Hale, *Indomitably Yours*, p. 255. This story is corroborated by a letter (if genuine) written by Rex Hardinge to his parents found on the Blakiana website, dated 20 September 1956, in which he states he was involved with Oscar Marmon (also mentioned by Hilda Hale) in setting up a network of contacts with the Communists in Peking.

11. Having lost further battles with the Vatican, in 1951 Teilhard went to live in New York where he died four years later.

12. Melby, *Mandate of Heaven*, p. 177.

13. Mary E. Ferguson, *China Medical Board and Peking Union Medical College*, New York: China Medical Board of New York, 1970.

14. Talati memoir.

15. Derk Bodde, *Peking Diary: A Year of Revolution*, New York: Henry Schuman, 1950, p. 18; 26 September 1948.

16. John Haffendon, *William Empson*, Oxford: Oxford University Press, 2005, vol. 2, pp. 118–19.

17. Quoted in Ibid., p.140; interview with Sybille van der Sprenekel.

18. See Ibid., pp. 140–1.

19. Quoted in Ibid., p. 124; Empson to Ian Parsons (Reading University Library), 29 February 1948.

20. *Life*, 3 January 1949.

21. Ibid.

22. Ferguson, *China Medical Board and Peking Union Medical College*, p. 208.

23. Ralph Lapwood and Nancy Lapwood, *Through the Chinese Revolution*, London: Spalding & Levy, 1954, p. 44.

24. Ibid., 'p. 45.

25. Bodde, *Peking Diary*, p. 74; 18 December 1948.

26. Ibid., p. 82; 25 December 1948.

27. Roy Rowan, *Chasing the Dragon*, Guildford, CT: Lyons Press, 2004, p. 142.

28. Dmitri Michael Horvath, memoir, private collection.

29. S.L. Tikhvinskii, *Diplomacy: Studies and Memoirs* (Diplmatiia: issledovaniia i vospominaniia), Moscow: Rossiiskai a akademii a naik, In-t rossiiskoi istorii, 2001, p. 221.

30. Lapwood and Lapwood, *Through the Chinese Revolution*, pp. 47–8.

31. Bodde, *Peking Diary*, pp. 79–80; 24 December 1948.

32. Ibid., pp. 96–7; 23 January 1949.

33. Tikhvinskii, *Diplomacy: Studies and Memoirs*, pp. 224–5.

34. Ferguson, *China Medical Board and Peking Union Medical College*, pp. 208–9.

35. Quoted in Haffenden, *William Empson*, vol. 2, p. 153.

36. Tikhvinskii, Diplomacy: Studies and Memoirs, p. 229.

37. On 29 April 1949, HMS *Amethyst* was sailing up the Yangtze towards Nanking when she came under attack from the Communists. Twenty-two men died and it was not until 30 July that the ship was able to escape down river to rejoin the British fleet.

38. David Kidd, *Peking Story*, London: Eland, 1988, pp. 85–8.

39. Ferguson, *China Medical Board and Peking Union Medical College*, p. 214.

40. Tikhvinskii, p. 234.

41. Ibid., p. 235.

42. William Empson, 'Red on Red', *London Review of Books*, 30 September 1999.

43. Kidd, *Peking Story*, p. 70.

SELECTED BIBLIOGRAPHY

Abrikosov, Dmitrii. *Revelations of a Russian Diplomat*. Seattle: University of Washington Press, 1964.

Acton, Harold. *Memoirs of an Aesthete*. London: Methuen, 1948.

——*Peonies and Ponies*. Oxford: Oxford University Press, 1983.

Airlie, Shiona. *Reginald Johnston*. Edinburgh: NMS Publishing, 2001.

Aisin-Goro Pu Yi. *From Emperor to Citizen*. Beijing: Foreign Languages Press, 1989.

Aitchison, Margaret. *Doctor and the Dragon*. Basingstoke: Pickering, 1983.

Aldrich, Robert. *Colonialism and Homosexuality*. London: Routledge, 2003.

Allen, Rev. Roland. *The Siege of the Peking Legations: Being the Diary of the Rev. Roland Allen, M.A.* London: Smith Elder, 1901.

Andrews, Roy Chapman. *Under a Lucky Star: A Lifetime of Adventure*. New York: Blue Ribbon Books, 1945.

Andrews, Roy Chapman, Granger, W., Nelson, N.C. and Pope, C.H. *The New Conquest of Central Asia*. New York: American Museum of Natural History, 1932.

Anon. *Where Chineses Drive: English Student-Life at Peking by a Student Interpreter*. London: W.H. Allen, 1885.

Arlington, L.C. *Through the Dragon's Eyes: Fifty Years' Experiences of a Foreigner in the Chinese Government Service*. London: Constable, 1931.

Arlington, L.C. and Lewisohn William, *In Search of Old Peking*. Oxford: Oxford University Press, 1987. First published by Henri Vetch, Peking, 1935.

Backhouse, Sir Edmund. *Décadence Mandchoue: The China Memoirs of Sir Edmund Trelawny Backhouse*. Edited by Derek Sandhaus (ed.), Hong Kong: Earnshaw Books, 2011.

Backhouse, E. and Bland J.O.P., *Annals and Memoirs of the Court of Peking*. London: Heinemann, 1914.

Ball, J. Dyer. *Things Chinese: Or Notes Connected with China*. Shanghai: Kelly & Walsh, 1925.

Barbour, George B. *In the Field with Teilhard de Chardin*. New York: Herder & Herder, 1965.

Barzini, Luigi. *Peking to Paris: An Account of Prince Borghese's Journey across Two Continents in a Motor-Car*. London: E. Grant Richards, 1907.

Becker, Jasper. *City of Heavenly Tranquillity*. London: Allen Lane, 2008.

Bell, Julian. *Essays, Poems and Letters*. London: The Hogarth Press, 1938.

Berg, Maxine. *A Woman in History: Eileen Power, 1989–1940*. Cambridge: Cambridge University Press, 1996.

Bickers, Robert. *Britain in China*. Manchester: Manchester University Press, 1999.

———*Empire Made Me: An Englishman Adrift in Shanghai*. London: Allen Lane, 2003.

Birch, John Grant. *Travels in North and Central China*. London: Hurst & Blackett, 1902.

Bisson, T.A. *Japan in China*. New York: Macmillan Co., 1938.

Bland, J.O.P. and Backhouse E., *China under the Empress Dowager*. London: Heinemann, 1910.

Bland, J.O.P. *Recent Events and Present Policies in China*. London: Heinemann, 1912.

Bodde, Derk. *Peking Diary: A Year, of Revolution*. New York: Henry Schuman, 1950.

de Bourboulon, Madame. *Shang-Hai à Moscou*. The Long Riders' Guild Press, thelongridersguild.com

Borel, H. *The New China*. London: T.F. Unwin, 1912.

Bowers, John Z. *Western Medicine in a Chinese Palace: Peking Union Medical College, 1917–1951*. New York: Josiah Macy, Jr. Foundation, 1972.

Bredon, Juliet. *Peking*. Shanghai: Kelly & Walsh, 1922.

———*Sir Robert Hart*. London: Hutchinson, 1909.

Bridge, Ann (aka Mary Anne O'Malley). *Peking Picnic*. London: Chatto & Windus, 1932.

———*The Ginger Griffin*. London: Chatto & Windus, 1934.

———*Four-Part Setting*. London: Chatto & Windus, 1942.

———*Facts and Factions*. New York: McGraw-Hill, 1968.

Brodsgaard, Kjeld Erik and Kirkebaek Mads, (eds). *China and Denmark: Relations Since 1674*. Denmark: Nordic Institute of Asian Studies, 2000.

Broomhall, Marshall. *Martyred Missionaries*. London: Morgan & Scott, 1901.

Brunero, Donna. *Britain's Imperial Cornerstone in China: The Chinese Maritime Customs Service, 1854–1949*. London: Routledge, 2006.

Buck, Pearl. *Letter from Peking*. London: Mandarin, 1990.

Bullock, Mary. *An American Transplant: The Rockefeller Foundation and Peking Union Medical College*. Berkeley: University of California Press, c.1980.

Burton, Margaret E. *The Education of Women in China*. New York: Fleming H. Revell, 1911.

Byron, Robert. *Letters Home*. Edited by Lucy Butler. London: John Murray, 1991.

Cadogan, Alexander, Sir. *The Diaries of Sir Alexander Cadogan, O.M.* Edited by David Dilks. London: Cassell, 1971.

Candlin, Enid Saunders. *The Breach in the Wall: A Memoir of Old China*. London: Cassell, 1973.

Carl, Katherine. *With the Empress Dowager in Peking*. London: KPI, 1986.

Casserly, Gordon. *The Land of the Boxers, or China Under the Allies*. London: Longmans, Green, 1903.

Ch'en, Jerome. *China and the West*. London: Hutchinson, 1979.

Cheng, F.T. *East and West: Episodes in a Sixty Years' Journey*. London: Hutchinson, 1951.

Clifford, Nicholas. *A Truthful Impression of the Country*. Ann Arbor, MI: University of Michigan Press, c.2001.

Coates, P.D. *The China Consuls: British Consular Officers, 1843–1943*. Hong Kong: Oxford University Press, 1988.

Croll, Elizabeth. *Wise Daughters from Foreign Lands: European Women Writers in China*. London: Pandora, 1989.

Cuénot, Claude. *Teilhard de Chardin*. Translated by V. Colimore. Baltimore: Helicon, 1965.

Denby, Charles. *China and Her People* (2 vols). Boston: L.C. Page, 1906.

Der Ling. The Princess. *Two Years in the Forbidden City*. New York: Moffat Yard & Co, 1911.

Dewey, John and Chipman Dewey, Alice. *Letters from China and Japan (1920)*. New York: E.P. Dutton, 1920.

Dickinson, G. Lowes. *Letters from John Chinaman*. London: Allen & Unwin, 1946.

Drage, Charles. *Servants of the Dragon Throne*. London: Peter Dawnay, 1966.

Easton, Robert. *China Caravans: An American Adventurer in Old China*. Santa Barbara, CA: Capra Press, 1982.

Elder, Chris. *Old Peking*. Hong Kong: Hong Kong University Press, 1997.

Elegant, Robert S. *China's Red Leaders*. London: Bodley Head, 1952.

Elleman, Bruce A. *Diplomacy and Deception: The Secret History of Sino-Soviet Diplomatic Relations, 1917–27*. Armonk, New York: M.E. Sharpe, c.1997.

Evans, Thomas, W.H. *Vanished China: Far Eastern Banking Memories*. London: Thorsons, 1956.

Fairbank, John K. *China's Response to the West*. Cambridge, MA: Harvard University Press, 1954.

—— (Ed.) *The Missionary Enterprise in China and America*. Cambridge, MA: Harvard University Press, 1974.

——*Chinabound*. New York: Harper & Row, 1983.

Fairbank, John K. and Goldman, M. *China: A New History*. Cambridge, MA: Harvard University Press, 2006.

Favier, Monsignor Alphonse. *Péking*. Paris: Desclée, de Brouwer, 1900.

Fenby, Jonathan. *Chiang Kai-shek*. New York: Carroll and Graf, 2004.

——*The Penguin History of Modern China: 1850–2009*. London: Penguin, 2009.

Ferguson, Mary E. *China Medical Board and Peking Union Medical College: A Chronicle of Fruitful Collaboration 1914–51*. New York: China Medical Board of New York, 1970.

Feuerwerker, Albert. *The Foreign Establishment in China in the Early Twentieth Century*. Ann Arbor: Center for Chinese Studies, University of Michigan, 1976.

Fleming, Peter. *One's Company: A Journey to China*. London: Jonathan Cape, 1934.

——*The Siege at Peking*. London: Readers Union, 1960.

Freeman-Mitford, A.B. *The Attaché at Peking*. London: Macmillan, 1900.

Fullerton, W.Y. and Wilson C.E., *New China: A Story of Modern Travel*. London: Morgan Scott, 1910.

Fussell, Paul. *Abroad: British Literary Traveling Between the Wars*. New York: Oxford University Press, 1950.

Franck, Harry Alverson. *Wandering in Northern China*. London: London University Press, 1924.

Gage, Sir Berkeley. *It's Been a Marvellous Party!* London: Limited edition, printed privately, 300 copies, 1989.

Gallenkamp, Charles. *Dragon Hunter: Roy Chapman Andrews and the Central Asiatic Expeditions*. New York: Viking Penguin, 2001.

Gamble, Sidney D. *Peking: A Social Survey*. New York: George H. Doran, 1921.

Gaunt, Mary. *A Woman in China*. London: T. Werner Laurie, 1915.

Gascoyne-Cecil, The Rev. Lord William. *Changing China*. London: James Nisbet, 1910.

Grant, Joy. *Stella Benson: A Biography*. London: Macmillan, 1987.

Haffenden, John. *William Empson*. Oxford: Oxford University Press, 2005–6.

——(Ed.). *Selected Letters of William Empson*. Oxford: Oxford University Press, 2006.

Hale, Hilda L. *Indomitably Yours*. Victoria BC: Hilda Hale, n.d.,

Hamilton, John Maxwell. *Edgar Snow: A Biography*. Bloomington, IN: Indiana University Press, c.1988.

Hart, Sir Robert. *These from the Land of Sinim*. London: Chapman & Hall, 1901.

—— *The I.G. in Peking: Letters of Robert Hart, Chinese Maritime Customs, 1868–1907*. Edited by John King Fairbank, Katherine Frost Bruner and Elizabeth MacLeod Matheson. Cambridge, MA: Belknap Press of Harvard University Press, 1975.

Hayter-Menzies, Grant. *Imperial Masquerade: The Legend of Princess Der Ling*. Hong Kong: Hong Kong University Press, 2008.

Hedin, Alma. *Mein Bruder Sven*. Leipzig: F.A. Brockhouse, 1925.

Hedin, Sven Anders. *My Life as an Explorer*. Washington: National Geographic Society, 2003.

Hewlett, William Meyrick. *Diary of the Siege of the Peking Legations*. London: Published for the editors of *The Harrovian* by F. W. Provost, 1900.

——*Forty Years in China*. London: Macmillan, 1943.

Hoare, J.E. *Embassies in the East*. London: Curzon, 1999.

Hoare, J.E. and Susan Pares. *Beijing*. Oxford: Clio Press, 2000.

Hoe, Susanna. *Women at the Siege Peking 1900*. Oxford: The Women's History Press, 2000.

Hood, Dora. *Davidson Black*. Toronto: University of Toronto Press, 1964.

Hooker, Mary. *Behind the Scenes in Peking*. Oxford: Oxford University Press, 1987.

Hooper, Beverley. *China Stands Up: Ending the Western Presence*. London: Allen & Unwin, 1986.

Hosie, Lady. *Two Gentlemen of China*. London: Seeley Service, 1924.

Howard, Harvey. *Ten Weeks with Chinese Bandits*. New York: Dodd Mead & Co., 1927.

Howell, Georgina. *Daughter of the Desert: The Remarkable Life of Gertrude Bell*. London: Macmillan, 2006.

Lo Hui-min (Ed.). *The Correspondence of G.E. Morrison*. Cambridge: Cambridge University Press, 1976–78.

Jeans, Roger B. and Lyle, Katie Letcher. *Good-Bye to Old Peking*. Athens, OH: Ohio University Press, 1998.

Jia Lanpo and Huang Weiwen. *The Story of Peking Man*. Translated by Yin Zhiqi. Beijing: Foreign Languages Press, 1990.

Johnston, Reginald F. (aka Lin Shao Yang). *Twilight in the Forbidden City*. Oxford: Oxford University Press, 1987.

Kates, George N. *The Years that Were Fat*. New York: Harper, 1952.

Keown-Boyd, Henry. *The Fists of Righteous Harmony: Boxer Rebellion*. London: Leo Cooper, 1991.

Keyes, Sir Roger. *Adventures Ashore & Afloat*. London: G.G. Harrap, 1939.

Kidd, David. *Peking Story*. London: Eland, 2008.

King, Frank H.H. *The Hong Kong Bank in Late Imperial China, 1864–1902. The Hong Kong and Shanghai Banking Corporation*, vol. 1, Cambridge: Cambridge University Press, 1987.

King, Louis Magrath. *China in Turmoil*. London: Heath Cranton, 1927.

Kish, George. *To the Heart of Asia: The Life of Sven Hedin*. Ann Arbor: University of Michigan Press, c.1984.

Knatchbull-Hugessen, Sir Hughe Montgomery. *Diplomat in Peace and War*. London: John Murray, 1949.

Kripalani, Krishna. *Tagore: A Life*. Published by the author, 1971.

Kruger, Rayne. *All under Heaven: A Complete History of China*. Chichester: John Wiley & Sons, 2002.

Kwan, Michael David. *Things that Must Not Be Forgotten: A Childhood in Wartime China*. Edinburgh: Mainstream Publishing, 2001.

Lamont-Brown, Raymond. *Tutor to the Dragon Emperor*. Stroud: Sutton Publishing, 1999.

LaMotte, Ellen N. *Peking Dust*. New York: Century, 1919.

Landor, Arnold Henry Savage. *China and the Allies*. London: Heinemann, 1901.

Lapwood, Ralph and Lapwood, Nancy. *Through the Chinese Revolution*. London: Spalding & Levy, 1954.

Lewis, Cecil. *So Long Ago So Far Away*. London: Luzac Oriental, 1997.

Little, Alicia. *Round About My Peking Garden*. London: T. Fisher, 1905.

Liddell, T. Hodgson. *China, Its Marvel and Mystery*. London: George Allen, 1909.

Lindsay, Hsiao Li. *Bold Plum*. Morrisville, NC: Lulu Press, 2007.

Loch, Henry Brougham. *Personal Narrative: Of Occurrences During Lord Elgin's Second Embassy to China, 1860*. London: John Murray, 1869.

Loti, Pierre. *Les Derniers Jours de Pékin,* Paris: Calmann Levy, 1902, reprinted in facsimile by Elibron Classics, 2006.

Lukas, Mary and Ellen Lukas. *Teilhard: A Biography*. London: Collins, 1977.

McAleavey, Henry. *A Dream of Tartary: The Origins and Misfortunes of Henry P'u Yi*. London: Allen & Unwin, 1963.

Martin, W.A.P. *A Cycle of Cathay*. Edinburgh: Oliphant Anderson and Ferrier, 1896.

May, Henry John. *Little Yellow Gentlemen*. London: Cassell, 1937.

Maynard, Isabelle. *China Dreams: Growing up Jewish in Tientsin*. Iowa City: University of Iowa Press, 1996.

Mazur, Allan. *A Romance in Natural History: The Lives and Works of Amadeus Grabau and Mary Antin*. Syracuse, NY: Syracuse University Press, 2004.

Melby, John F. *The Mandate of Heaven: Record of a Civil War, China 1945–49*. London: Chatto & Windus, 1969.

Morrison, Hedda. *A Photographer in Old Peking*. Oxford: Oxford University Press, 1985.

Moser, Michael J. and Wei-chih Yeone, *Foreigners Within the Gates: The Legations at Peking*. Chicago: Serlinda Publications, 2006.

Nash, Gary. *The Tarasov Saga: From Russia through China to Australia*. Kenthurst, NSW Rosenberg Publishing, n.d.

Norris, Rev. Frank L. *China*. London: Mowbray, 1908.

Northcliffe, Alfred Harmsworth Viscount. *My Journey Round the World*. Lord Robert Cecil and St John Harmsworth (eds), London: John Lane, 1923.

Oliphant, Nigel. *A Diary of the Siege of the Legations in Peking*. London: Longmans, Green, 1901.

O'Malley, Owen St Clair, *The Phantom Caravan*. London: John Murray, 1954.

Oudendyk, William J. *Ways and By-Ways in Diplomacy*. London: Peter Davis, 1939.

Paine, S.C.M. *Imperial Rivals: China, Russia, and Their Disputed Frontier*. London: M.E. Sharpe, c.1996.

Pakula, Hannah. *The Last Empress: Madame Chiang Kai-shek and the Birth of Modern China*. London: Weidenfeld & Nicholson, 2010.

Payne, Robert. *Journey to Red China*. London: Heinemann, 1947.

Pearl, Cyril. *Morrison of Peking*. Sydney: Angus & Robertson, 1967.

Peck, Graham. *Through China's Wall*. London: Readers Union, 1945.

Pennell, Wilfred V. *A Lifetime with the Chinese*. Hong Kong: South China Morning Post, 1974.

Perckhammer, Heinz von. *Peking*. Berlin: Albertus, 1928.

Phillips, Clifford H. *The Lady Named Thunder: A Biography of Dr. Ethel Margaret Phillips (1876–1951)*. Edmonton: University of Alberta Press, 2003.

Power, Brian. *The Ford of Heaven*. London: Peter Owen, 1984.

——*The Puppet Emperor*. London: Peter Owen, 1986.

Power, Desmond. *Little Foreign Devil*. West Vancouver: Pangli Imprint, 1996.

Preston, Diana. *The Boxer Rebellion*. London: Robinson, 2002.

Rand, Peter. *China Hands*. New York: Simon & Schuster, 1995.

Rea, Kenneth W. and Brewer John C., *The Forgotten Ambassador: The Reports of John Leighton Stuart, 1946–49*. Boulder, CO: Westview Press, 1981.

Read, Donald. *The Power of News: The History of Reuters*. Oxford: Oxford University Press, 1992.

Ready, Oliver G. *Life and Sport in China*. London: Chapman & Hall, 1903.

Reinsch, Paul Samuel. *An American Diplomat in China*. New York: Doubleday, Page & Co., 1922.

Reischauer, Edwin O., Fairbank John K., Craig Albert M., *East Asia: The Modern Transformation*. Boston: Houghton Mifflin, 1965.

Rennie, David Field. *Peking and the Pekingese: During the First Year of the British Embassy at Peking*. 2 vols. London: John Murray, 1865. Reprinted in facsimile by Elibron Classics, 2005.

Robb, Graham. *Strangers: Homosexual Love in the 19th Century*. London: Picador, 2003.

Rowan, Roy. *Chasing the Dragon: A Veteran Journalist's Firsthand Account of the 1949 Chinese Revolution*. Guilford, CT: The Lyons Press, 2004.

Roy, Claude. *Into China*. Translated from the French by Mervyn Savill. London: Sidgewick & Jackson, 1955.

Russell, Bertrand. *The Problem of China*. London: Allen & Unwin, 1922.

——*The Autobiography of Bertrand Russell*. London: Allen & Unwin, 1967–9.

Russell, Dora (née Black). *The Tamarisk Tree*. London: Elek Pemberton, 1975–81.

Russo, John Paul. *I.A. Richards*. London: Routledge, 1989.

'Saint-Jean Perse (aka Alexis Leger), *Letters of St-John Perse*. Translated and edited by Arthur J. Knodel. Princeton: Princeton University Press, 1979.

Schurman, Franz and Orvill Schell (eds). *Republican China*. London: Random House, 1967.

Segalen, Victor. *René Lys*. London: Quartet Encounters, 1990.

Serebrennikov, Ivan and Serebrennikov, Aleksandra. *The Diaries of Ivan and Aleksandra Sebrennikov, 1919–34*. Moscow-Stanford: ROSSPEN, 2006.

Seton, Grace Thomas *Chinese Lanterns*. London: John Lane Bodley Head, 1924.

Shapiro, Sidney. *An American in China: Thirty Years in the People's Republic*. Middle Island, NY: New World Press, 1979.

Sharf, Frederic A. and Harrington Peter, *The Boxer Rebellion: China 1900*. London: Greenhill Books, 2000.

Sheean, Vincent. *Personal History*. London: Hamish Hamilton, 1969.

Shulman, Nicola. *A Rage for Rock Gardening: The Story of Reginald Farrer, Gardener, Writer and Plant Collector*. London: Short Books, 2001.

Sitwell, Osbert. *Escape with Me*. London: Macmillan, 1939.

Smedley, Agnes. *China Correspondent*. London: Pandora Press, 1984.

Smith, Arthur H. *Chinese Characteristics*. New York: Fleming H. Revell, 1894.

Snow, Edgar. *Red Star Over China*. London: Gollancz, 1937.

———*Journey to the Beginning*. New York: Random House, 1972.

Snow, Helen Foster. *My China Years*. London: George Harrap, 1984.

Spence, Jonathan D. *To Change China*. Boston: Little Brown, 1969.

———*The Gate of Heavenly Peace*. New York: The Viking Press, 1981.

———*The Chan's Great Continent: China in Western Minds*. New York: W.W. Norton, 1998.

———*The Search for Modern China*. New York: W.W. Norton, 1999.

Sproxton, Vernon. *Teilhard de Chardin*. London: S.C.M. Press, 1971.

Strand, David. *Rickshaw Beijing: City People and Politics in the 1920s*. Berkeley: University of California Press, 1989.

Stuart, John Leighton. *Fifty Years in China*. New York: Random House, 1954.

Sun Shuyun. *The Long March*. London: HarperCollins, 2006.

Tan, Chester C. *The Boxer Catastrophe*. New York: Columbia University Press, 1955.

Teichman, Eric. *Affairs of China*. London: Methuen, 1938.

Teilhard de Chardin, Pierre. *Letters from a Traveller*. London: Collins, 1962.

Thomas M., King, S.J., and Wood Gilbert Mary, (eds). *The Letters of Teilhard de Chardin and Lucile Swan*. Scranton: University of Scranton Press, 2001.

Thompson, Peter and Macklin, Robert. *The Man Who Died Twice: The Life and Adventures of Morrison of Peking*. Crows Nest, NSW: Allen & Unwin, 2004.

Thorbecke, Ellen. *People in China*. London: George Harrap, 1935.

Tikhvinskii, S.L. *Diplomatii a: issledovanii a I vospominanii* [Diplomacy: Studies and Memoirs]. Moscow: Rossiiskai a akademii a naik, In-t rossiiskoi istorii, 2001.

Tipton, Laurance. *Chinese Escapade*. London: Macmillan, 1949.

Townley, Lady Susan. *My Chinese Note-Book*. London: Methuen, 1904.

Trevor-Roper, Hugh. *A Hidden Life*. London: Macmillan, 1976; later re-published as *The Hermit of Peking*. Harmondsworth: Penguin, 1978.

Tuchman, Barbara W. *Stilwell and the American Experience in China, 1911–45*. New York: Grove Press, 1985.

Varè, Daniele. *The Last of the Empresses*. London: John Murray, 1936.

———*Laughing Diplomat*. London: John Murray, 1938.

Vishnyakova-Akimova, Vera. *Two Years in Revolutionary China, 1925–1927*. Translated by Steven I. Levine. Cambridge, MA: East Asian Research Center, Harvard University, distributed by Harvard University Press, 1971.

Vologodskii, Petr Vasilevich. *A Chronicle of the Civil War in Siberia and Exile in China*. Compiled, edited and introduced by Semion Lyandres and Dietmar Wulff. Stanford: Hoover Institution Press, 2002.

Wang, Jessica Ching-Sze. *John Dewey in China*. New York: State University of New York Press, 2007.

Weale, Putnam B.L. *Indiscreet Letters from Peking*. London: Hurst and Blackett, 1907 and Gloucester: Dodo Press, 2005.

West, Philip. *Yenching University and Sino-Western Relations, 1916–52*. Cambridge, MA: Harvard University Press, 1976.

Wingate, Col. A.W.S, *A Cavalier in China*. London: Grayson & Grayson, 1940.

Wood, Frances. *Did Marco Polo Go to China?* London: Secker & Warburg, 1995.

———*No Dogs and Not Many Chinese: Treaty Port Life in China, 1843–1943*. London: John Murray, 1998.

———*The Lure of China*. Hong Kong: Joint Publishing (H.K.) and Yale University Press, 2009.

Woods, Dr Grace E. *Life in China: From the Letters of Dr. Nancy Bywaters*. Braunton, Devon: Merlin Books, 1992.

Xu, Guoqi. *China and the Great War*. Cambridge: Cambridge University Press, 2005.

Young, Ernest P. *The Presidency of Yuan Shi-k'ai: Liberalism and Dictatorship in Early Republican China*. Ann Arbor: University of Michigan Press, 1977.

Yuming Shaw. *An American Missionary in China: John Leighton Stuart and Chinese-American relations*. Cambridge, MA: Council on East Asian Studies, Harvard University. Distributed by Harvard University Press, 1992.

INDEX